JEWISH ISSUES IN ARGENTINE LITERATURE

JEWISH ISSUES
IN ARGENTINE LITERATURE

From Gerchunoff to Szichman

Naomi Lindstrom

University of Missouri Press
Columbia, 1989

Copyright © 1989 by
The Curators of the University of Missouri
University of Missouri Press, Columbia, Missouri 65211
Printed and bound in the United States of America
All rights reserved

Library of Congress Cataloging-in-Publication Data

Lindstrom, Naomi, 1950–
    Jewish issues in Argentine literature : from Gerchunoff to Szichman /
Naomi Lindstrom.
        p.   cm.
    Bibliography: p.
    Includes index.
    ISBN 0–8262–0708–1 (alk. paper)
    1. Argentine literature—Jewish authors—History and criticism. 2. Argentine
literature—20th century—History and criticism. I. Title.
PQ7634.J48L56   1989
860'.9'8924—dc19   88–27635
                                                                         CIP

∞™ This paper meets the minimum requirements of the American National Standard
for Permanence of Paper for Printed Library Materials, Z39.48, 1984.

TO FREDERICK AND ISAAC

ACKNOWLEDGMENTS

Support for research and writing of this book came from a Faculty Research Assignment from the University Research Institute of the University of Texas at Austin; an Andrew W. Mellon Foundation Grant awarded through the Institute of Latin American Studies of the University of Texas at Austin; and the Dallas TACA Centennial Fellowship in Liberal Arts, 1987–1988.

Quotations from the literary works under discussion are from the original Spanish, with English translations supplied in parentheses. Quotations from critical works are given in translated form only. All translations are my own.

My thanks go to Seth L. Wolitz, for telling me to write this book; to David William Foster and L. L. Johnson, for their encouragement; and to Nora Glickman, for her careful reading of the work.

N.L.
December 1988

CONTENTS

Acknowledgments, vii

Introduction, 1

1. Alberto Gerchunoff: Rhapsodizing a Jewish New World, 51

2. César Tiempo: Worldly Lyricization of the
Urban Jewish Experience, 61

3. Bernardo Verbitsky: Toward a Critical Discussion
of Jewish Argentine Issues, 79

4. David Viñas: The Novelistics of Cultural Contradiction, 88

5. José Rabinovich: A Poetics of Disputation, 102

6. José Isaacson: An Open Letter to Spinoza, 113

7. Marcos Ricardo Barnatán: The New Novel as
Access to Kabbalah, 130

8. Mario Szichman: A Questioning Eye on
Jewish Argentine History, 146

Postface, 158

Notes, 169

Selected Bibliography, 185

Index, 201

INTRODUCTION

This examination of Jewish Argentine literature centers on the analysis of eight selected works whose publication dates range from 1910 to 1977, half of them from the 1970s. The eight texts have been chosen to represent the diversity of the literary treatments accorded Jewish Argentine issues over a period of swift and profound historical change. Whereas some of the works claim attention by offering an account of historical issues, it is also important to recognize the more hidden and oblique ways in which literature implies a commentary on aspects of society. To give these subtler forms their due, this study will examine poetry, typically more veiled in its presentation, and a novel of seemingly abstract aestheticism, as well as novels overtly concerned with social history.

This introductory chapter surveys major tendencies in Jewish Argentine literature together with the events of Argentine social history that most affected Jewish writers, their work, and its reception. The eight featured authors are introduced through a narrative designed to emphasize the way in which they form part of a developing literature and a changing society. This chronological account combines elements of social events, literary history, and a description of the careers and original contributions of the eight, as well as briefer discussion of major representative figures and a sampling of works that indicate the chief tendencies in Jewish Argentine literature. Following the eight chapters of commentary on the selected works, a postface will survey Jewish Argentine writing as it has developed since the mid-1970s. Its recent past is distinguished by two phenomena: the exile literature that arose during the repressive military regime of 1976–1983 and, with the 1983 return to civilian government, the renewal of overt social criticism in internal intellectual discussion and literary expression.

Jewish Argentine writing has potentially a great deal to reveal about history: Argentine social history, the history of attitudes toward cultural variety, the history of Jewish thought, and other factors that have changed rapidly over the course of the century. Yet the writers of this literature have at times been reluctant witnesses, leaving unsaid or denying the most powerful statements their work might have made. Though circumstances have given these authors a significant vantage point, their testimony may be cryptic, vague, or distorted, betraying a deep-seated and understandable fear of arousing hostility by appearing unenthusiastic about the Argentine nation. The dilemma that results from this insecurity—an exceptional capacity for criticism, inhibited by a tenacious disinclination to criticize—is one of the principal concerns of this study.

Also traced is an allied secondary development: the gradually increasing freedom with which Jewish Argentine authors may display cultural *particularism,* to use the term long associated with the issue. Jewish immigrants to Argentina had received encouragement, both through the official rhetoric of patriotism and through the general culture, to diminish those features of their identity that distinguished them from the long-standing, largely Catholic Mediterranean population. The earliest Jewish authors provide reassurance that these newcomers are less other than they might seem and growing less so. In subsequent generations, writers show a sense that they must speak for a group whose identity is undeniably marked. They come to concede a long-avoided point: that certain Jewish ways are ineluctably strange to those outside the group and cannot, without surrender and falsification, be diminished to minor variants on Christian patterns. It becomes increasingly acceptable to bring to the discussion of national problems, which have proven refractory to established forms of analysis, help from Jewish traditions of critical thought. To do so means to overcome the old anxiety that a discussant whose outlook is identified as Jewish will be perceived as insufficiently Argentine to speak of national affairs.

Whether to achieve a salutary frankness as critics of society or to manifest confidence in the group's entitlement to distinctive traits and intellectual resources, these authors have had to overcome a set of attitudes crudely but effectively summed up in the question "Can a good Jew be a good Argentine?" From its inception, Jewish Argentine literature has had little choice but to respond in some fashion to this potentially paralyzing dilemma. For the earliest writers, the problem was essentially one of answering the question in the terms in which it was posed. Later authors challenged the presuppositions behind the question and suggested that it served to discourage groups other than the dominant one from expressing their needs and views.

Before there could be a Jewish Argentine literature and, indeed, before the above question could even arise, there had first to exist a Jewish population substantial and visible enough for its role in national life to be a matter of public discussion. Such a situation came about only early in the present century. To be sure, Jews had always been among the Europeans arriving in what is now Argentina. But since Jewish immigration into the New World colonies was forbidden, as was also any deviation from Catholicism in land under the Spanish crown, these early Sephardic arrivals were understandably quick to blend into the general population. The Jewish immigrants who succeeded this shadowy Sephardic presence were not the result of any organized movement or campaign but rather of scattered journeys from various countries, especially France, Germany, and England. Partly because of their isolation from European ties and partly because they represented an emancipated, considerably secularized Western Jewry, the members of this community made no strenuous effort to retain Jewish religious ways, legal thought, or other areas of special knowledge or forms of behavior. By the time of the massive immigration of Eastern European Jews—the group that would give Argentina its markedly Jewish population—the long-standing Sephardic presence consisted of perhaps a few hundred individuals who offered, in many cases, little contrast to the dominant culture. They did maintain a temple, appoint a rabbi, and establish Jewish social services, but to the next Jewish immigrants, the Eastern European arrivals of 1881–1910, all these existing institutions appeared to be mere vestiges of a virtually abandoned Judaism.[1]

The Jewish immigration that gave rise to a distinctive community cultural life and, eventually, to a literature was the result of the Argentine government's drive to settle and regulate the pampas. The longtime population of the area, composed in large part of Indians and racially mixed gauchos, was deemed innately unequipped to help the nation progress. Contemporary racial theories held that Europeans, particularly those from cold climates, possessed the greatest industry and capacity for orderly development. In addition, the government was eager to eliminate fully the nomadism and communal land tenure typical both of the culture of the Indians and that of the gauchos, fierce defenders of open range during the government's drive to fence the pampas. European immigrants would devote themselves to the settlement and cultivation of assigned lands and would have no choice but to uphold this "modern" system against the continuing hostilities of the displaced natives.

Although immigration and land-assignment policies originated at governmental level, their implementation was the work of a complex and sometimes disorganized web of public, philanthropic, and profit-making agencies. In the case of Eastern European Jewry the Bavarian-born Maurice de Hirsch (1831–1896) was most responsible for the promotion of immigration to Argentina. Concerned over the renewed anti-Jewish activities in Russia beginning in 1881, the baron arrived at the conclusion that the Argentine plains would offer not only a refuge from pogroms but also, eventually, a new Jewish homeland. The many variants of Zionism in nineteenth-century Jewish thought were far from unanimous in urging the return to

Palestine; Hirsch supported the Palestine effort but believed that Zion could be equally well established in Argentina. The equation of Argentina with the new Zion came to enjoy almost official status as part of the nation's patriotic rhetoric owing in large measure to its promulgation through the writings and statements of Alberto Gerchunoff (1884–1950), the first Jewish Argentine to achieve prominence as a man of letters.

The baron was not the initiator of the immigration of Jews from Europe to the Argentine interior; indeed, there is evidence of scattered settlements at least as early as the 1860s. But it was Hirsch's Jewish Colonization Association that systematized the process. In 1891, Hirsch underwrote his first settlement, populating it with the survivors of an ill-fated previous attempt.[2] The founding of this colony, Moisésville, is generally considered to mark the beginning of the massive Jewish immigration to Argentina that diminished only when, in 1914, World War I impeded virtually all immigration. Different statistics illustrate various aspects of the phenomenon, but an especially indicative figure is the count of 158,167 Russian immigrants entering Argentina between 1889 and 1914. Whereas Argentina did not necessarily prove to be the final destination for these arrivals, their large number, together with the historically justified assumption that most of them were Jewish, is impressive.

These events, and the interpretation of them favored by the Argentine government, supply the subject matter of the earliest work of Jewish Argentine literature to claim a broad readership, still the best-known example of this literature as well as the first text analyzed in this study: Gerchunoff's *Los gauchos judíos* (*The Jewish Gauchos,* 1910; English translation, *The Jewish Gauchos of the Pampas,* 1955), first published beginning in 1908 in the prestigious Buenos Aires newspaper *La Nación.* Its sumptuous style reflects the ideal of the harmonious, self-consciously artistic prose inherent in Modernism, the dominant literary mode in contemporary Buenos Aires.

Los gauchos judíos offers, in its way, a participant's account of life in the colonies, where the author had spent his childhood: arriving from Proskuroff, Russia, Gerchunoff's family had first been assigned to Moisésville, later moving to Rajil in Entre Ríos province. Yet, two factors distance this retelling from the documentary realism one might associate with an involved witness to history. First, the lyricized version of life in the agricultural settlement is in startling contrast to the harshness of the actual events. The elegant prose portrays life on the pampas as the realization of a rapturous dream and as the way Jews could best become part of the Argentine nation's existence and the creators of Zion. The novel accords a complex poetic treatment to social realities not inherently amenable to such rhapsodizing. The commentary on *Los gauchos judíos* contained here will center on its insistent lyricization and the underlying motives of the rhetoric, rooted largely in contemporary Eastern European Jewish thought.

However, the element of artistic distortion tends to disconcert present-day readers less than does the deformation arising from the author's nationalistic ideology and acritically progovernment stance. The work assumes that the long-standing Hispanic Catholic population of Argentina are the hosts, whereas the new Argentines coming from Eastern European Jewry are guests who must take care not to disrupt preexisting national life with their alien ways. Russian Jews appear to be refugees sheltered by a magnanimous nation, rather than immigrants recruited from their longtime homes by representatives of various interested parties.

The glorification of Argentine immigration policy and its implementation is not surprising given the author's deep gratitude toward the nation and the circumstances under which his novel appeared. *Los gauchos judíos,* offered in homage to the Argentine nation on its centennial, could not do other than promote an agreeable vision of the country. By transforming the settlers' experiences to suit aesthetic and tendentious motives, *Los gauchos judíos* stands far from the artlessness of testimony (a point made plain when aging settlers began to write or dictate their recollections for the historical record). Further, the novel is so removed from the raw material that provides its subject matter because its author had distanced himself from his rural background, mastering the cosmopolitanism of Buenos Aires.

The urbanity of the novel as literary art and of its author as man of letters testifies to a shift already profoundly affecting Jewish Argentines and their place in the nation's life. Though *Los gauchos judíos* proclaims the mission of these new Argentines to be the tilling of the soil, Gerchunoff had to become part of the metropolis not only to write such a work but also to see it to successful publication. Inevitably, to participate fully in national life, this population would need to shift toward the capital, with its centralized resources for cultural activities, public affairs, and the achievement of visibility. Concentration in Buenos Aires was a prerequisite to Jewish entry into national cultural life, as seen in the route Gerchunoff traveled between the experiences described in his famous novel and the successful launching of that work.

In 1895, the young Gerchunoff left the settlements to make his way to Buenos Aires. There he held jobs in workshops and factories and was a street vendor. He came to the attention of Enrique Dickmann, a member of the active and prominent Dickmann family. The Dickmanns were the first

Eastern European Jewish Argentines to win major public office, albeit not as "identified" Jews, for the Socialist party opposed all religious affiliation. As the Dickmanns rose to national prominence, they continued to take an interest in the Jewish population of Buenos Aires and its most promising members. Although the concern of some publicly prominent Jews was with strengthening bonds of Jewish community, the Dickmanns were more eager to draw the group toward participation in socialist politics and the progressive cultural and literary scene.

It was Enrique Dickmann who brought Gerchunoff into the Socialist party and introduced him to its founder and leader, Juan B. Justo (1865–1928). Whereas Dickmann avoided the extremes of socialist antiparticularism, Justo took his antiparticularist and antireligious position to such an extreme that many of his statements on Jewish issues are difficult to distinguish from those of an anti-Semite. Its leader's excesses apart, the Socialist party had a clearly enunciated position on the role Jews were to play in national social history. Because of their relative sophistication—many were skilled industrial proletarians and had been exposed to contemporary radical tendencies—Jewish Argentines were considered especially useful recruits in building a progressive movement. However, their potential utility could be tapped fully only, according to this line of thought, if they were willing to leave behind their religious culture.[3]

The young Gerchunoff benefited from his connections with major non-Jewish figures on the leftist cultural scene: Francisco Grandmontagne, Alfredo J. Palacios, Roberto J. Payró, an important mentor, and Leopoldo Lugones (1874–1938), who would shortly gain a leading role in the cultural establishment and who would become Gerchunoff's most important mentor. In 1900, Gerchunoff began publishing humorous sketches in the widely distributed magazine *Caras y Caretas* (*Faces and Masks*) and developed a reputation as a lively, Bohemian asset to literary life.[4]

Admission to the writing staff of the elite newspaper *La Nación* in 1908, then considered consecration for a man of letters, distanced Gerchunoff from his youthful radicalism and high spirits. Gerchunoff was designated to write the official centennial portrait of Argentine Jewry through his friendship with Lugones, who took a profound, if erratic, interest in Jewish matters. As organizer of cultural commemorations, Lugones encouraged Gerchunoff to write a specifically Jewish entry; he himself was composing the *Odas seculares* (*Centennial Odes*, 1910), which celebrated in pastoral verse the nation-building labors of various ethnicities. Current-day readers may be troubled by Gerchunoff's and Lugones's appropriation of the immigrant experience to produce a likeness pleasing to the dominant group.

Nonetheless, one should consider that before these strenuously agreeable works, the only major Jewish character in Argentine literature was the sinister dealer Glow in *La Bolsa* (*The Stock Market*). The exact target of this 1891 novel by Julián Martel (1867–1896, real name José María Miró) has been the subject of critical debate: The work may blame Jews specifically for Argentina's involvement in high-stakes capitalistic ventures, or it may express a more general fear that new immigrant groups were coarsening, cheapening, and commercializing the nation.[5] Whether anti-Jewish or xenophobic, *La Bolsa* exposed considerable numbers of readers to a negative and pessimistic vision of immigrants and their impact on the country. Liberal Argentines, among whom Lugones then numbered, found such notions embarrassingly unworthy of an enlightened nation. The dogmatically celebratory centennial writings hastened to supplant this type of outlook with its inverse. Lugones, who had long been interested in Gerchunoff's simultaneous Jewishness and adaptability to mainstream ways, spotted the younger man as a useful source of positive and unchallenging images of Argentine Jewry.

The designation of Gerchunoff as the centennial figure of patriotic Argentine Jewishness raises a set of interrelated issues that, with the passage of time, have come to make the author seem problematic as a progressive force in the nation's cultural climate. With some necessary simplification, the problem could be summed up as follows: Had Gerchunoff, having achieved a prominence unprecedented for a Jew, become a writer and public figure more beneficial to the non-Jewish establishment than to the Jewish community for whom he appeared to speak? To raise this question is not to cast doubt on the decency of Gerchunoff's intentions. Those critics of his words and actions who have ventured to reconstruct the underlying motives have deemed Gerchunoff a sincere man led to regrettable stances by such factors as the "longing to join [the elite]" and the "misdirected sense of gratitude and loyalty to his adopted country," which Saúl Sosnowski diagnoses.[6] Leonardo Senkman has conducted the most detailed inquiry to date into the forces that impelled Gerchunoff to assume his various, and often tortuous, positions on Jewish Argentine issues. Though undisguisedly repulsed by many of this celebrated figure's statements and implications, Senkman finds Gerchunoff a well-meaning man struggling under such constraints as his perceived debt of loyalty to Lugones and the latter's insistence on a positive view of national matters.[7]

Intentions apart, words Gerchunoff wrote or spoke, considered together with the occasion of their publication or utterance, tend to suggest an author eager to reach and please a non-Jewish public. Looking at Gerchunoff's early career, one may be struck perhaps too easily by his reliance on the Hispanic Catholic establishment. Whereas this could suggest indifference to reaching the Jewish community and an obsession with winning the approval of a non-Jewish audience, the contemporary cultural resources available must be taken into account. Although it is true that Gerchunoff was an advocate of Jewish entry into mainstream cultural life, his integrationist beliefs were not the only motive for his early pattern of publication and association. At the time *Los gauchos judíos* appeared, Jewish cultural life in Buenos Aires had few coordinating organizations. Gerchunoff would have been hard pressed to reach a specifically Jewish readership of significant size. There were certainly many organizations within the contemporary Jewish community, but many of these were localized or were concerned with providing such services as burial or charity or with spreading utopian, socialist, anarchist, or Zionist thought. For example, the association that would later become the wide-ranging Asociación Mutual Israelita Argentina was, at its 1894 inception, simply the burial society; by 1940, when it became AMIA, it was the most important vehicle for coordinating Jewish Argentine philanthropic, educational, and other agencies and programs. During the 1900s and accelerating during the 1910s, larger associations began to form, in many cases to unite pockets of radicalized Jews into voting blocs and to maintain relations with the Socialist party, whose candidates often attracted such support. Yet cultural life lagged in its organization. The 1908 Federación Israelita Argentina, an attempt at coordination, illustrated in its short life the difficulty of such a task.[8]

Even such outlets as Yiddish newspapers, which now seem an inseparable part of the history of Jewish Buenos Aires, tended to serve limited functions—often advocacy of a political tendency—with the great community papers still to come. *Di Yidishe Tsaitung,* foremost among these (1914–1972), was yet to be founded by the active organizer and entrepreneur Jacob Simón Liachovitzky. *Di Presse* was founded in 1918 by Pinie Katz, who would become a friend and colleague of Gerchunoff's and who would translate *Los gauchos judíos* into Yiddish.

Publications in Spanish, more directly germane to Gerchunoff's case, had not yet come to include periodicals focused on Jewish affairs. Especially significant is the 1923 launching of the long-running weekly *Mundo Israelita,* whose famous editor—the philosopher, student of Jewish thought, and community leader León Dujovne—would become another close Gerchunoff associate.

Such notable magazines as *Juventud (Youth)* and *Vida Nuestra (Our Life)* would, during their relatively brief lifespans, perform an important service in bringing together dispersed sources and channels of information within the community.⁹ But in 1910, the city's fragmented Jewish population was difficult to reach by any means. The large umbrella organizations, which would later spread word of cultural and social activities and speak on behalf of Jewish Argentines, would emerge over the course of the century.

Even given the lack of Jewish outlets in the 1910s, Gerchunoff was not alien to a Jewish audience. One should be careful not to be too categorical in calling *Los gauchos judíos* a work for a non-Jewish public. It is true that Lugones initially promoted the novel through mainstream channels and that it explains Jewish allusions to its readers and omits any "ungrateful" mention of the less exalted motives behind the welcoming of immigrants. But *Los gauchos judíos* was an object of commentary in Jewish circles as well. The flourishing career of its author and his public statements were of great interest to members of the Jewish community who looked to Gerchunoff for representation.

Gerchunoff's desire to see Jews benefit from assimilation, and his fear lest the chance to join the Argentine nation be lost, motivated many of his actions and positions. A clear example was his unusually persistent reluctance to voice support for the Jewish state in Palestine. Gerchunoff was the most prominent contributor to Argentine public discussion of Zionism and related issues. Yet his anxiety lest he offend Argentine nationalists and his concern for the sensitivities of his non-Jewish public made him too cautious to represent the community with due force. For example, when the revived discussion of a Palestine homeland, culminating in the Balfour Declaration (1917), stirred fresh controversy over the issue of a Jewish nation or people, it was Enrique Dickmann, from his position as a Socialist party congressman and as the most prominent Jew in public affairs, who gave addresses defending the compatibility of international socialism with Zionism. Gerchunoff, with his wide influence in the cultural realm, maintained that Argentina should be the homeland for all except a few ultrareligious Jews. In the years to follow, Enrique and his brother Adolfo Dickmann, also a congressman and leading figure of socialism, frequently argued in favor of a traditionally situated Jewish homeland. Yet until the establishment of modern Israel, Gerchunoff either kept silent or held to the view that Jewish Argentines could best find Zion on Argentine soil.¹⁰

There were many signs that strict melting-pot ideology was losing the hold it had had during the period of massive immigration. For example, Justo, the Socialist party leader who was one of Gerchunoff's first sponsors and mentors, had set as policy that Jewish socialists renounce their religious or cultural identity; time proved, though, that this rigid principle could not be uniformly implanted on the Argentine Left. Socialist candidates often relied on members of Zionist associations who, though particularistic, constituted a valuable pool of voters with an understanding of the platform. The breakdown of the antiparticularistic line became especially evident after Alfredo Palacios's 1915 split with Justo's Socialist party and Palacios's founding of a variant Argentine Socialist party. Palacios was consistently friendly to the Jewish community, seeing in it a reservoir of advanced social thought. His version of socialism was distinguished, among other things, by a programmatic and well-articulated defense of Argentine Jews and a willingness not merely to draw support from but to express admiration for an ethnically marked group. This stance did not replace antiparticularism, but demonstrated an alternative.

Gerchunoff does not seem to have fully appreciated the relaxation of rigid assimilationism; as the 1920s approached, he was still cautious about any remark that might sound too categorically Jewish. Though Gerchunoff was extreme in his reticence, there were still good historical grounds for uncertainty. Jews had many reminders of their less than complete acceptance in Argentine society. One of the most deeply traumatic was the anti-Jewish violence of the Semana Trágica, the "Tragic Week" of 7–12 January 1919. These disturbances began with the repression of a strike at the Vasena metal-working plant and the government's efforts to cast blame on anarchist and socialist immigrants from Russia. *Ruso* (Russian) was a term popularly applied to all Eastern European Jews, and in the general perception, all Russians were easily imagined to harbor revolutionary tendencies. Vigilante actions quickly became widespread, resulting in the burning of Jewish-owned businesses and violence against members of the Jewish community. Lugones, as spokesman for Argentine culture, criticized the anti-Jewish actions but considered them no cause for profound concern. He pronounced them an anomaly, not part of Argentine life and unlike the anti-Semitism of the Old World. Gerchunoff's unprecedented success in penetrating mainstream cultural institutions put him in a good position to make a significant statement, but he was restrained in his comments. Even as Enrique Dickmann and many others denounced the events of the Tragic Week, Gerchunoff accepted Lugones's analysis and declined to acknowledge prejudice as a feature of Argentine society.

The events of the Tragic Week prompted many non-Jewish intellectuals, especially those of liberal or leftist tendency, to express public solidarity with the Jewish community and its right to distinctive ways. Such affirmations appear in the two issues (Nos. 7 and 8 of 1919) that *Vida Nuestra* dedicated to commentary on the still recent disturbances. Lugones and socialist leader Palacios were among the public figures who made a dual assertion by extending their support from the pages of a Jewish Argentine periodical.

Amid this widespread recognition by influential figures that the Jewish community needed special support, Justo found Argentine anti-Semitism no reason to diminish his attacks on Jewish particularism. In a famous position statement of 1923, Justo expressed offense at the request to write a piece for *Vida Nuestra,* which often solicited commentary from prominent non-Jewish figures on issues of concern to its readership. Justo responded with an editorial explaining why the invitation, and indeed why the existence of such a periodical, disturbed him. The resulting position statement, "Por qué no me gusta escribir en una hoja que se dice israelita" ("Why I Don't Like to Write for a Publication that Calls Itself Israelite") sums up the antiparticularistic stance that has long held its place on the Argentine Left.[11]

The delicate pioneering role Gerchunoff played underwent changes as more Jewish Argentines achieved national recognition in the arts and humanities. Though still anomalous in his membership in elite media and literary circles, he no longer bore alone such responsibility for exemplifying in his person the Jewish Argentine presence. Now Gerchunoff could serve as the most generally recognized member of a nucleus of prominent Jewish intellectuals and professionals concerned with leading the community toward a more polished and cultivated collective identity and toward better relations with the non-Jewish cultural and social organizations. Able to rely on Jewish colleagues for support and no longer singled out as the sole figure representing the community on the cultural scene, Gerchunoff began to relax, in various ways, his earlier rule that Jewish Argentines must live prepared to sacrifice their particularistic ways. His involvement with the Sociedad Hebraica Argentina, to be discussed shortly, and his fascination with figures from Jewish cultural history are two signs of this growing sense of freedom to be unmistakably Jewish in one's pattern of associations and intellectual style.

Despite the greater ease with which he publicly displayed his distinctively Jewish identity, Gerchunoff remained inhibited about voicing opinions that might stir fresh suspicion concerning Jewish Argentines' patriotism or their belonging to the nation. Eagerness to promote fraternity and to secure for the Jews a firm place in Argentine society led Gerchunoff to employ Christian references, even to Jewish audiences who at times found this accommodation disturbing. For all his impressive access to both elite and popular publics, his ability to speak for the Jewish population was marred by his persistent overstatement of the compatibility of Christianity and Judaism.[12]

Further complicating his situation, Gerchunoff maintained friendships with two non-Jewish cultural leaders whose views on national identity were undergoing confusing transitions. Lugones and the novelist Manuel Gálvez (1881–1962) were becoming staunch defenders of traditional Argentine values, that is, those from the Hispanic Catholic past. Both were moving toward spectacular renewals of their Catholicism and were growing politically conservative. Lugones would eventually, in the period leading up to his 1938 suicide, adopt an apocalyptic fascist vision. Yet both men retained from their progressive pasts (Lugones had been an anarchist and Gálvez a reform-minded liberal) the notion of including Jews in national life. Gálvez drew a friendly caricature of Gerchunoff in his 1922 novel *El mal metafísico* (*The Metaphysical Malaise*) and frequently considered, in both his narrative work and his journalism, what the Jewish presence meant to the nation.[13] Though Gálvez has been charged with perpetuating a number of stereotypical notions about Jews, he considered himself to be welcoming members of this recently arrived group into national intellectual and artistic life.

For purposes of this brief overview, the Jewish cultural figures who came to share the public attention that earlier had focused on Gerchunoff can be divided into two categories. Most generally known were the young writers and editors, most of them born around the turn of the century, whose primary association was with the Buenos Aires experimentalist and social literature movements of the 1920s. These literary newcomers, with their youthfully rebellious image, will be discussed during the presentation of César Tiempo (Israel Zeitlin), the most prominent Jewish participant in the movement. Gerchunoff developed friendly relations with this new cohort of writers; however, Gerchunoff's own writing only fitfully reflected the literary innovations of the young writers. He did strive to be part of the changing literary times, as shown by such actions as his 1931 resignation from the chair accorded him in the Argentine Academy of Letters. His belief that academy membership would imply an endorsement of unchanging use of language shows him to have understood at least part of the 1920s cultural rebellion.[14]

More similar to Gerchunoff in their image and actions were the distinguished intellectuals and professionals on whom the famous writer came to depend for support as he increased his involvement with the Jewish community and his liaison work between this group and the general cultural establishment. These associates of Gerchunoff's did not constitute an assemblage either as literary or as generally known as the youthful avant-gardists. Gerchunoff remained unique in his generation. He never had a contemporary creative writer from his background, although many of his Jewish colleagues, such as Dujovne, were in publishing.

Dujovne, who shared Gerchunoff's concern for ties between the Jewish community and non-Jewish intellectual and political figures, would become known for his diplomatic and learned persona and his ability to represent the Jewish community in many public roles, as well as for his editorial work. His essays and addresses, which continue to be reissued, provide valuable testimony to a style of thought and expression typical of the 1920s–1940s.[15]

In 1926 the Sociedad Hebraica Argentina was founded. Gerchunoff was among the number of prominent Jewish intellectuals involved with this project. He elicited expressions of support from many non-Jewish cultural figures. With his excellent network of intellectual friendships, and buoyed by the progressive 1920s intellectual culture, Gerchunoff was able to draw leading writers and thinkers. No earlier Jewish organization had approached the scale of the SHA or its extensive relations with major figures of national life. The encouraging presence of non-Jewish figures was a typical feature of the book-signing parties, commemorative events, and other ceremonial functions of the SHA. Gerchunoff's eagerness to make Jewish Argentine culture fully part of national life determined the SHA's orientation. Though the SHA was noted for the creative artists and performers associated with it, its administrative roster tended to be drawn from the liberal professions, from scholarship, and from the networks of finance and commerce. Its first president was Marcos Satanowski, an expert in commercial law who personified the original SHA plan by his success both in gaining access to the mainstream and in organizing Jewish community undertakings.

In recent times, the SHA has had a less than bold image, owing in part to caution prompted by resurgences of anti-Jewish activities, in part to what is sometimes perceived as an emphasis on local social life. Nonetheless, the public announcement of its initial premises—that Argentine Jews could be part of the nation while maintaining distinctive forms of community—was, for its time, a daring move requiring forethought and diplomacy. Also worth bearing in mind is the SHA's long record of preserving information concerning Argentine Jewry and Jewish issues generally; although its library is the most visible evidence of this effort, the SHA has also sponsored or cosponsored a number of research and documentation projects.

After the SHA was launched, Gerchunoff's bonds to the Jewish community became more clearly marked. In 1933 José Mendelsohn produced, with the author's cooperation, a Yiddish translation of Gerchunoff's novelized biography of Spinoza; the SHA published this version. There were other signs of Gerchunoff's lessened fear of provoking hostility by the public display of Jewish community ties. He published in such Jewish cultural journals as *Judaica* (1933–1946; Salomón Resnick, ed.), which stressed both world and national Jewish literature, and *Davar,* which appeared in 1945 under the editorship of Bernardo Verbitsky, a man Gerchunoff mentored and the third author considered in this introduction.

By the 1930s, Gerchunoff's career was less that of an imaginative writer than that of a statesman, giving addresses and carrying out liaison work between cultural agencies and associations. He continued to earn his live-lihood in journalism, much of his work consisting of brief items giving national and international cultural news, with fewer extended original pieces. He wrote many obituaries, salutations to visiting intellectual dignitaries, and words of homage for commemorative occasions—in short, texts meant to meet the needs of a given moment. With his prefaces to other people's books and his friendly book reviews, Gerchunoff at times seemed more eager to present lesser-known writers than to continue his own career.

Gerchunoff remained highly influential in the SHA, whose valuable library today bears his name. His son-in-law Manuel Kantor, himself a writer, became Gerchunoff's literary executor and oversaw the production of posthumous collections of occasional pieces.

* * *

César Tiempo (Israel Zeitlin, 1906–1980) is the second major figure of Jewish Argentine literature considered here. Tiempo is best known for his enthusiastic participation in the Buenos Aires literary avant-garde of the 1920s and 1930s. While still in his teens he helped to organize events for both the experimentalist and the social-literature factions of the decade's younger writers. In 1926 he perpetrated the famous Clara Beter hoax, convincing many among the literary public that he had discovered a pros-titute-poet and her collection, *Versos de una . . .* (*Verses of a . . .*), which quickly ran through five editions before the public learned that it was Tiempo's own work.[16] With Pedro-Juan Vignale, he coedited the 1927 *Exposición de la actual poesía argentina (1922–1927)* (*Exposition of Contemporary Argentine Poetry, [1922–1927]*), the historically valuable compilation of poetry and position statements by young writers of both camps.[17] He was editor of the social-literature *Vanguardia.* Self-consciously literary and cosmopolitan, Tiempo and his work clearly represent a later, more self-assured, moment of the Jewish Argentine experience. However, his is early work in an important sense. Tiempo still expended great effort to reassure non-Jewish Argentines that the Jewish immigrants were not an alien, incomprehensible, and potentially risky people residing in their country but rather were fellow Argentine patriots sharing a large number of characteristics with the majority population.

Tiempo had arrived at two years of age from Ekaterinoslav, the Ukraine, to live in Buenos Aires. Tiempo's father was known as a theatrically expressive man unable to retain a job for long; his mother was exceptionally literate. To maintain themselves, the members of this household took up, among other employments, acting, miscellaneous theatrical and newspaper jobs, and the printing and selling of books. This early background, intricately tied up with the city's cultural life, gave Tiempo a sense of sureness. He fascinated the avant-gardists by having at his disposal a repertory of cultural information new to them despite their typically elite education. Tiempo had little in the way of organized studies, whereas established men of letters, as indeed avant-gardists, usually had a high level of education; many held professional credentials.

Tiempo's cycle of Sabbath poems is his most sustained effort toward a new Jewish Argentine writing. This verse, centered on the topics of the Sabbath and Buenos Aires ghetto life, appears in four linked volumes published between 1930 and 1952. The publication dates are misleading, for Tiempo's Sabbath cycle was already making its impact in the 1920s as individual poems appeared. Even subsequent poems maintained their 1920s ambience through allusions to Buenos Aires as it had been during that decade. Of the collections, *Sabatión argentino* (*Great Argentine Sabbath,* 1933), the second work analyzed here, best coordinates all the heterogeneous aspects of the cycle: secular, pious, modern, traditional, social realist, and avant-garde.

The author's allusions range from the great Jewish sages and poets to such popular figures as Al Jolson and Charlie Chaplin. Tiempo was eager for the Jewish community of Buenos Aires to constitute a culturally aware and sophisticated public, drawing full advantage from a multicultural background. *Sabatión argentino* often urges readers to know world Jewish culture even while caught up in the life of the Argentine capital. An example is a much-cited poem in the 1938 collection *Sabadomingo* (*SabbathSunday,* also translatable as *SaturdaySunday*). "Arenga en la muerte de Jaim Najman Biálik" ("Harangue on the Death of Chaim Nachman Bialik") reproaches the Jewish community of Buenos Aires for its indifference to the landmarks of Jewish literature, here epitomized by the revival of Hebrew as a poetic language, and for its fixation on local social news. Tiempo posits an ideal community that enjoys neighborly intimacy and the easy pleasures of popular culture yet is able to appreciate the intricacies of Jewish cultural history and twentieth-century innovations. By extension, Tiempo promotes this goal for all those, whether Jewish or not, who have the pluralistic modern city at their disposition.

Although he could become fascinated with religious culture, like most prominent Jewish Argentine writers Tiempo was not formally religious and did not anticipate that his readership would be. He took care not to posit traditional Judaism's superiority to the Christian and secular culture with which it coexisted in Buenos Aires. The Sabbath poems celebrate the prospect, in the cosmopolitan setting of Buenos Aires, for interfaith and interethnic exchange. The thematic focus of the Sabbath was chosen, in great measure, because the consecration of one day of the week is common to Christians and Jews. Other shared characteristics, such as certain words and phrases of liturgical and biblical origin, appealed to Tiempo as recognizable to readers of both religious traditions. In emphasizing these common bonds, however, Tiempo never went so far as to assert, as had Gerchunoff, that Jews could accept Christian language and practices whose purpose was to affirm the messianic status of Jesus. He did not delude himself or his readers that essential differences could be willed away through good feeling.

Frequent allusions to real-world events mark *Sabatión* as poetry of the 1920s. This was the last decade of Argentina's sanguine progressive period, before the military coup of 1930 and the world depression undermined national confidence. The economy appeared solid, however fragile its underpinnings would prove, and open expression of ideas was taken for granted. Under these relatively relaxed circumstances, Tiempo called for the maintenance of whatever Jewish ways provided greatest personal satisfaction, together with a freedom to experiment in the culturally open environment of Buenos Aires. Tiempo's use of the term *ghetto* could have alarmed nationalists unwilling to see parallels between the situation of Jews in the Old World and their status in the New, where all citizens were to be strictly Argentine. The allusions to a ghetto, though, are complicated with irony, since the inhabitants were free to enter other parts of the city at will. Indeed, this anomaly is crucial to those poems that emphasize the inhabitants' excited forays in search of non-Jewish women and adventures off limits to the truly ghetto-bound Jews of Eastern Europe. Even as Tiempo's ghetto poems appeared in collections, Jewish residents once concentrated in particular blocks of Buenos Aires were already becoming dispersed. Tiempo's ghetto really refers to a stage in Jewish Argentine history: lower-middle-class Jews, now urbanized, establishing an ethnic enclave in Buenos Aires, still poor but sufficiently assured of survival to devote time to the frivolous pleasures of city life.

Tiempo the poet is seldom overtly a social critic, but his selection of subject matter implies a populist stance tinged with cultural radicalism. He is particularly eager to relax the constraints of decorum, typically tightened by authors uncertain of their welcome. Consider the limits of the expression of sexuality in the diffident *Los gauchos judíos:* young women settlers described with an emphasis on hearty wholesomeness rather than on any seductive allure. Tiempo's references to the element of flirtation inherent in everyday interactions and to explicitly forbidden behaviors have the lighthearted, bemused tone with which the avant-garde characteristically treated these sensitive issues. He joins the avant-garde's attack on the general primness of Argentine letters while demonstrating that writers need no longer be so cautious as to show Jews invariably as figures of dignity. He celebrates both classical and vernacular forms of Jewish culture, in contrast to Gerchunoff's preference for such elevated manifestations as biblical allusions and fragments of prayer-book Hebrew. Tiempo demonstrates enough assurance to display elements of Jewish culture concerned with show business, commerce, the skilled trades, and raillery. The use of Yiddish—a language strictly unacknowledged in *Los gauchos judíos*—is perhaps the foremost sign of Tiempo's daringly informal populism.

On the whole, Tiempo's poetry moves toward a sense of freedom to be as Jewish as one wishes without fearing to seem less than Argentine. Yet the poetry is characterized by omissions and reticences that betray its genesis in uncertain times. Most notably, the existence of Argentine anti-Semitism is nearly denied, putting the best face on interethnic matters. Tiempo recognizes the poverty of the Jewish ghetto, but he treats it with unremitting cheer.[18]

Sabatión's extraordinary optimism may have resulted both from the spirit of the age and from the ease with which its author had gained access to the sparkling cultural high life of 1920s Buenos Aires. Tiempo was constantly on stage as a representative of Argentine Jewry. His creative writings and public statements were subject to scrutiny by observers eager to monitor the Jewish community's satisfaction with Argentina and willingness to join mainstream national life. Implications concerning the status of Jews in Argentine society certainly abound in Tiempo's poetic representation of the ghetto, and readers were quick to draw inferences on this topic. Reading between the lines and second-guessing were invited by the poetry's tantalizingly oblique and metaphorical allusions to a matter of widespread concern and curiosity: the relation of the new Jewish population to Buenos Aires. Tiempo's reluctance to offer direct statements on this set of issues was not simply the result of caution or uncertainty, though these may have been factors. The 1920s avant-garde held that any social commentary in literature should be masked and unobtrusive.

Though the literary public perceived Tiempo as the paradigmatic Jewish figure of his generation, he was by no means isolated, as the young Gerchunoff had been. There was a sizable Jewish contribution to the 1920s scene, with its avant-garde and social-realist movements and new surge of interest in foreign literatures. Several of the Jewish participants were known more for their editing and publishing than for their writing. Manuel Gleizer, through the publishing house that bore his name, brought out editions of innovative and sometimes difficult-to-promote works. He was closely associated with the Florida group of experimental writers, whom he befriended and promoted through his publishing house and bookstore. Gleizer published works, both Jewish and non-Jewish, that he considered in the forefront of current literary and social thought. He ran a special series, "Jewish Topics," of both imaginative writings and essays on Jewish issues by an international selection of authors. He was one of Gerchunoff's publishers in the 1920s, brought out the 1930 *Libro para la pausa del sábado* (*Book for the Sabbath Pause*) by Tiempo, and published the first reissue of *Los gauchos judíos* in 1936. Samuel Glusberg (1898–1987; also known as Enrique Espinoza) directed the publishing house B.A.B.E.L. (Biblioteca Argentina de Buenas Ediciones Literarias). Although chiefly known as an avant-garde concern, B.A.B.E.L. also reached out to Jewish authors and readers. For example, throughout the 1920s B.A.B.E.L. maintained titles by Gerchunoff in its catalogue.

Glusberg's creative writing won notice in 1924 with the publication of his *La levita gris* (*The Gray Frockcoat*), "Jewish stories set in Buenos Aires" as the subtitle characterizes them. Among these are stories centering on issues of special concern to contemporary Jewish Argentines. One narrative deals with the situation of the Jewish child in a classroom in which Catholic religious instruction is compulsory; another chronicles the life of a hard-working immigrant, culminating in his killing in the 1919 disturbances. In contrast to this critical view, the lyrical, patriotic celebration of Jewish immigrant life characterizes Glusberg's *Ruth y Noemí* (*Ruth and Naomi*), which B.A.B.E.L. published in 1934.

Glusberg was a part of the now legendary camaraderie of 1920s Argentine literary life and was a friend of such luminaries as Lugones and Ezequiel Martínez Estrada. He and his brother and colleague, Santiago, were famously supportive of the imaginative but troubled short-story writer Horacio Quiroga. The tabloid *Martín Fierro* (1924–1927; Evar Méndez, ed.), crucial to the avant-garde, had Glusberg as printer and technical advisor. Jacobo Samet, who flourished in the same period, published a number of avant-garde poets. Many other Jewish men of letters contributed to 1920s literary activity through their expertise in editorial work and the book trade.

The most profoundly avant-garde of the Jewish poets of this generation is Jacobo Fijman (b. Bessarabia, 1898; emigrated to Argentina, 1902; d. 1970). He first emerged as one of the poets associated with *Martín Fierro* and with the search for new metaphors. However well he fit in with the 1920s youth movements that renewed literary Buenos Aires, Fijman stood out as being more personally than aesthetically fixated on irrational juxtapositions and images. His attraction to the extremes experienced by Christian mystics and to their metaphorical conventions, as well as to the writings of the church fathers and the scholastic philosophers, led to his 1929 baptism. Whereas Fijman's move toward Catholicism may seem a bizarre action, spectacular conversions and renewals of piety were a relatively common occurrence in contemporary cultural life, as witness the celebrated examples of Lugones and Gálvez. Indeed, Fijman entered religious instruction with close friends, though his Jewishness and difficulties in dealing with life made his case more complex. He became progressively disorganized and was hospitalized during his last years (1945–1970), in part simply as a way of caring for the now destitute and unemployed poet. Fijman is the prototype of Samuel Tessler, the wild, sarcastic, and critically aware philosopher of Leopoldo Marechal's famous novel *Adán Buenos-ayres* (1948).

Fijman produced only three collections of poetry: *Molino rojo* (*Red Mill*, 1926), *Hecho de estampas* (*Made Up of Images*, 1930), and *Estrella de la mañana* (*Morning Star*, 1931). Until the 1960s movement to rediscover neglected figures of Argentine literature, Fijman was for many years scarcely more than a legend of literary Buenos Aires. In the late 1960s, the poet Vicente Zito Lema sought out Fijman and persuaded him to break his long silence. Zito Lema's edition of his tape-recorded sessions with Fijman appeared in 1970 as *El pensamiento de Jacobo Fijman; o, el viaje hacia la otra realidad* (*The Thought of Jacobo Fijman; or, The Journey to the Other Reality*), the poet's only expression during his last four decades. This collection of aphorisms, self-explanations, and free-form meditations encouraged readers to look for the overall program of ideas that unifies Fijman's writing.

It is too easy to view this poet's work as simply a prolonged attempt to deal with disturbed thoughts and images and an obsession with religion. Fijman's metaphorical innovations, his cryptic pronouncements, and his efforts to reach the mystical side of Catholicism from a Jewish basis all can look demented and chaotic. Nonetheless, the effort toward a new mystical expression provides the orienting principle of the poetry. As Zito Lema has emphasized, Fijman's experimentation was organized by an identifiable system of thought. Of the issues raised by Fijman's life and work, that of his Christianity continues to be one of the most complex. Clearly, many of the elements of Fijman's mystical poetic language were patterned on the work of Catholic poets, especially St. John of the Cross. Yet Fijman emphasized to Zito Lema that his conversion had in no way diminished his Jewish self, and he gave as one of the clues to his thought "el misterio de la unidad divina" (the mystery of divine unity) whose source was "el pueblo de Israel" (the people of Israel).[19]

In another area of 1920s innovation, that of theatrical experimentation, Tiempo's friend Samuel Eichelbaum (1894–1967) especially deserves mention as a prominent creative figure who maintained certain Jewish elements in his public identity. He followed the development of Jewish culture and on occasion wrote on Jewish themes, although he is associated more with the theatrical depiction of psychological states. His 1926 play *Nadie la conoció nunca* (*No One Ever Knew Her*) touches on the prostitution of Eastern European Jewish women in Buenos Aires, the anti-Semitism that surfaced during the Tragic Week, and the eagerness of some Jews to mask their origin. These themes come together in the story of an elegant kept woman who, shaken by her lover's participation in the anti-Jewish actions of 1919, reveals her past as a poor Jewish prostitute.[20] A less-noted Eichelbaum play from the same year, *El judío Aarón* (*Aaron the Jew*), also features a Jewish protagonist forced to confront issues of identity when those around him display anti-Semitism.

More readily associated with Jewish subject matter is Lázaro Liacho (Jacobo Simón Liachovitsky, 1898–1969), the poet and essayist who gave a classically bucolic treatment to the idea of the Argentine interior as the site of the new Zion in *Siónidas desde la pampa* (*Odes of Zion from the Pampa*), collected in 1969 with his *Sonata judía de Nueva York* (*Jewish Sonata of New York*).[21] At the same time that Liacho spread a pastoral vision of Jewish immigrant life in one thematic current of his verse, in another mode he celebrated the long-standing *criollo* culture of Buenos Aires, maintaining the biculturalism that characterized his career.

Carlos M. Grünberg (1903–1968), who held a degree in philosophy and one in law, was one of the first of the university-educated, professionally trained Jewish intellectuals to come to prominence in Argentina. Grünberg, one of Tiempo's generation of younger, experimental poets, was probably the most identified with Jewish Argentine themes. Grünberg's verse of the 1920s and 1930s typically laments the disadvantages suffered by Argentine Jews. Yet his verse cannot qualify as social criticism in any comprehensive sense, since anti-Semitism is treated in isolation from the tensions that bring it forth in a society. In 1940 Grünberg's Jewish-theme poems were issued as a volume entitled *Mester de judería* (*Minstrelsy of the Jewish People*), to which Jorge Luis Borges wrote an encomiastic preface.[22] As do many early Jewish Argentine texts aimed at a general audience, this work vigorously expresses loyalty to the Argentine nation and asserts that Jews find it a worthy home. A number of poems reassure the reader that however persistent the signs of anti-Semitism are in the here-and-now country of Argentina, these lapses do not represent or diminish the view of Argentina as the *patria* or homeland.

In a notable shift of outlook, Grünberg's 1965 collection *Junto a un río de Babel* (*By a River of Babel*) expresses a sense of not belonging to any land.[23] It reflects Grünberg's disappointment over the years that had elapsed between the two books of poetry. Despite his enthusiastic work as an advocate and official spokesman for the state of Israel, Grünberg publicly acknowledged that he could never feel at home there. The poems reiterate with nearly obsessive insistence an inability to overcome the feeling of foreignness, either in Argentina or in Israel.

The drive in the 1920s to break away from the publishing industry's predictable patterns of acquisition, in which French literature dominated the lists of translations, was aided by the new knowledge brought by Jewish editors, translators, and consultants. Slavic and Germanic languages, with their associated literatures, were naturally more apt to fall within the expertise of literary intellectuals of Eastern European background. Grünberg, for instance, translated the work of Heinrich Heine, a poet who enjoyed a considerable vogue in *entreguerre* Buenos Aires, owing partly to the efforts of Gerchunoff. Max Dickmann (1902–), whose social realist novels were the subject of much commentary during the 1930s, specialized in the translation of English-language works, including the still less-than-prestigious writings from the United States. In the previous generation, Gerchunoff, Dujovne, and Katz were active in the spread of Germanic- and Slavic-language literatures. In addition to these and other celebrities, many less-visible Jewish Argentines carried on the translation and liaison work that made Buenos Aires an international literary capital. Spanish-to-Yiddish and Yiddish-to-Spanish translation became, of necessity, a local specialty.

Tiempo, in particular, had a hand in the selection and preparation of foreign acquisitions. He was involved in the editorial effort to spread the discussion of contemporary social thought, often limited to immigrant and, in many cases, Yiddish-language circles, to a broader Spanish-language population. Interest in these tendencies and the literary work that reflected them had been heightened by the reorganization of Soviet society. Tiempo collaborated with radical publishing concerns toward this end. The dramatic events in Soviet society and the great vogue of the new "proletarian" literature (translations from both the Russian and the Argentine social literature promoted by the Claridad publishing house) were relayed to the Argentine public in part through Tiempo's efforts.

Tiempo's combination of editorial, journalistic, theatrical, and creative skills enabled him to flourish through the 1930s, when fewer could live from cultural activity and when experimental writing was less in favor. During this period, Tiempo continued to publish collections of the Sabbath poems, with their typically 1920s ambience and manner, but his commentary on the present day appeared in his work for the theater. Because Tiempo was identified as a representative of both Jewishness and literary daring, and was visible to diverse publics, his new undertakings of the 1930s often elicited responses symptomatic of attitudes toward the Jewish presence in Argentina. An example is the controversy stirred by Tiempo's 1933 play *El teatro soy yo* (*I Am the Theater*). The topic of ethnic and racial prejudice here appears through the story of a black playwright and his Jewish rival. It is a complicated, meditative play that generates a number of statements about racial and ethnic prejudice. The Jewish playwright learns, among other things, that blacks, whose "otherness" is evident, suffer graver disadvantages than Jews and that she should take pride when her work is cited for its embodiment of a Jewish outlook. Seen from a present-day perspective, the work seems tentative in presenting the issue of Argentine anti-Semitism. Nonetheless, a number of critics at the time reacted strongly to the very suggestion of prejudice in Argentina. Senkman's survey of contemporary reviews shows that, in both Jewish and general-public periodicals, commentators were eager to deny the existence of or the severity of Argentine anti-Semitism.[24] Such refutation, which often dominates the reviewer's response to the play, reflects the persistent belief that Argentina would offer a new beginning and a melting pot to all peoples and testifies to Tiempo's daring in suggesting otherwise.

With the emergence in the 1930s of fascism and renewed anti-Semitism, a number of Jewish leaders and intellectuals began to show a greater readiness to admit publicly that the Argentine Jewish community needed special care and advocacy beyond the general protection offered by the pluralism of the national melting pot. The DAIA, Delegación de Asociaciones Israelitas Argentinas, founded in 1936 as an umbrella association through which Jewish groups could express concern over anti-Semitism, evolved from the 1933 Comité contra el Antisemitismo y el Racismo, with Simón Mirelman as president. Whereas the original committee's purpose was to oppose European anti-Jewish activity, the organization soon focused on Argentine problems as well. In 1935 it assumed its present name as a sign of concern over matters in the New World. The aim of this large, active group is to encourage sensitivity to needs and entitlements of Jewish Argentines and Jewish populations elsewhere. It has taken up such issues as Israel, incidents of anti-Semitism, and compulsory Catholic instruction in the public schools. Historically, this organization has been more cautious in its criticism of anti-Jewish occurrences within Argentina than elsewhere. This pattern reflects a reluctance to contradict the long-favored belief that there could be no Argentine anti-Semitism, though the decadent influence of the Old World could contaminate the New.

In 1937, Tiempo provoked another rush to interpret his statements about the role of Jews in Argentine society. The occasion was the success of his play *Pan criollo* (*Homegrown Argentine Bread*), which won the National Theater Prize and enjoyed a notable run. This work shows a Jewish judge accommodating to the absorption of his family by the larger society. The central character suffers crises of assimilation: his daughter marries a Christian, and Jewish litigants in his court face difficulties in adapting to the Argentine environment. Nonetheless, it was the protagonist's ultimate acceptance of assimilation that left the greatest impression. The play was greeted as an endorsement of the need to abandon Jewish particularism to enter fully into national life. It is notable that Tiempo's earlier, much less sanguine dramatization of a similar theme, the 1935 *Alfarda* (an archaic word for penalties levied from the Jewish population of Moorish Spain), failed to achieve the wide success of *Pan criollo*.[25]

In 1938, Tiempo set forth his frankest statement yet on anti-Semitism. In a pamphlet published by *Mundo Israelita*, Tiempo responded to two novels of 1938, *El Kahal* (*The Kahal*) and *Oro* (*Gold*), that had seized the popular imagination with lurid fictional revelations of a vast Jewish conspiracy. Alarmingly, these novels were the work of Gustavo Martínez Zuviría (1883–1962, pen name Hugo Wast) a solid member of the establishment. The notion of a worldwide Jewish conspiracy followed a pattern of defamation already familiar from European fascism and *The Protocols of the Elders of Zion.* The title of Tiempo's response, *La campaña antisemita y el Director de la Biblioteca Nacional* (*The Anti-Semitic Campaign and the Director of the National Library,* 1938), pointed to a deliberate and organized anti-Semitism, not the isolated outbreaks of interethnic tension widely cited as the motive for the Tragic Week some twenty years earlier, and to the disturbing fact that the anti-Jewish novels were known to be the pseudonymous work of the director of the National Library. In fact, from this post and his seat in the Argentine Academy of Letters, Martínez Zuviría drew a prestige that augmented his power as a writer with a mass readership. He was also able, both as an elected legislator and as a political appointee, to exercise governmental power. In 1943, Martínez Zuviría would assume the cabinet post of Justice and Public Schooling, which he would use to strengthen compulsory instruction in Catholic doctrine.

The polemical reply to Martínez Zuviría marks the virtual end of Tiempo's boldness as a writer. From the early 1940s onward, he grew involved with the burgeoning Argentine film industry, for which he wrote or co-wrote a great number of screenplays. His essays and journalism became whimsical and nostalgic. Only one more significant work appeared, the 1955 *Sábado pleno* (*Full Sabbath*), completing the cycle of Sabbath poetry. Its date of publication, though, suggests that it was one of the numerous previously composed works belatedly made available in the 1955–1956 rush to display pluralistic and critical views. This and other effects of the 1946–1955 Peronist regime, with which Tiempo maintained affable but guarded relations, will be discussed in the characterization of the 1940s and 1950s Jewish Argentine intellectual culture. On the whole, Tiempo steadily drew away from activities that could enmesh him in public debate and conflicts, leaving this endeavor to the next generation of discussants.

* * *

The third work analyzed, the 1941 *Es difícil empezar a vivir* (*It's Hard to Start Living*) brought in this new wave. The first novel of Bernardo Verbitsky (1907–1979), it reflects the uncertainty and questioning that marked Argentina as the 1930s wore on without improvement in the economic or political climate. *Es difícil* brought Verbitsky to prominence as a novelist, won him the Losada Prize, and helped the Jewish-theme Argentine novel to move away from an acritical and often ahistorical vision of society. However, it would be a mistake to think of Verbitsky as a figure of harsh opposition. A literary critic for some time before *Es difícil*'s publication, he always discussed Gerchunoff and his literary work with approval and respect. His own career, though, brought him considerably less into contact with powerful, often nationalistic-conservative cultural leaders than was the case with Gerchunoff or Tiempo. Verbitsky's wide appeal was based partly on his view that the traditional elite had faltered in its pursuit of European high civilization and had allowed the country to sink into economic depression and a stagnating military government. He represented the tastes of a socially conscious readership revolted by excessive gentility.

Verbitsky presented an alternative to the genteel critics of the past not by a more aggressive or polemical tone but largely by virtue of the authors on whom he chose to focus. During the 1920s, European literature concerned with formal innovation tended to receive considerable attention in Argentina, whereas only certain movements and works of socially conscious writing had previously roused the interest of Argentine critics. Verbitsky ranged widely in his search for social criticism in literature. He built on the 1920s vogue for Russian and Soviet writing to expand Argentines' awareness of literature written in Russian. Among native Argentine enthusiasts of this writing, he was one of the few to read it in the original and keep current on Soviet cultural life through readings and travel. In Argentine literature as well, Verbitsky, essentially a realist, had a pattern of preferences. Formal experimentation or stylistic brilliance carried less weight than ability to provoke insight into human character and society.

Although Verbitsky's essays show his vision of society and its problems, he does not articulate this understanding in his novels. Instead, he takes readers through his characters' struggles to perceive the pattern of social history in the confusing welter of events. A typical Verbitsky hero is sensitive to and deeply affected by the grave and disturbing news with which the media assault him. Such characters gradually emerge as critical thinkers as they take a skeptical look at the accepted account of how Argentine, and world, society functions. This novelistic design, evident in the work examined in this study, can make Verbitsky's writing look tentative, since his characters are seldom confident in their assessment of society. Nonetheless, these hesitant and tongue-tied protagonists often are blundering toward a new freedom to criticize. For example, the hero of Es difícil, through his vacillations and missteps, is learning to question the assimilationism that is unthinkingly practiced in his environment. The late thirties shake his belief that anti-Semitism belongs to the past or to nations less progressive than Argentina.

Verbitsky's novelistic career overlapped those of several other prominent writers with concern for social ethics and with Jewish backgrounds that only occasionally surface in their work. Max Dickmann, mentioned earlier, with his socialist position and concern for immigrant proletarians, continued his extraordinarily lengthy and productive life as a realist novelist. Samuel Eichelbaum, cited as a member of the 1920s theatrical scene, remained active, still mixing psychological exploration and realistic presentation of social environments. These long-standing figures were joined by newer contributors to Argentine social writing. For instance, Bernardo Kordon (1915-), like Verbitsky, observed an Argentina that had lost its ability to offer opportunities to newcomers. These realists treat issues that are part of but not exclusive to the Jewish experience in Argentina: the relations of immigrants and their Argentine-born children; the shift of the population from rural areas to the city; the difficulty of maintaining a professional or artisan's status during the depression. Only here and there in their writings do these questions directly entail that of Jewish identity.

Kordon's short story "Kid Ñandubay," collected in his 1971 *A punto de reventar* (*Just About Had It*), exemplifies the way in which social realism made Jewish subject matter serve to convey more general statements about society.[26] Its protagonist is a second-generation Jewish Argentine who, during the thirties, finds no place in the working class and becomes an itinerant boxer. Because of his childhood experiences of anti-Semitism and his conviction that a boxer should have an aggressive "homeboy" persona, the hero fights under a name suggesting both U.S. popular culture and the much mythified indigenous past. Kordon's story follows Kid Ñandubay through a crisis, brought on by late-1930s anti-Jewish activities and by diminishing earnings and status, that impels him to reclaim his name. With the name restored, the boxer begins to regain his dignity and to see Jewishness as compatible with a hardy and rugged image. The point made about Jewish identity remains ancillary to a statement concerning the need for critical thought. To recover, the boxer must abandon the notion that unquestioning capitulation to the prejudices of his society might bring him into the land of opportunity promised to immigrants.

Another example is Pablo Palant (1914-), the dramatist and lawyer whose 1939 play *Jan es antisemita* (*Jan Is an Anti-Semite*) not only helped to secure his reputation as a social dramatist but also was important as a public statement of concern over the rise of anti-Jewish activity. This message play is in essence a warning against racial and ethnic bias, with Jews the timely case in point. There are possible explanations for the low frequency of Jewish allusions in the works of these social writers. The authors may have been uncertain of their ability to make bold and frank statements about the situation of Jewish Argentines, or uncertain of their readers' willingness to absorb such assertions. Perhaps more likely, given contemporary progressive social thought, is that these writers chose to concentrate attention on problems whose origins lay in the class structure and the distribution of material resources rather than on problems of a particularistic group. Every movement toward realism in literature includes an agenda of topics considered most urgent. The treatment of specific ethnic and religious groups was not in the program of Argentine social literature. Only with authors born in the 1940s does one find a belief that the specific treatment of Jewish identity could further, rather than detract from, the analysis of unfolding social history.

Verbitsky's Jewishness became more evidently a part of his literary career when, in 1945, he was named editor of *Davar,* the journal produced by the Sociedad Hebraica Argentina. Editorial policies reflected in many ways the SHA's double emphasis on Jewish cultural unity and relations with mainstream figures. Under Verbitsky's editorship, *Davar* included imaginative writing as well as discussion of Jewish issues. As was usual SHA policy, the participation of distinguished non-Jewish intellectuals was encouraged. One result of this policy was that *Davar* became a valuable repository of literary treatments of Jewish themes and characters by Argentine writers who were not themselves Jewish.

Although it is common to think of Bernardo Verbitsky as the novelist and his brother Gregorio as the journalist and historical essayist, the former continued all his life to write and edit literary journalism, editorials, reflections on politics, and other nonfiction work. Working for the paper *Crítica* (*Criticism*), he provided much relied-upon reportage on cultural affairs. Having been a student of law, medicine, and literature at various times, he was well acquainted with the university system and was able to comment on the often intricate issues of university governance and educational policy. New developments in Argentine political culture, especially efforts to supersede traditional parties and campaigning, occupied his attention. A present-day reader, surveying Verbitsky's essays and literary journalism, may find them difficult to appreciate as being groundbreakingly progressive. Though coherent in his own social thought, Verbitsky is slow to criticize the contradictions of others and tends to praise even confused and inconsistent writers, so long as a desire to show social problems is evident. He showed a respect for elders—most notably, for Gerchunoff—that would today be astonishing from a discussant of Verbitsky's youth and political convictions. Only in the post-1955 period does one find extensive public criticism of Gerchunoff from Jewish Argentine writers, who, willingly or not, are his heirs. In comparison to the more aggressive manner of the post-1955 generation, Verbitsky's approach seems uncertain. Nonetheless, the choice of authors treated and the relative attention accorded writers of pronounced social tendency constitute a dramatic statement.

Verbitsky assumed the editorship of *Davar* as a crucial period was getting under way. No account of twentieth-century Argentine life can omit mention of the 1946–1955 presidency of Juan Domingo Perón. Peronism is notoriously difficult to characterize by allusion to other political systems because it is so intricately bound up with the specifics of Argentine history and with two individuals, Perón and his charismatic wife, Eva. The long period of Peronist rule affected Jewish Argentine life and letters, and all other national matters, in ways that remain difficult to assess. Peronism's positive and negative effects on the Jewish community provide an inexhaustible theme for debate. With its populist programs and determination to redistribute national wealth and open high posts to nonelite appointees, Peronism won support from Argentine Socialist party members, Jewish and otherwise, who had grown impatient with the latter group's progress in transferring power from the country's elite to outsider groups.

Yet despite isolated cases of pro-Peronism, on the whole Jewish Argentine intellectuals, like their non-Jewish counterparts, had an uneasy time under Peronism. (Tiempo's editorship of a Peronist-owned publication, the most public link between Perón and a Jewish intellectual, has excited decades of rumor and conjecture.[27]) Perón had poor relations with the intellectual community for a number of reasons, the most important being his administration's inhibiting effect on open discussion. Fearing reprisals or the many forms of censorship, most writers were careful either to exclude their opinions on public affairs from their work or to convey them through allegorical and allusive modes. Given this set of circumstances, it is understandable that Argentine imaginative writing and essays of this period should be poor in direct critical discussion of social problems. However, *Davar* and *Comentario* (1952–1971) treated a variety of matters, with emphasis on the Jewish contribution to current culture.

* * *

The post-Peronist era is represented by the noted 1962 novel *Dar la cara* (*Making a Stand*) by David Viñas (1929–). Viñas has been a public figure since his twenties, setting a new style of hard-hitting social criticism and polemic and writing influential works of history, literary studies, fiction, and theater. He first made his name as a leader in the student anti-Peronist underground. In 1953, he founded and coedited *Contorno* (*Context*), the magazine that came to emblematize a generation of aggressive young intellectuals and their confrontational, or—to use the designation that Emir Rodríguez Monegal popularized—*parricidal,* criticism.[28]

After Perón's fall in 1955, Viñas quickly emerged as the most charismatic young contributor to the newly open discussion of social problems. He organized and headed the Argentine Movement of National Liberation, intended to move beyond traditional party politics. These public activities gave him a high visibility; his bluntness, undisguised anger over injustice, and criticism of national cultural heroes aroused controversy on many occasions. His two main goals were a revisionist interpretation of the nation's development, including the growth of its literature, and the maintenance of a climate of open intellectual discussion. He was quick to recognize that his personal identity and history summed up sensitive aspects of Argentine society, and he accordingly made rhetorical use of his image. Important features included his half-Jewish status, his identification with the Jewish tradition of dialectic and disputation, and his evaluation of social history against ethical standards. However, Viñas's individual distinctions were less significant than the new critical tendency he signaled.

The writers associated with *Contorno* were not predominantly concerned with Jewish matters, although Jewish Argentines were well represented in the group's composition. Rather, the parricides' massive effort to understand the processes at work in the formation of Argentine society entailed the examination of Jewish issues. Of particular interest were the relations of the Jewish population both with the long-standing *criollo* (that is, of Iberian ancestry) elite and with those working- and middle-class non-Jews with whom the Jews directly interacted and competed. The point of this type of discussion was to obtain an overall picture of Argentine society and of the rival groups striving for access to wealth, power, and status. The question of Jewish identity and its maintenance became part of the larger issue of becoming aware of the historical processes at work in society and avoiding a mindless accession to them. For example, Jewish traditions of critical social thought and commentary were considered valuable as an alternative to the Argentine liberalism that the parricides distrusted. Assimilationism came in for harsh questioning because of the ideological presuppositions it contained and helped to mask. However, an interest in Jewish ways and concepts as such was little encouraged.

Viñas's interpretation of Argentine history includes the idea that the country's Jews, as other less-prestigious immigrants and their descendants, are in a special position to question its development as a nation, once they overcome their hesitancy to speak out. He has drawn attention to the significance of the 1880s and 1890s, when elite liberalism became entrenched and immigrant workers were sought. For the descendants of these Jews to raise issues about the dogmas of the late nineteenth century and the results is a doubly meaningful act of assertion. In 1958 Viñas brought these ideas together in a novel that gave him a major literary success and brought a great deal of controversy. *Los dueños de la tierra* (*The Owners of the Land*) provides a thorough challenge to official interpretations of Argentine history. It succeeds, among other things, in broadening what has sometimes been isolated as "the Jewish question" into one aspect of the analysis of the nation's development. This celebrated novel relates an anarchist-led ranch hands' strike in the far south of Argentina. Immigrant groups appear both among the strikers (radicalized newer Spanish emigrés, Italians, and Jews) and among the opposing forces—the government representatives and the landowners (Germans and British). The heroine represents the secularized Eastern European Jewish intellectual, dedicated to critical analysis of society and culture. This background enables her to identify the Radical government's bad faith in dealing with the striking ranch workers. Her husband, schooled in traditional Argentine values, has great difficulty comprehending the collusion between government and ranchers. The novel, in effect, recommends that Argentines develop the critical scrutiny of social arrangements that is a hallmark of the politicized forms of Eastern European Jewish thought. The work contains a graphic reminder that Indian tribes were exterminated to make way for "advanced" immigrant populations. Hence all the currently competing factions—including the scions of long-established Hispanic families—are relative newcomers vying for the benefits of the land. The novel offers an unambiguous political analysis and interpretation of the events surrounding the Patagonian strikes, with special emphasis on the roles played by groups of varying ethnic origin and date of immigration.

The 1962 *Dar la cara,* the novel discussed in detail here, reflects Viñas's support of the Radical presidential candidate Arturo Frondizi and his disappointment over the latter's post-victory compromises and party politics in general. The aggressive realism of this novel breaks many of the conventions of good taste that had been widely observed in Argentina's sometimes surprisingly prim literature. Its rough language is a statement of entitlement far exceeding that found in Tiempo's poetry. Both in its choice of thematic material and in its novelistic construction, the work serves to heighten awareness of the cultural contradictions of the society under critical scrutiny. It not only brings social and cultural problems to the fore and diagnoses them but also proposes a detailed historical interpretation of their origin. Its analysis of national perplexities includes examination of the confusion surrounding Jewish identity.

Around the time *Dar la cara* was published, the outlines of Viñas's literary activity altered. Previously he had been known as the author of lengthy realist novels containing fairly explicit, discursive explication of Argentine history. Though he continued to produce novels, Viñas increasingly turned to other forms. His 1964 *Literatura argentina y realidad política* (*Argentine Literature and Political Reality*) launched the reaction against Gerchunoff's centennial version of Jewish Argentine history. The rhetoric employed might seem more fiery than required to reveal the idealizing, progovernmental tendencies of a novel without pretensions to realism and unabashedly part of a patriotic celebration. Yet such force was, in a sense, called for, considering the hold the novel's vision still exerted. For many years, Argentine intellectuals had refrained from criticizing a work with which they could scarcely be in sympathy. A persistent vein of writing has perpetuated the rosy outlook of 1910, as witness the dates of such Gerchunoff-style works as Natalio Budasoff's 1962 *Lluvias salvajes* (*Savage Rains*) and Pablo Schvartzman's 1967 *Cuentos criollos* (*Downhome Argentine Tales*), the latter exceptionally euphemistic in its suppression of evidence of ethnic conflict.[29]

The move away from the centennial version of events did not necessarily take forms as vehement as Viñas's work. A gently lyrical corrective to Gerchunoff's work appears in the novels *Dios era verde* (*God Was Green*) of 1963 and the 1967 *Pueblo pan* (*People of Bread*) by José Chudnovsky (1916–1966).[30] Chudnovsky, who was from Gerchunoff's area, had grown up hearing of the events narrated in *Los gauchos judíos*. He brought to the task of retelling this story a revisionist's sense of history. For example, *Los gauchos judíos* transforms the murder of Gerchunoff's father by a drunken gaucho into an occasion for understanding acceptance; Chudnovsky reminds readers that the Jews lynched the murderer. In his frank new version, immigrant settlement is a profitable as well as an idealistic undertaking, with Jews delivered to designated sites by labor-contracting agencies. Though full of such reminders of the exploitation, grief, and disappointment immigration entailed, the novels suggest that a hard look at the past can initiate a reinvigoration of Jewish Argentine life.

During this period, a work of theater succeeded in arousing discussion of Jewish interpersonal issues in contemporary national life. This drama was the 1964 *Réquiem para un viernes a la noche* (*Requiem for a Saturday Night*), the widely debated drama by Germán Rozenmacher (1936–1971).[31] *Réquiem* drew attention not only because it showed Rozenmacher to be a young Jewish-theme playwright of promise but also because it highlighted the sensitive issues of intermarriage and abandonment of Jewish observance by a younger generation. In this case, Sabbath ritual makes no sense to a young man who has taken up his peers' habit of socializing on weekend evenings. The father's struggle to return his son to Jewish ways succeeds only in convincing the young man that Judaism is constraining and repressive. By the play's end, the young character is announcing with relief his intention to marry a young Christian woman and to place even more distance between himself and the ritual requirements of Jewish law.

As Sosnowski has noted, Rozenmacher's play in many ways denigrates the maintenance of Jewish ways. Though the father is shown with sympathy, his notion of how a Jew should live appears abhorrently dull, and Jewish family life has little appeal.[32] When writing analyses of Argentine political culture, Rozenmacher was quick to identify unexamined assumptions and their ideological implications. Yet he brings little of this critical awareness to his literary treatment of Jewish themes. Sosnowski suggests that this disturbing separation is symptomatic of Rozenmacher's general inability to see Jewish life as part of, and as an eloquent sign of, the nation's social history or, indeed, to see himself simultaneously as a Jew and as an Argentine. Despite these negative features, the work was frequently performed in Jewish centers, seeming to attest to a general shortage of contemporary cultural works capable of sparking discussion over the central dilemmas of Jewish life in Argentina. The work would have been more effective for this purpose, though, if it had raised a larger question than the family conflict presented: What social forces would drive young people like the hero of *Réquiem* to perceive their inherited traditions as a stigmatizing burden?

Rozenmacher also produced a number of short stories; as Sosnowski's analysis shows, he began to move away from the facile rejection of Jewish life. His early death in a motor accident prevented further extension of the path he appeared to be taking toward a more comprehensive view of Argentine Jewry.

In the discussion of public affairs, Jewish issues assumed sudden prominence at various moments during the 1960s. For example, Adolf Eichmann's 1960 apprehension in Buenos Aires, with the resulting friction between Argentina (whose officials complained of lack of due consultation) and Israel, raised a flurry of commentary. A longer-running and more thoughtful debate occupied the politically aware public during the last years of the 1960s and the first half of the 1970s. A fresh outbreak of the old polemic over the compatibility of Zionism, or "particularism," and a progressive political position was rekindled by the Six-Day War of 1967. The Israeli occupation of previously Arab-held territory, together with the newly popularized concept of a Third World struggle for liberation from capitalist and capitalist-backed countries, gave rise to a massive questioning of the propriety of liberal and leftist support for the Jewish homeland in Palestine.

The most obvious effect of this shift in the political climate was the spread of a new variant of anti-Zionism based on the association or equivalence of pro-Israeli sentiment with colonialism and a desire to see capitalism penetrate the Third World. However, the debate over Zionism almost inevitably entailed the old question of whether Jews' loyalty to their cultural identity might not interfere with their ability to perceive universal questions of social justice. In Argentina, there was a suddenly renewed distrust of the retention of what might be considered markedly Jewish behavior and outlook. Increasingly, associations and coalitions on the Left pressed Jewish colleagues to disassociate themselves not simply from the defense of Israel but from their Jewishness. As the rhetoric escalated, concern over the occupied lands and their inhabitants escalated to anti-Zionism, antiparticularism, and in some cases outright distrust of Jews. Jewish intellectuals on the Left were driven to devise rejoinders to demonstrate that Jewish thought should properly augment, rather than diminish, a progressive stance on social issues. A line of critical argumentation developed, eventually producing such essays as those carried in the journal *Nueva Presencia* (*New Presence*; 1977–1981, 1983–). Nonetheless, many Jewish Argentines, especially younger ones and those immersed in campus life, capitulated to contemporary trends and detached themselves from the Israeli cause and their own cultural identity.

Among the parricidal critics was León Rozitchner (1924–). Rozitchner merits discussion here for his 1967 essay *Ser judío* (*To Be a Jew*), a stimulus to thought and commentary on the situation of Jewish Argentines and the reflections on the general society.[33] The essay combines existential thought with an essentially Marxist examination of social history and the new concern with colonized attitudes. Developed during the post-Peronist ferment of social criticism in Argentina, the arguments presented in *Ser judío* continue to be stimulating to discussants seeking a larger historical framework for Jewish Argentine issues. *Ser judío* is, among other things, an assertion of the Jews' entitlement to be part of Argentine national life and of national territory. Rozitchner observes that when he is singled out as "a Jew," distinct from the scene around him, he is made discontinuous with national territory. He then can claim as his own no more than the room taken up by his own body. He must regain the right, enjoyed by others, to belong to the land and to extend his space beyond his physical self.

Rozitchner owes a clearly acknowledged debt to the Tunisian Albert Memmi (1920–), known for his engagement of Jewish social ethics with such present-day issues as cultural autonomy and dependency.[34] *Portrait d'un juif* (1962; English translation, *Portrait of a Jew*, 1971), and even more so his further commentary in the essay *La Libération du juif* (1966; English translation, *The Liberation of the Jew*, 1966), not only are models for situating the "Jewish question" as part of overall social history but also are especially interesting as treatments of Jewishness in a society removed from areas that are thought of as centers of Jewish culture. Though it was Rozitchner who expanded Memmi's concerns and applied them to the Argentine context, he was by no means an isolated case of influence. Memmi's *La Libération du juif* provoked considerable discussion in Argentina; Argentine editions of this and others of his essays have been successfully marketed by firms aimed at a general intellectual reading public (Ediciones de la Flor) and by those with a typically Jewish distribution (Candelabro, Ediciones O.S.A.).

From the same generation of social critics as Viñas and Rozitchner is Juan José Sebreli, editor of the 1968 *La cuestión judía en la Argentina* (*The Jewish Question in Argentina*).[35] Although this work is an anthology of diverse texts with little critical commentary, the selection indicates the issues that concerned these writers. The debate on the Left over whether Jewish identity diminishes dedication to socialism receives substantial attention. Sebreli also displays examples of old-line Liberal rhetoric, with its unquestioned assimilationism and expressions of confidence in Argentina's ability to transcend the ethnic conflicts of the Old World. Right-wing nationalism and its extension into anti-Semitism also appear in the exemplary texts. Notably lacking is a type of writing that would fully emerge only during the 1970s: meditations on Argentine society that reveal an interest in Jewish identity, thought, and outlook uninhibited by anxiety over appearing narrowly parochial or, to use the long-standing word, particularistic.

Of the many contributors to Zionist discussion, two of the most prominent were literary men: Verbitsky and the psychoanalyst and writer Marcos Aguinis (1935–). The Six-Day War and new anti-Zionism spurred Verbitsky to a vigorous effort that spilled over from his public statements and journalism to his fiction. His efforts to reconcile Israel's new situation in the Middle East with his general outlook appear in his journalistic writings and public remarks. Readers of Verbitsky's novels can gain an idea of his polemical exertions from his 1972 *Etiquetas a los hombres* (*Labels on*

Men). It contains long, dialectical exchanges in which a Jewish intellectual representing the old Left defends Israel against the fashionable, unexamined anti-Zionism of the young.

Marcos Aguinis enters the debate from a considerably different background. He brings to his work a much cooler analysis of historical processes and an application of psychoanalytic thought. Like Rozitchner, he is influenced by Albert Memmi. Aguinis works with many of the parricide ideas but is as tactful as the parricides were aggressive; he is the great diplomat of progressive Jewish social thought in Argentina. He has especially sought to spread an understanding of the idea of a Jewish homeland in Palestine, using the terms most current among younger discussants. In essays and fiction that examine the Palestine question, Aguinis reviews the history of this uneasy region and points out that a number of parties—capitalist, socialist, and nonaligned nations among them—have had occasion to benefit from the perpetually volatile situation. Aguinis develops a view of the matter that is sympathetic to the Palestinian Arabs, whom he considers to have been poorly treated by both European and Arab countries, but that at the same time retains the principle of Israel's right to exist.

There is a common purpose to Aguinis's novel *Refugiados,* first published in 1969 and reissued in revised form in 1976 as *Refugiados: Crónica de un palestino* (*Refugees: The Chronicle of a Palestinian*), and his 1974 essay *La cuestión judía vista desde el Tercer Mundo* (*The Jewish Question Seen from the Third World*). Through critical argument and the presentation of historical evidence, these two works defend the idea of a Jewish homeland in the Palestine area (though not necessarily all actions taken by Israeli officials) to those uncertain of its validity.[36] At the same time, these writings provide readers already sympathetic to Israel with an articulate set of arguments for their position. The novel has as its narrator a young displaced Palestinian on scholarship in Europe. He falls in love with a young woman whose early history is intricately involved with the Holocaust and the founding of the modern state of Israel. Through his friendship with her and with a learned mentor, he comes to perceive modern Israeli history as part of, rather than an impediment to, the struggle for Third World liberation. The work's lengthy dialogues reflect the conflicting world opinion over the Six-Day War and Israel's changed relations with its Arab neighbors. The essay is not only about conflicts in the Middle East, however. It is also about how to sustain an Argentine position that might be considered Jewish or pro-Jewish in a political culture grown hostile to such an outlook. Aguinis was concerned that intimidation might prevent Jewish Argentines, and others who might support Israel's right to exist, from stating their views.

* * *

The last four works studied in detail were chosen to show the diversity of Jewish Argentine writing as the 1970s progressed. The first two are by poets: José Rabinovich (1903–1978) and José Isaacson (1922–). The work of the immigrant Rabinovich, even after crossing over to a Spanish-language readership, represents a historic Yiddish-language literature and journalism in Buenos Aires, preserved in the 1970 *El violinista bajo el tejado* (*The Fiddler Under the Roof*). Isaacson, of Sephardic ancestry, stands out for his skillful composition of Jewish-theme verse and his integration into mainstream Argentine poetry. His 1977 *Cuaderno Spinoza* (*Spinoza Notebook*) exemplifies veiled, allusive forms of social commentary often published under constraining circumstances.

José Rabinovich was born near Bialystok, West Russia (later Polish national territory), a center of transportation and commerce and hence of the fusion of cultural and ideological tendencies. He emerged from an intellectual scene in which Yiddish was the operant medium and discussion drew freely on both religious and secular forms of thought. However dramatically respect for Yiddish culture has risen in recent years, the intellectual framework and rhetorical style on which *El violinista* relies are coming to require preservation, increasing the importance of Rabinovich's work as testimony to a cultural milieu and an intellectual style. The collection of his poetry examined here includes texts that comment, as would a newspaper editorial, on contemporary events, as well as on issues of a more meditative and timeless nature. This poetry, though original to Rabinovich, shows a readily identifiable set of cultural sources: interpretive and moralizing commentary on texts and anecdotes, rabbinical-style disputation, biblical conventions of speech (the prophetic harangue), and the passionate debates about society that once characterized Eastern European intellectual life.

Rabinovich emigrated to Argentina in 1924, remaining until his death. He first came to the attention of literary figures through his poems, short stories, and journalism published in *Di Presse* and other Yiddish outlets. Today his name evokes an era when Buenos Aires harbored an active, still youthful Yiddish cultural scene with lectures, musicals, melodramas, revues, commemorative celebrations, polemics between political tendencies, and such fabled celebrities as the actress Berta Singerman. Although there is documentation through such institutions as the YIWO (Yidisher Wisnshaftlecher Institut) Archives and Library, the Yiddish culture of 1920s–1940s Buenos Aires is known largely through legend.[37]

Rabinovich is the most famous Argentine Yiddish writer, but he owes his fame to his successful crossover into Spanish-language letters. Argentine realists of the early 1940s discovered him, admired his direct way of infusing literature with social commentary, and persuaded him to reach out to a Spanish-language audience, first through a translator and then by writing directly in Spanish. Since the proletarian literature movement of the 1920s, realists had worried that Argentine social-consciousness writing was too literary, that is, too lyrical, picturesque, and concerned with aesthetics. Rabinovich brought a bluntness more typical of oral disputation, editorials, open letters, and other nonliterary forms. Not only was his style of commentary, dialectic, and disputation new to Spanish-language Argentine letters, but so also was his use of these undisguised forms of rhetoric in poetry and narrative prose.

Rabinovich was overtly interested not only in the uses of Jewish expository style but also in Jewish characters as representatives of society's disadvantaged strata. A characteristic concern in Rabinovich's prose and poetry is the ability of outcast groups to withstand the humiliations society inflicts. The title of his *Tercera clase* (*Third Class*), the 1944 collection of short stories promoted by the social realists, hints at one aspect of this theme. Many of the characters in these narratives have, after years of degrading treatment, come to feel that they are inherently third class; they have ceased to demand a more dignified status and better conditions. The narrators and characters of these stories, however, are explicit in attributing this defeatism to, among other factors, the long history of Jewish persecutions.

Although such treatment of Jewish themes is among the most evident features of Rabinovich's work, his admirers among the social realists were little concerned with ethnicity, celebrating instead the discovery of a proletarian writer. Elías Castelnuovo and his colleagues took a great interest not only in the social class of Rabinovich's characters but also in the class background of the author. He incarnated the ideal, widespread among the Russophile social realists, of a radicalized industrial proletarian. Senkman places Rabinovich as part of the wave of Jewish Polish proletarians and craftsmen who, beginning in the 1920s, entered the Buenos Aires labor force in such areas as the manufacture of textiles, garments, and furniture and the printing trade. These arrivals were characteristically from such highly industrialized cities as Lodz, Warsaw, or Krakow (the last, in Rabinovich's case) and were sophisticated in their skills and knowledge.[38] More than any previous type of immigrant, this skilled laborer fit an image the social writers had admired in Russian literature: the industrial proletarian who, if not radicalized, was at least familiar with socialist-anarchist thought.

Moreover, Rabinovich was still a member of this group while producing the literary work that so interested the social realists. Ricardo Baeza's 1947 introduction to the Spanish version of Rabinovich's *Los acusados* (*The Accused*) draws attention to the circumstances of its composition, with its author working long hours setting type and only writing on Sundays and holidays.

The particular emphasis of the social realists gave Rabinovich the image of a writer concerned only with the documentation of social realities, and it turned attention away from his form of expression. Critical discussion of his work tended to make Rabinovich's literary activity, whether short stories or poems, more socially than artistically important. Luis Emilio Soto, for example, notes Rabinovich's "piercing realism" and foregoes discussion of the author's mode of presentation in favor of consideration of the subject matter.[39]

The realists' discovery of Rabinovich as a proletarian cultural worker launched his career in Spanish-language letters but did not sustain public interest for long. It was not until the late 1960s that Rabinovich's work had a second discovery and a flurry of new and reprinted editions. To these rediscoverers, Rabinovich no longer appeared as the street-corner agitator that the realists had promoted. Now interest arose in his ability to represent, through his subject matter and rhetorical style, a nearly lost portion of cultural history. There was a greater acknowledgment that Rabinovich possessed a fund of cultural information acquired through study, whereas his radicalized outlook received less attention. Rabinovich's freethinking humanism seemed, with the passage of time, more likely to produce nostalgia than revolution. His work began to appear in such publications as the literary supplement of *La Nación,* known to favor cultural and aesthetic issues over social ones.

The 1960s revival of interest in Rabinovich has several implications. On the one hand, it is a move away from the often scant representation of diasporic culture in Jewish education in Argentina and, in many cases, in the presentation of Jewish culture to the non-Jewish public. Yiddish and Eastern European Jewish culture have been important in real life, but their significance has often been downplayed in favor of the more prestigious traditions of Palestine-area antiquity. This tendency was exacerbated with the founding of the state of Israel and the establishment of modern Hebrew, which could then supplant the already faltering Yiddish in Jewish education. It becomes inherently a populist statement to extend recognition to a poet rooted in local Yiddish journalism with its fiery editorials, invective-filled debates, and impassioned responses to current events.

Rabinovich's renewed acclaim may also be linked to what Dorothy Seidman Bilik calls post-Holocaust consciousness, referring to concern over the loss of cultural resources. Such a preoccupation, in the literary world, is expressed by giving high significance to the unique ways of European Jewish immigrants. Rabinovich promoted a strengthening of interest in the preservation of Yiddish culture. Bilik states that "renewed concern for the Jewish immigrant and immigrant-survivor reflects the delayed expression by Jewish American writers of a post-Holocaust consciousness."[40] As the significance of the events became clear, so did the importance of Jewish ways and traditions that were in danger of extinction.

In his last major undertaking, Rabinovich appears to have recognized and validated the more aesthetic and cultural concerns of his second wave of Spanish-language readers. The boyhood memoir *Sobras de una juventud* (*Leftovers of a Youth,* 1976) gives an insistently unsentimental account of early-twentieth-century Jewish Russian life. Rejecting the popular idealization of a unified, pious *shtetl,* Rabinovich takes care to note the diverse and often improvised Jewish life in the region near Bialystok where he spent his youth. His own family included Jews who either were simply not religious or developed their own forms of piety outside religious law. These freethinkers excited his admiration but so did the rabbinical thought also found in the family. Rabinovich, moving away from his image as a realist indifferent to expressive questions, in this work publicly considers the sources of his style. Though essentially a freethinker, he learned cantoring and biblical recitation and with them the stylistic conventions of biblical discourse. His account of how this expressive tradition can convey secular meanings helps to illuminate his own poetry, whose adaptation of biblical modes will be examined in detail in the chapter on Rabinovich.

José Isaacson in *Cuaderno Spinoza* (*Spinoza Notebook,* 1977), which presents its statements in an artful and allusive form, raises the issue of a masked, cryptic approach to social and cultural commentary. The inclusion of a work by Isaacson in this study might, at first glance, seem to represent a turning away from the critical frankness that distinguishes some of the most notable Jewish Argentine writing. Yet subtle and covert commentary on social and cultural issues characteristically accompanies an era of great caution—as indeed was the case here.

Argentine political life had become progressively disorganized following the victory of one of Perón's loyalists in the presidential election of 1973. Perón himself had come back from exile, and he assumed the post quickly vacated by the winner but was too infirm to regularize the new government. After his death in 1974, his widow, Isabel, presided until 1976 when the military instituted its rule, alleging a state of national emergency. The years of this second Peronist regime featured relatively little inhibition of the expression of ideas and encouraged a climate of intellectual experimentation. Difficulties arose not from official constraints but from the social disintegration whose most disturbing sign was the rise of guerrilla militias specializing in urban actions, as well as right-wing vigilante, parapolice, and paramilitary operations. The diverse factions resorting to political violence generated a chronic state of undeclared or, in the contemporary phrase, "dirty" war.

These circumstances did not result in such obvious consequences as the massive exile of intellectuals, particularly Jewish intellectuals, that occurred during the subsequent military regime. Yet they made it difficult to practice social criticism drawing on the resources of Jewish thought. The Radical Left continued to distrust signs of Jewishness, associating them with Zionism and hence with imperialism, as well as with a possible check on revolutionary loyalty. If identifiably Jewish style was often suppressed among social critics, so was social criticism among those identified with the Jewish community. Jewish Argentine associations had long been cautious in commenting on national affairs, and the disorder of the early 1970s and the subsequent repression exacerbated this tendency. The community, aware of the widespread tendency to equate Jewishness with dissent, pursued a strategy of attempting to distance and disassociate itself from the crisis wracking Argentine society. Though understandable, this effort cannot be considered very efficacious, since the Jewish population, especially young adults, proved exceptionally vulnerable during this period, constituting an especially high proportion of the suspected subversives who were detained and later disappeared. The postface to this study, which examines exile literature during the military regime and the writing that accompanied redemocratization, considers the attempt to remedy this unnatural separation of critical social thought from Jewish cultural life.

In 1977, the year of *Spinoza*'s publication, the American Jewish Committee announced that it was forced to close its office in Buenos Aires because of anti-Semitic activity. The undisguised preoccupation with problems of personal identity and with their aesthetic expression in *Spinoza,* published amid the terror and disorder of Argentine society, suggests the refuge taken in private concerns. Moreover, Isaacson's public persona as a man of letters lacks a confrontational, challenging style, tending instead toward the comfortable integration into establishment circles sought earlier by the prototype of an undisturbing cultural Jewishness, Gerchunoff. For example,

Isaacson is a regular contributor to the *La Nación* literary supplement, in which *Los gauchos judíos* originally appeared.

These very considerations are reasons to examine Isaacson's poetry of this period. It would be misleading to suggest that forthright criticism is the only route open to the further growth of Jewish Argentine writing. The alternative, flying under essentially establishment colors while delivering a diffuse and veiled set of comments, also continues to serve well certain purposes. Isaacson remained in and published in Argentina during a period when frankness about questions of public concern was ill-advised. This circumstance distinguishes Isaacson's approach from that of contemporary exile writers. *Spinoza* provides such strategies as an ostensible retreat into private obsession; these can help maintain a conduit for critical reflection and discussion.

The examination of Isaacson's work also offers a salutary reminder that poetry, including the skilled and refined poetry that wins Isaacson mainstream acclaim, continues to be a vehicle for the expression of beliefs about and attitudes toward real-world problems. The explicitness of recently prominent novelists, especially Mario Szichman (1945–), Alicia Steimberg (1933–), Gerardo Mario Goloboff (1939–), and Pedro Orgambide (1928–) in the second part of his career, owes much to the conventions of their chosen genre, in which a great deal can be stated "in so many words." Steimberg, Cecilia Absatz (1943–), and Nora Glickman, whose work began to win notice in the 1970s, will be discussed in this introduction along with Szichman. Work by Goloboff and Orgambide is discussed in the postface along with that of others whose writing careers flourished somewhat later.

Spinoza is an apt text to read because its avowed subject matter— Isaacson's thoughts on reading Spinoza—raises the suspicion that writing is a way of treating issues one can neither confront nor dismiss. Isaacson takes Spinoza's words as a displaced statement on the Sephardic past, the varieties of diaspora, the outcast status, and the relations between the individual's cultural identity and the well- or ill-functioning social mechanisms that should allow this identity to coalesce. In so doing, he invites in turn a similar between-the-lines scrutiny of his own poetry. Isaacson's reliance on cryptic allusions and metaphors inevitably also stands for a contemporary reticence, and the need for it, that have become painful to remember.

Of interest too is Isaacson's public persona. He has characteristically worked within organizational patterns in his participation in both the literary world and Jewish community activities. He has contributed to the poetic scene not only by his own work but also with anthologies of Argentine poetry that help to consolidate readers' understanding of the traditions and innovative tendencies at work. His cooperation with organized Jewish efforts is typified by his work on yearbooks of the Argentine community (see bibliography). This persona makes Isaacson distinctive among the recent Jewish Argentine writers examined here, the others all assuming, in various ways, alienated or countercultural stances.

* * *

The last two writers selected, both born in the mid-1940s, provide a remarkable contrast. Marcos Ricardo Barnatán (1946–) is a writer concerned with formal experimentation and subject matters that may seem too ethereal to permit social commentary. Part of the interest of his work, though, is that on examination it reveals profound continuities with Argentine literature and, in its oblique fashion, generates statements about Jewish tradition and its possibilities as part of modern culture. The work of Mario Szichman is indicative of the paths being taken by other young Jewish Argentine writers. It is Szichman who clearly continues, adapted to a new generation, Viñas's project of reconsidering, through fiction, the patterns and motivations behind Argentine social history.

Marcos Ricardo Barnatán might seem to be, of the eight authors, the one least concerned with the issues whose treatment is traced in this study. To cite an obvious biographical circumstance, Barnatán, born in Argentina in 1946, has lived primarily in Madrid since 1965. His novel discussed here, the 1971 El laberinto de Sión (The Labyrinth of Zion; the first in a trilogy including the 1973 Gor and the 1982 Diano), portrays a Jewish Argentine family whose shifts of residence have weakened its attachment to real-world countries, leaving only a mythified homeland in Jewish Spain. Whereas the other authors refer to social history, Barnatán prefers to speak overtly only of the development of cultural forms. His historical understanding of society is expressed in oblique ways that are easy to overlook amid the apparently ethereal aestheticism of his novel, as is the case with poetry. Adding to the effect of detachment from Jewish Argentine issues is the image Barnatán presents, that of an otherworldly individual disengaged from public issues in order to pursue art and veiled forms of knowledge.

Nonetheless, Barnatán is a Jewish writer, and an Argentine one, in ways that justify his inclusion. First, it is important to recognize that commentary on Jewish Argentine issues can arise from a novel that is oblique in its reference to real-world matters and that is wide-ranging in its cultural allusions. (The similar case of Mario Satz, born in 1944 in Argentina and a resident of Spain since 1976, will receive brief consideration in the post-face.) Second, Barnatán covers aspects of the Jewish Argentine experience seldom touched on by authors more easily identified with this subject matter. Together with Isaacson and Humberto Costantini, he is one of the few writers to supply a Sephardic subject matter little presented in Jewish Argentine writing. Reconstruction of the Sephardic past, often fragmentary and interested accounts, has been a significant and delicate task for scholars and imaginative writers in Spanish-speaking countries. In *El laberinto de Sión,* Barnatán has joined this effort through an exceptionally risky experiment, working with information he clearly does not have under expert control and using as much gossip and speculation as he does verifiable material. By the author's own testimony, the 1971 novel was an extreme case of construction out of uncertain and incomplete information; he wrote it at a time when his knowledge of Kabbalah was tenuous indeed.[41] The resulting precarious web of hearsay and imaginings contrasts with the documentary foundation relied on by authors treating Eastern European immigration.

Barnatán also touches on other less-noted aspects of the Jewish Argentine experience: for example, that many immigrants to Argentina, far from constructing Zion or "making America," found only a provisional home. Further, Barnatán treats Jewish elites, who fail to interest either early authors with a sentimental, populist concern for the perseverance of the Jewish poor or later ones eager to study Jews as a group struggling up the class ladder.

Particularly interesting for this study, which traces the slow overcoming of inhibitions on the part of Jewish Argentine writers, is Barnatán's willingness to draw attention to those aspects of Jewish history most apt to be perceived as exotic and alien to mainstream ways. One should appreciate the distance traveled from Gerchunoff's and Tiempo's anxious efforts to reassure Christian readers that Jews are transparently similar to the dominant population, uncomplicated by hidden lore or intricate private codes. In contrast to this display of wholesomeness, Barnatán conflates his literary Judaica with the oracular revelations of the pagan mystery cults and the black knowledge of medieval necromancers. His collections of poetry, the 1973 *Arcana mayor* (*Major Arcana*) and the 1984 *El oráculo invocado* (*The Oracle Invoked*), place Jewish-theme texts under volume titles referring to dangerous secrets, whereas *Diano,* the last novel in the trilogy, is boldly named to evoke the hermaphroditism prized by devotees of mystery cults.

In his relation with the literary tradition too, Barnatán represents certain tendencies deserving attention. Of the eight authors, he is the only one to draw significantly on the Bohemian subcultures of this century and to give countercultural qualities to his literary version of Jewishness. An expert on such movements as *fin-de-siècle* decadence, the Beats (whom he has anthologized), and late-1960s street culture, Barnatán has merged these currents with certain subcultural aspects of Jewish life, such as the schools of Kabbalism and the Jewish theatrical milieu of the *belle époque*.

Barnatán's literary criticism also confirms his belonging to Argentine letters. His understanding of the possible meanings of Jewish identity is closely tied to his way of reading and discussing Argentine and, more generally, New World writing. Barnatán has written several commentaries on the work of Jorge Luis Borges, emphasizing how the latter recognizes literature's debt to forms of Jewish thought (see bibliography). Although Borges, famous for giving Argentine literature a Kabbalistic tinge and for popularizing Jewish themes, has most often drawn Barnatán's critical scrutiny, Barnatán's other efforts as a critic and anthologist also tend to portray literature as a transformation of mysticism.

Barnatán's literary concerns also indicate a preoccupation with the New World's perspective on the long-running cultural continuities of Europe and the Eastern Mediterranean. In this respect too, Borges has been his essential reference, with other Latin American and U.S. writers also coming in for study. Such a shift of attention toward the Americas, often occurring in subtle ways, is typical of Barnatán's novel as well. Despite the frequency of European settings, characters who are unproblematically European arouse little interest, whereas transatlantic figures and the culture they devise for themselves offer considerable material for exploration. In showing European scenes as registered by immigrants doubly transplanted, Barnatán is altogether part of Argentine literature, a valuable source of commentary on the New World's reencounter with the Old. The expatriate Barnatán is the only one of the eight authors studied to bring this set of concerns to Jewish Argentine literature.

In Barnatán's literary vision, Latin American new narrative becomes itself a way of extending mystical concerns into the realm of aesthetic elaboration. *El laberinto de Sión,* as a work of imaginative writing with an implicit element of literary criticism, promotes the notion that Latin American *nueva narrativa* bears such a resemblance to Jewish linguistic mysticism as to provide a point of entry for those seeking an initial understanding of this occult tradition. The coming together of Barnatán's Kabbalistic preoccupations and his distinctive perception of Latin American narrative expression is the focus of the reading of *El laberinto* included here.

* * *

Mario Szichman has been chosen to represent those fiction writers who, in works published during the 1970s and 1980s, have been unflinchingly frank in their depiction of Jewish Argentine life and the social forces that have shaped it, at times unattractively. For these authors, of whom Gerardo Mario Goloboff and Alicia Steimberg are also prime examples, exposure of less than admirable aspects of the Jewish presence in Argentina reveals the social processes being played out as Jews were first entering various sectors of national life. Having barely attained access to prestigious forms of livelihood and association, the Jewish characters throw themselves into a frenzy of contradictory behaviors, alternating mimicry of Christian ways with an awkwardly sporadic retention of Jewish patterns. Goloboff, early known as a poet, would eventually integrate the above-described concerns, among others, into one of the most accomplished works of 1970s exile literature. This outstanding text, the 1976 *Caballos por el fondo de los ojos* (*Horses in the Depths of the Eyes*), will be discussed in the postface along with other eloquent writings of exiled intellectuals.[42]

Part of this examination of Jewish life in Argentine society came from women writers able to present a fresh view through the eyes of articulate, disillusioned female characters. Of these women, Steimberg is the most clearly established as part of contemporary Argentine writing. Whether directly engaged with Jewish issues or not, her writing has been exceptionally able to represent the contemporary moment, both in its formal construction and in its insights into society. She embeds her critical commentary in seemingly pitiless revelations concerning the lives of women in middle-class Jewish Argentine households. Especially distinctive are two novels—*De músicos y relojeros* (*Musicians and Watchmakers*) and early passages of *Su espíritu inocente* (*Your Innocent Spirit*)—giving the outlook of a girl who is precociously wise to the maneuvers of the women she observes yet is childish in her confusion over growing up Jewish in a Christian environment.[43] In the former novel, the sharp-eyed child narrator details the advantage-seeking rules that determine when the women of her family disguise traits distinguishing them from non-Jewish contemporaries and when they display these features. Games of one-upmanship between Jews and Christians and between those who play down their Jewishness and those who emphasize it come in for an undisguisedly resentful portrait. The result is an aggrieved refutation of the mindless celebration of ethnic and religious diversity. The 1981 novel shifts the scenario in which cultural and religious identity is stage managed, concentrating on the child as she presents herself to teachers and schoolmates. Its first sections relate an elaborate masking of her Jewish background to rise in the hierarchy of her school.

Another participant in the frank depiction of Argentine Jewish family life is Cecilia Absatz. She has developed a distinctive female variant of the first-person account of postimmigrant Jewish Argentine life. Although her success in mass-circulation magazines and her sometimes flippant tone might seem to mark her as a "pop" writer, she has developed original texts composed of narratives by worldly-wise—to the point of being jaded—urban Jewish adolescent girls and women. Absatz, who has a long record in women's magazine work, made her name known when she launched and edited the first *Playboy*-type magazine in Argentina, *Status*. She quickly became known as an exponent of a less-decorous norm of expression. Her own work draws attention to itself for its uninhibited exposition of the confused sexuality of female adolescents, especially in the title story of the 1976 *Feiguele y otras mujeres* (*Feiguele and Other Women*) and in the short novel of 1982 *Té con canela* (*Tea With Cinnamon*).44 Another noteworthy specialty is her versions of detached, city women who are aggressively sexual beings. The wry heroines are Jewish, giving a sharp detachment to their outlook and an added complication to the personal issues they must manage.

Although Steimberg and Absatz have been singled out here for their distinctive ways of bringing together women's and Jewish issues in literature, many other writers have worked toward such an integration. Tamara Kamenszain (1947–), who has a strong record of adapting new literary theory in her creative writing and commentary, was early in her career known for coordinating Jewish cultural repertories with her textual experimentation.45 In the 1980s, she expressed a renewed concern with the marks that Jewish identity inscribes in literature. This preoccupation, shared by a number of contemporaries, will be discussed in the postface. Eugenia Calny (1928–), in her 1972 novel *Clara al amanecer* (*Clara at Dawn*), exposes conventional notions of courtship and marriage as they prove treacherous to a present-day Jewish Argentine woman.46 U.S.-based Nora Glickman evokes both the settlements and the present-day urban confusions in the stories that, in 1983, were collected as *Uno de sus Juanes* (*One of Her Juans*).47

Of fiction following the above-described tendencies, Szichman's novels, and particularly his 1971 *Los judíos del Mar Dulce* (*The Jews of the Fresh-Water Sea*), stand out as most directly in the progression begun with *Los gauchos judíos.* One may see the work of Tiempo, Verbitsky, and Viñas as constituting, in various ways, rejoinders to the centennial novel. Each of these authors strives to inject into Jewish Argentine writing qualities most disturbingly absent in the founding text of 1910: criticism, frankness, historical accuracy, and the acknowledgment of such human realities as sexuality, ambition, urbanity, and loyalty to one's source of identity. Gradually the bucolically high-minded Jewish gauchos, unquestioningly ready to sacrifice their long-standing ways, are replaced by Jewish characters who suffer disillusionment in their new country, seek out urban satisfactions, voice dissent, and maintain various forms of Jewish thought and behavior. Viñas becomes especially direct in countering the statements and inferences of *Los gauchos judíos.* Whereas the 1910 work assures readers of the Jews' eagerness to discard any traits that might bring them into conflict with the custom of the land, Viñas's *Dar la cara* closes by affirming the Jewish tradition of critical thought as a force to disrupt regressive tendencies in society.

Los judíos del Mar Dulce has been chosen from Szichman's novels chronicling, through the story of the contentious Pechof family, Jewish Argentine and national history from the 1910s to the 1950s. His novels are, in effect, variations on the same fictional family saga and episodes from national history. The 1972 *La verdadera crónica falsa* (*The True False Chronicle*) reworks material from the 1971 novel and the 1969 *La crónica falsa* (*The False Chronicle*). *A las 20.25, la señora entró en la inmortalidad* (1981; English translation, *At 8.25, Evita Became Immortal,* 1983), one of the many contemporary Argentine works published in exile by authors critical of society, adds further twists to the Pechofs' complicated family history. Of these versions, *Los judíos del Mar Dulce* most directly reprises *Los gauchos judíos.* Its very title reiterates the name of the 1910 novel, altered to refer now to the urban setting (*Mar Dulce,* or *Fresh-Water Sea,* an early term for the River Plate, mocking Gerchunoff's reliance on elevated-sounding anachronisms). The framing device with which the novel opens, the screening of an unsuccessfully lyricized pseudodocumentary on Jewish immigration, again proclaims the need to challenge this euphemistic account to achieve a historical understanding of the events.

In placing Szichman in this line of increasingly bold Jewish Argentine expression, one may perhaps be too easily impressed by his debt to the historical insights formulated by Viñas and the generation of the parricides. Szichman acknowledges Viñas's critical vision of Argentine history through such tributes as the dedication to *La verdadera crónica falsa* and his 1972 interview of Viñas, in which he shows a thorough knowledge of the older writer's thought. Szichman's refutation of the patriotic version of Jewish Argentine immigration is, in a sense, the novelistic counterpart of Viñas's polemical essay "Gerchunoff: Jewish Gauchos and Xenophobia."

New to Szichman and his generation, though, are certain displays of audacity with no precedent in the critical essays and fiction of Viñas and his colleagues. The most evident of these is an uninhibited expression of interest in the questions of Jewish identity and of recognizably Jewish modes of thought and expression. As the Pechof family struggles to present its identity and background to greatest advantage, it encounters difficulties specific to Jews in a predominantly Christian society. Its problems are not necessarily, as in the previously prevailing treatment of the question, problems common to some larger segment—such as immigrants, members of a given social class, or all marginalized groups. There is a frank admission that Jews differ more profoundly from the old Hispanic Catholic norm than do other immigrant groups and, moreover, that their difference in itself deserves examination. The more specifically Jewish focus is signaled by such markers as the characters' free use of Yiddish and the narrator's black humor. The persistence of these and other signals serves to drive home the idea that an unmistakably Jewish novel can be a commentary on the entire nation's social history.

Szichman is worth including too for the stance and persona he brings to the consideration of sensitive social issues, whether as a novelist or a discussant. As the "angry young" Viñas did in his generation, Szichman contributes to intellectual exchange a personal style that is itself a statement concerning culture and society. Among the features of this style is a talent for raucous mimicry, especially of the self-serving and all-accommodating rhetorics that have arisen as evasions of the need to confront and analyze the course of national life. *Los judíos del Mar Dulce* showcases this ability, particularly in Szichman's burlesque of the old-line Liberal talk of opportunity for all, the rhetoric that ushered in Jewish immigration.

In his citations of history, Szichman makes good use of a detailed knowledge of the most shameful episodes in national life, such as the more disreputable tactics employed in the recruitment and delivery of immigrant labor, the prostitution network that once flourished in the Jewish community of Buenos Aires, and the massacre of working-class detainees in the vindictive euphoria that followed the fall of Perón. Szichman brings a new detachment to the depiction of Perón's decade of rule, treating these matters with a detached mockery not found in the preceding generation. His recourse to mundane vulgarity also distinguishes his critical expression from the sober anger with which the parricides set forth their historical thought.

* * *

As the story of Jewish Argentine writing approaches the 1980s with works published by Szichman, Barnatán, Rabinovich, and Isaacson, a question arises: What do these works indicate about the possibilities still open for the future development of this literature? Conversely, what tendencies have begun to lose their potential for further elaboration, either because they belong to a vanishing cultural orientation or because they represent attitudes and concepts from which current writers are pulling away? Two of the works from the 1970s—Rabinovich's and Isaacson's—represent currents that have already begun to lose vigor. In Rabinovich's case, the reason for the decline is the attrition of the generations with firsthand knowledge of Eastern European Jewish life and thought of the late nineteenth and early twentieth centuries and their continuation in Argentina. The exhaustion of a different type of tradition is suggested by Isaacson's *Cuaderno Spinoza*. For all the craft apparent in this cycle of poems, one cannot easily imagine a younger writer taking it as a guide to the writing of Jewish Argentine literature. The reserve with which it expresses social commentary runs somewhat counter to the current drive toward plain, or even painfully bald, statement. Certainly Isaacson's reticence shows an impressive independence of mind when compared to the avowals of indebtedness toward official Argentina that today strike Gerchunoff's readers as abject. Nonetheless, it is a reminder of the historical pressures to remain silent on sensitive issues and of the decades during which Jewish Argentine writers often masked their most important assertions and as such is likely to be put aside while the right to insistent boldness is established.

Barnatán's writing, though it could hardly be called a direct form of expression, is daring in ways that engage it with the present cultural moment. It frequently alludes to conventionally hidden aspects of sexuality. For example, the protagonist, in drawing close to his aunt, in some sense becomes the captive of a powerfully charged lunar goddess or priestess, whereas less ethereal characters have connections to the elegant demimonde. Just as modern as the allusions to the variant forms of sexuality is Barnatán's drive to display issues of religious, ethnic, and national identity in all their bewildering complexity. This theme permeates his treatment of cultural history, beginning with the acknowledgment of the embarrassingly pagan strains in Judaism and continuing up to the era of fast travel and mass communications, where personal identity may easily be tailored to the most prestigious model. Although no writer can be called Barnatán's counterpart, the exploration of the more baffling realms of sexuality and identity, carried out by a writer with Jewish concerns in mind, is far from exhaustion. In the postface to this work, one newly prominent writer, the expatriate Edgardo Cozarinsky, is discussed for his work along these general lines.

Szichman's 1971 novel, though, is the work most illustrative of the major tendencies Jewish Argentine writing will pursue in subsequent years. From the outset, the work makes it clear that the Jewish experience is undergoing a fresh scrutiny in the hope of understanding history, particularly its distressing and bewildering aspects. The language is rough, bitter statements are made flatly, and the satirical treatment often deprives the characters of their dignity. These severe and brutal tones are in reaction to the conventions that have often blunted the ability of Jewish Argentine literature to generate insights into the processes at work in culture and society.

1 ALBERTO GERCHUNOFF

Rhapsodizing a Jewish New World

Los gauchos judíos (*The Jewish Gauchos*) is, as noted in the introduction, the novel to which Alberto Gerchunoff (1884–1950) owes his fame and is as well the work of Jewish Argentine literature most widely read and best accepted as part of the national literature. Yet present-day critics find it difficult to appreciate.[1] The book's ideological presuppositions have drawn adverse commentary from David Viñas, Saúl Sosnowski, Gladys Onega, and others. They object to rhetorical features of the novel that betray its effort to recount Jewish Argentine immigration in a way favorable to official national policy.[2]

A major complaint about Gerchunoff's work is that it inaccurately shows Eastern European Jewish immigrants receiving an unreserved welcome and adapting easily to Argentine life. Gerchunoff omits historical realities that would add a negative note. He understates the conflicts between Jewish settlers and the long-standing population. At the same time, he exaggerates the human ability to discard, without ill effects, behaviors that help sustain personal and group identity. His characters cheerfully abandon Jewish observances and folkways. Criticism has also pointed to the flattering portrayal of Argentine immigration policy. The novel exalts the benefits of immigration for the Jews but masks the government's eagerness for European farmers to settle and "civilize" lands that previously were the open range of the gauchos. In the novel, these recruited immigrants, who often came as contracted labor, are the recipients of charitable refuge. (No author of the period, however, dealt adequately with these issues.)

This officially approved picture of immigration is really less a work of representation than of celebration. In the most literal sense, the novel is part of the patriotic commemoration of the Argentine centennial, to which it is overtly dedicated. Less evidently, it is the rhapsodic treatment of one variant of the Zionist ideal that had gained such a hold on the Eastern European Jewish intellectual imagination. Immigration to Argentina appears not as a fortunate relocation but as the natural fulfillment of the Zionist dream, a blissful adventure, and a great gift to the Jews from an uncorrupted New World nation.[3]

It is possible to recognize the novel's bias and inaccuracy yet still find it to be valuable literary proof of the transfer of Eastern European cultural

tendencies to the Argentine scene and of their adaptation to local ideological needs. Kessel Schwartz provides a point of departure. Without holding
the work to criteria of verisimilitude, Schwartz calls it "romantic" and
"idyllic."[4] These terms suggest that *Los gauchos judíos,* unreliable as documentation of social conditions, may offer testimony to the dreams that
shape social thought.

To pursue this insight, one should remember that *Los gauchos judíos* is
not only an Argentine centennial novel.[5] It is also a projection of the
intellectual and expressive tendencies that swept through Eastern European
Jewry during the late nineteenth and early twentieth centuries. As a reference to this context, the novel is here examined jointly with a poem by Saul
Tchernihowsky (1875–1943). Juxtaposition of the two authors' works is
intended only to make evident significant commonalities of background
and outlook and not to deny the differences between their approaches. The
celebrated Hebrew-revival poet was a rebel who frequently set out to shock.
Gerchunoff is known for the sedative qualities of his novel, in which even
the rejection of tradition is presented gently.

These divergences notwithstanding, Tchernihowsky and Gerchunoff
share important concepts. They celebrate a radical transformation occurring, or about to occur, among oppressed Eastern European Jewry. The
great renewal demands an intensely lyricizing literary treatment. The drear-
iness of pogrom-ridden Russia contrasts with the vitality of the New World.
The remade Jewish realm may be the messianic era, the restored Jewish
homeland, or Tchernihowsky's neopagan utopia. It is the fruition of some
great ideal, some project capable of recreating all things for the Jewish
people.

For an example of these common elements, it is helpful to place the
speech a village rabbi gives in Gerchunoff's opening chapter beside Tchernihowsky's "They Say There Is a Country . . ."; this is the exalted language
Tchernihowsky uses to evoke a land of promise:

They say there is a country
A land that flows with sunlight
Where is that country?
Where is that sunlight?

They say there is a country
Where seven pillars are
There bloom on every hilltop
Seven wandering stars

A land where is fulfilled
All a man can hope
Everyone who enters—
Akiba must approach

"Shalom to you, Akiba
Peace be with you, Rabbi
Where are they, the holy?
Where are the Maccabee?"

Answers him Akiba
Says to him the Rabbi
"All Israel is holy,
You are the Maccabee."[6]

This visionary moment is close to the rabbi's rousing description of Argentina. In lyrical prose, the rabbi exhorts the shtetl population to emigrate to Argentina: "Es una tierra donde todos trabajan y donde el cristiano no nos odiará, porque allí el cielo es distinto, y en su alma habitan la piedad y la justicia" (It's a land where everyone works and where the Christian won't hate us, because there the heavens are different and in the soul dwell piety and justice) (15).

Although the rabbi has a pragmatic goal—a move to the Argentine pampas—his oratory rises to a level of abstraction similar to the "all Israel is holy" of Tchernihowsky's poem. The rabbi says he now sees that Zion can exist anywhere; the Jewish homeland transcends the specifics of history and geography. He argues against a return to either Palestine or the urban high civilization typified by the Sephardic Golden Age in Spain. As in Tchernihowsky, Jewish exile is to end through collective self-renewal, not external circumstance. For the rabbi, leaving pogrom-beset Russia is not the goal of emigration. To flee oppression is only the first step toward a revigorated peoplehood.

These themes, similar in Gerchunoff and Tchernihowsky, arise from an environment abounding in projects for Jewish transformation. The situation in post-1881 Russia convinced many that it was time to remake Jewish life. This notion surfaced as one of a number of contemporary tendencies of thought, among them the varieties of Zionist, socialist, anarchist, and utopian programs and Jewish apocalypticism. Tchernihowsky's neopaganism and Gerchunoff's belief in salvation through agriculture are only two examples of a larger phenomenon. Each author represents, in his way, the ferment of (broadly speaking) Zionist activity:

The ground for the pioneering spirit in Israel was fertilized first by Jewish thinkers like Dr. Leo Pinsker (1821–1891), author of the famous treatise, *Auto-Emanzipation* (1881) in which he proposed a plan for a Jewish homeland, be it in Palestine or somewhere else, a territory inhabited by Jews and governed by them as the only solution to the Jewish problem. . . . The atmosphere was pervaded with the idea of national regeneration through self-help.[7]

The two authors describe natural life according to their ideologies of transformation. For Gerchunoff's rabbi, "the heavens are different" because a new life is possible. In Tchernihowsky's poem "There bloom on every hilltop / seven wandering stars" as a sign of the new age. In this reading of *Los gauchos judíos,* the portrayal of nature will receive special examination for what it can reveal about the currents of thought that went into the novel, giving it a distinctive form.

Gerchunoff at first seems intent on directing attention from the inherent wonders of nature toward the goodness of agriculture. This is a characteristic of the rabbi who serves as his spokesman. Arguing against a Zion in Spain, he faults the Golden-Age Sephardim for their urban, commercial ways. After evoking the horrors of the Inquisition, he notes: "Fué en España donde los judíos dejaron de cultivar la tierra y cuidar sus ganados" (It was in Spain that the Jews ceased to cultivate the land and raise their herds) (16). The rabbi stops just short of saying that urban worldliness brought God's wrath upon the Spanish Jews. This is the first of many passages that invoke the authority of Jewish tradition, alternatively biblical, talmudic, and vaguely folkloric, to support an agricultural imperative. The narrator, like the rabbi, favors the notion that rural settlement and farming have been the norm in Jewish life. His historical allusions are chosen to give the impression of a people almost continuously engaged in working the land. He avoids the tradition of urban Jewish life and thought, from the highest moments of Jerusalem to, in Gerchunoff's day, the intellectual ferment of the Central European capitals. This distortion of history is by no means peculiar to Gerchunoff; as Irving Louis Horowitz notes, the rural settlement program was accompanied by effort to "reconstitute the myth of the Jew as a man of the soil as an answer to anti-Semitic charges of the 'commercial Jew.'"[8]

The rabbi's evocation of farming as the glorious fulfillment of Jewish destiny dominates the first segment of the novel, the only segment set in the

Old World. His speech establishes a framework for understanding the entire work. The rabbi is providing his congregation with postulates to make sense of the experience of the pampas. The shtetl dwellers, beyond any doubt, find comfort and guidance in the rabbi's interpretation of nature and their relation to it. For the reader, though, their leader's insistence that nature means agriculture is not altogether useful in understanding the presentation of the natural world in *Los gauchos judíos*.

Viñas's observations are helpful in examining the inconsistencies in the depiction of nature. For this analysis, the features Viñas notes are positive characteristics of the text. They increase its complexity and bond it to an Eastern European imaginative tradition, thus creating an innovative fusion with Argentine literature. For Viñas, though, these traits are negative in that they provide false reassurance and give an impression of peace while describing a historically conflictive movement of peoples.

Viñas observes that nature is often shown as motionless. Not only is agricultural work often nowhere to be seen, but all activity seems magically to cease during lyrical passages. In Viñas's analysis, depicting nature in absolute repose conveys a pantheistic sense of the world: "smells, above all the smells of nature, identified and embodied, bring to mind perfumes or ritual aromas permeating space. . . . All of nature thus acquires something of the character of a temple: calm, sumptuous, fragrant and brimming full, tepid or warm, but never for a moment losing its harmony. And ponderous, because for Gerchunoff peace, as well as being religious, is slow."[9]

The type of passage to which Viñas refers, in which the narrator speaks of "ritmo tranquilo" (tranquil rhythm) and "margaritas en denso plantío" (thickly clustered daisies), illustrates another point. The description of ornamental (from the point of view of the settlers) elements of nature— nonagricultural plants and animals, stars, clouds, fragrances—moves the reader away from the notion of the earth as something the Jews must work. The fact that nothing is being accomplished, not even a crop passively ripening, confers on the world a religious or magical quality. The reiteration of such terms as *bañar* (*to bathe*) and *saturar* (*to saturate*), criticized by Viñas for too strong a suggestion of "relaxation" and "peace," falls into this same pattern.[10] These words, conveying the image of something (sunlight, fragrance) penetrating the natural world, imply that pantheistic forces pervade the countryside and bring it into harmony. This supernatural wholeness is entirely independent of the efforts of the Jewish settlers. The Jews' struggles to survive, to earn their welcome in Argentina, and to transform their lives have no place in this effortless perfection. The narrator's favored term *beatitud,* to which Viñas objects, is the proper one to account for the peace unobtainable by human striving. Only a special working of numinous powers can bring it about.

The scenes of pantheistic stillness mark a veering away from the novel's announced program of ideas. After the rabbi has propounded a doctrine of nature as the scene of regenerative work, a very different figure of nature appears in the lyrical descriptions. Still, the magical notion of nature does not displace the principle of self-renewal through labor. The two ideas compete for dominance throughout the novel, neither succeeding in upstaging the other for long.

As well as numerous passages of the type Viñas considers nature worship, the novel offers descriptions exemplary of the bond between nature and redemptive farm work. For instance, when the narrator observes that "un sol fuerte nos ahogaba y desparramaba su llamarada por la campiña segada, que parecía un inmenso cepillo de oro" (a strong sun was drowning us and spreading its flames all through the newly mown countryside, which looked like an immense golden bristle brush) (33), the glory of the fields is the effect not only of reflected sunlight but also of the just-finished harvest. The narrator takes a more than aesthetic pleasure in the scene. He is one of the harvesters admiring the evidence of their industry. The passage highlights the marks agriculture leaves on nature:

Era un día caluroso y limpio. A ambos lados de la aldea, los sembrados verdeaban en las eras inmensas, onduladas levemente por un viento suave. En el vasto potrero que separaba las dos hileras de casas, los muchachos apartaban el ganado para conducirlo al pastoreo.

(It was a warm, clean day. On both sides of the village, the planted soil was sprouting green in the immense vegetable plots, stirred slightly by a gentle wind. In the vast enclosure that ran between the two rows of houses, the boys were separating out the cattle to take them to pasture) (36).

When the fieldwork is that of neighboring gauchos, not Jewish settlers, the praise of agriculture is most salient. The narrator describes in detail the house and grounds of Don Estanislao Benítez, a rich gaucho friendly to Jewish neighbors. Far around the man's house, "su campo se extendía surcado en arroyos y manchado de cardales" (his land stretched out furrowed with gulleys and splotched with thistle bushes) (83). The emphasis on this vast farm property, whose thornbushes betray its recent wildness, links Don Estanislao's personal value to his triumphant wresting of farmland from open range. Don Estanislao sides with the Jewish newcomers largely through this shared bond. Like him, they derive personal worth from farming lands they have won from savagery. Just as the *gauchos judíos* are superior to Jews who, forsaking talmudic precepts, neglected agriculture (16), so Don Estanislao is better than nomadic gauchos.

In *Los gauchos judíos,* visual evidence of fieldwork betokens the remade world where "el cielo es distinto" (the heavens are different) (15). Spiritual regeneration through farming has spread from Jews, for whom (in Gerchunoff's thought) it was mandated, to gauchos, who thus become colleagues of the Jews. To achieve this picture of land-rooted interethnic community, the novel must deny the nomadism central to gaucho culture.

Even as he insists that the good gaucho works the land, Gerchunoff delights in the romantic figure of the gaucho, whose panache derives from his roaming life. The immigrants find it exciting to wear the typical garb and accoutrements of the gaucho, invested as these articles are with the glamour of freedom. References to gaucho tradition, especially its decorative elements and legends, thrill the Jewish settlers.

Clearly, Gerchunoff is benefiting both from a concept of nature in which stability and cultivation are most valued and from the contradictory ideal of nature as wild freedom. Jorge Luis Borges, in his irascible remarks on the novel, draws attention to this duality: "That book by Gerchunoff, *Los gauchos judíos,* has a title that doesn't fit the text. Because, when you read the book, you realize that those immigrants weren't gauchos, but rather farmers. And that's apparent in the very chapters, which are entitled 'Plowing,' 'Threshing,' etc. That has nothing to do with the gaucho, who was a horseman, and not a farmer."[11]

Borges makes a valid point, albeit through overstatement. To be just, he should have mentioned chapter titles that move away from the agricultural theme. "La lechuza" ("The Owl") and "Las brujas" ("The Witches"), for example, refer to magical entities. If these chapters appear isolated as short stories—as "La lechuza" at times does—the resulting texts are fantastical literature. "La lechuza" offers a further swerve into wildness. The characters, disturbed by events in their environment, seek explanations from both Jewish and gaucho lore. The former source at first appears safer:

Graznó otra vez la lechuza, y miró a las mujeres, en cuyo espíritu sus ojos produjeron la misma sugestión agorera.
—Dicen que es de mal agüero.
—Dicen así, pero no creo. ¿Qué saben los campesinos?
—¿No decimos nosotros, los judíos, que el cuervo anuncia la muerte?
—¡Ah, es otra cosa!

(The owl screeched again, and looked at the women, its eyes arousing the same sense
of foreboding in all their spirits.
"They say it's an ill omen."
"They say so, but I don't believe it. What do the peasants know?"
"Don't we Jews say that the crow announces death?"
"Oh, that's a whole different matter!") (66).

In the end, though, gaucho legend—superstition—offers the most satisfac-
tory account of matters. The story endorses values that are far from the
rational work and European-style civilization that it overtly celebrates.

These fantastical tales confer a new meaning on the term *gauchos judíos*.
Usually, the phrase refers to the Jews' adoption of useful items from the
gauchos' cultural repertory. Here, though, the Jews find the gauchos' imaginative products stimulating. These episodes bring relief from the novel's
insistence on hard work and discipline. They honor a world beyond civi-
lized regulation. This other world is undisguisedly that of the pre-European
pampas. The eruption of its magical strength promotes the notion that the
Jewish settlers are involved in an enthralling adventure as they create Zion
in a New World full of unknown beings and forces.

By such shifts, the novel continues to support a doctrine of work and
stability yet allows enjoyment of fantasy, magic, and the pleasingly irrational. One perhaps obvious explanation for these fluctuations is that *Los
gauchos judíos* works to draw the reader into a fascinating imaginative
realm of ritualism, a central point in Viñas's complaint against the novel.
According to this line of thought, the text lyricizes and embellishes historical realities the better to lull readers into accepting a falsified version. A
less imaginative rendering would not require such vigorous demythification
by critics because readers could easily spot and reject its ideological distortions.

Although the persuasive function of *Los gauchos judíos* is certainly
significant, its vacillations also stem from its origins in the contemporary
notion of Jewish renewal. Things become possible that would previously
have been too much to hope for. Among these possibilities is the reconciliation of a natural, free-roaming life with the settlement of farmlands. It is
well known that the real-life gaucho population suffered violence to its way
of life when government programs sought to fence and develop the pampas.
This unhappy circumstance need not appear in *Los gauchos judíos* because
the novel presents a world in which conflicts need not be such. However
long-standing the conflict between wildness and stability or between open

rangers and farmers, it is dissolved when life undergoes transformation into a seamless, harmonious whole.

The novel's fluctuation between the praise of farm work and the worship of wild nature is only one of its vacillations. A duality also exists between assimilation and retention of Jewish behaviors and outlook. Again, the dissensions that could arise from competing claims are lyrically smoothed over. Schwartz has remarked on Gerchunoff's admiration for talmudic learning and argumentation as a factor keeping him from complete assimilationism.[12] *Los gauchos judíos* shows the abandonment of Jewish observance and draws the conclusion that Jewish tradition must cede before the practical necessities of Argentine life. Yet the novel dedicates an entire chapter to the celebration of Jewish legal thought and practice, as the deliberations for the granting of a divorce are given in detail. Admiration for the subtlety and flexibility of Jewish legal tradition is the dominant note. This chapter is exempt from the novel's official tenet that immigrants should learn to follow the customs of their new land. The granting of a divorce under religious law—not an annulment but the dissolution of a properly contracted bond—is shown as a just and ethical solution. Yet Argentina's legal code made no provision for civil divorce, and the Roman Catholic church considered such legislation an incitation to moral decline. Again, passages of the novel enjoy an exemption from the dominant message that gratitude to the Argentine nation should inspire patriotic sacrifice of particularistic ways. Such rules can be suspended in the remade world, with its ability to make all things possible.

As a result of these shifts and "magical" exceptions to its own ideological rules, *Los gauchos judíos* is more complex than the single-minded centennial celebration of immigration that is its most evident aspect. It owes this complexity, in great measure, to the infusion of constituents originating in the Eastern European Jewish culture of the late nineteenth and early twentieth centuries. These components engage with the novel's Argentine elements—the lyrical prose of Modernism and the prodevelopment, melting-pot rhetoric of traditional liberalism. The resulting fusion presents an impressive innovation in Argentine literature and lightens the ideological burden the work carries by introducing a rapturously utopian vein of thought and expression.

Whereas *Los gauchos judíos* offers these notable literary features and bears valuable witness to the continuation of Eastern European thought in Argentine culture, it is still a problematic beginning place for Jewish Argentine literature. Its progovernment apologetics are tempered with fantasy and imagination and are embedded in an unusually variegated novelistic construction. Yet the work's statements discourage readers from questioning the government's noble intentions in recruiting Jews to settle the pampas. The omission of portions of history, such as the expropriation of these lands from the original Indian population and the open-ranging gauchos, is less disturbing than the novel's implications about Jewish immigrants in Argentine society. These new arrivals appear as the objects of charity, as guests who ought not to disturb the existing arrangements of the household or criticize its governance. As the subsequent development of Jewish Argentine writing shows, overcoming the presuppositions embodied in *Los gauchos judíos* required a lengthy and painful effort.

2 CÉSAR TIEMPO

Worldly Lyricization of the Urban Jewish Experience

It is easy to be struck by the celebratory treatment that César Tiempo (1906–1980) accords to Jewish immigrant life in Argentina. To say that his work is positive and cheerful, though, does not convey the full originality of Tiempo's poetic good news. Other writers had depicted excellent prospects for the new immigrants; particularly vivid examples are the two bucolic centennial works on this theme, Leopoldo Lugones's *Odas seculares* and Gerchunoff's *Los gauchos judíos*. A significant contrast emerges between these pastoral visions and Tiempo's hoped-for future. Tiempo develops a characteristic poetic to promote a belief in the compatibility of life in the Argentine capital and the maintenance of Jewish life.

This chapter focuses on strategies in Tiempo's 1933 *Sabatión argentino* (*Great Argentine Sabbath*), which incorporates also the contents of the 1930 collection *Libro para la pausa del sábado* (*Book for the Sabbath Pause*).[1] Analyses of selected poems emphasize the use Tiempo made of poetic innovations pioneered in Argentina by the 1920s avant-garde. This is not to claim for Tiempo a cultural radicalism equivalent to that of a Macedonio Fernández or an Oliverio Girondo. Rather, it is to note that Tiempo could maintain his traditional interest in poetry as lyrical expression, his social interest in proletarian poetry, and his role as Jewish poet without foregoing the exuberant and often playful new approach of the avant-garde poets.

Tiempo, like many poets of the 1920s, believed that poetry needed a new language to maintain its importance as a human activity. As the "Manifesto de Martin Fierro" (published in the tabloid review of that name in 1924 and authored by Girondo) put it, the vanguard poet needed "new eyes," "new sensibility," "new expression," and the ability to convey through his poetic language that "all things are new under the sun."[2]

This obsession with new expressive systems coincided with Tiempo's search for a poetry that would both affirm identity for the Jewish community in Argentina and help to create bonds of understanding between this special group and the much larger population of Argentine non-Jews. As well as carrying a message of brotherhood in the overt, traditional sense, the poetry was to form a space between the two cultures where this communality, or set of shared cultural characteristics, might be made manifest.

Following these ideas, Tiempo worked to devise a language that would emphasize what the Jewish and the mainstream Christian population held in common while not disregarding the distinctive features of the former. He did so by looking for signs that would carry an essentially equivalent semantic weight for both groups (most typically, the Sabbath) as well as signs that could be used in contrasting patterns. By appealingly displaying these charged signs, or symbols, in his poetry, he sought to convince readers that the bicultural situation was a salutary one, affording both human communalities and an aesthetically pleasing variegation.

Tiempo often relies on the reader's understanding of elements of both Christian and Jewish culture. As much as possible, he avoids explanatory material, such as glosses or in-text comments. Such assistance would draw attention to the fact that Christian readers really do not know many things about Jewish life. Tiempo prefers to proceed as if the Argentine (or any Spanish-language) reader ought to be comfortable with references to both traditions.

Secondary to this Christian-Jewish conjunction is a pattern of borrowing from other mythic, magical, and religious traditions. For example, one poem draws on the Central European lore of vampires and werewolves, paradoxically and amusingly grafted onto Christian hagiography. Other allusions bring into Tiempo's eclectic system borrowings from gaucho, peasant, and Native American cultures.

The most obvious explanation for the juxtaposition of diverse cultural elements is that Tiempo is a poet of universal fraternity. But beyond the topic of brotherhood, Tiempo is working with the avant-garde idea of assembling a new medium not dependent on old orthodoxies yet capable of expressing the supernatural or transcendental dimension of experience.

The astrological-Kabbalistic-Catholic languages of Xul Solar (Alejandro Schulz Solari), Oliverio Girondo's collection of totems and fetishes, and Norah Lange's presentation of herself as a mythic being of Scandinavia are all examples of avant-gardists' efforts at a new religious and mythical synthesis. Luis Borges's famous, ironic fascination with systems of belief emerged from this milieu.[3] On the whole, such eclecticism was a trait of a number of the more profoundly avant-garde contemporary poets and painters, whereas those colleagues who favored a particular system tended to aesthetic caution (as the overtly Catholic poet Eduardo González Lanuza).

* * *

In rejecting the supposed dichotomy between Jewish and Argentine loyalty, Tiempo questions other presumed incompatibilities. The implication is that many forms of civilization have already begun to mesh and become synthesized. The task now is not to bring cultures together but to increase readers' awareness of a process of coalescence already under way.

Sabatión leaves unanswered a question that may well arise in the minds of readers: How literally should one understand the allusions to the most traditional concepts of Judaism? At times, *Sabatión* appears to espouse such time-honored notions as a personal deity who intervenes in human affairs, a Jewish people or nation with an exceptional place in the creation, the absolute significance of every occurrence in Jewish history, and the necessity of performing ritual or cultic commandments. It would be contrary to good sense to see *Sabatión* as any absolute endorsement of traditional, particularistic beliefs. Tiempo was part of the worldly culture of Buenos Aires and was an experimentalist who tested the limits of literary propriety. *Sabatión* contains many elements of secular culture and modern Jewish-Christian rapprochement. Tiempo's modernity does not, however, preclude his poetically entertaining traditional concepts. It is of importance that Tiempo gives equal and conjoint representation to beliefs that are, in great measure, irreconcilable under real-world circumstances.

Sabatión most clearly manifests its variable, indeterminate stance in the treatment of the religious. However great his absorption in the modern world, Tiempo is drawn to Judaism as a religious civilization developing through history (Mordecai M. Kaplan's celebrated definition is especially appropriate in this case).[4] This concern sometimes intermingles with an interest in Judaism as religion or cult. However, the two outlooks are not opposed to or evaluated against one another. Tactfully, *Sabatión* does not urge on readers a single approach to Judaism. The poems go no further than the artistic display of aspects of Jewish tradition. The implicit recommendation is that readers appreciate and examine the full variety but respond by their own lights.

Before a detailed analysis of the poems "Noche hiemal en el ghetto" ("Winter Night in the Ghetto") (87–88) and "Sabatión porteño" ("Great Buenos Aires Sabbath") (49–50), three of Tiempo's strategies will be discussed and exemplified. The first is a form of humor that subtly demonumentalizes the heights of piety. A second procedure is the poetic evaluation of the lives of Jews faithful or unfaithful to their heritage. Shifts in tone and register of speech are central to the third technique.

* * *

A prankish, irreverent style characterized avant-garde humor. *Sabatión* modifies this boisterous mode. A change is necessary because the avant-garde tends to make tradition and old age automatic targets of scorn. In the "Manifiesto de Martin Fierro," for example, mockery of the literary establishment shows a horror of aging and of convention. The elder poets are said to suffer from hardening of the arteries, both in their persons and in their work. Such an outlook would not serve in a collection of poems celebrating the accumulation of tradition and learning that built up Jewish civilization.

Sabatión resolves this dilemma by avoiding direct satire of figures representing piety. For example, an item of traditional Judaism may be paired with a modern-day equivalent. The juxtaposition is in itself humorous because unexpected, but more important, it is the modern element in the pair that receives any overtly mocking treatment, leaving the traditional item apparently unscathed. Though Tiempo undoubtedly finds something comical in the utter dedication of scribes and judges, such an observation never becomes overt in the text. "Méier Dréier Ave Negra" ("Meier Dreier, Legal Eagle") shows how this displacement works. It is not the devoted, learned scribe who receives the parody but rather the modern lawyer who shares his zealous application. Such sly humor hints that one need not feel awe at human accomplishments. Parallels with trivial matters make the feats of holy men less intimidating. Another juxtaposition pairs a patriarch with modern lottery-ticket vendors. Although both are able to wield power over the community, deal with matters of fortune and destiny, and devote themselves to their work, only the lottery-ticket vendors are direct targets of satire.

If humor allows a lighthearted look at piety, it can also promote traditional religious virtues. Just as Tiempo avoids actually mocking holy men, he uses figurative displacements to escape preaching in verse. This indirectness characterizes "Versos para nosotros dos y mis amigos" ("Verses for the Two of Us and My Friends") (71–72). The speaker in this poem is courting a restaurateur's daughter. He feigns approval of her father's establishment while knowing it does not give customers good value. This simple, understandable case of hypocrisy becomes complicated because of the metaphorical language used by the suitor. He involves the issues of faith and skepticism, which emerge as the real themes of the poem. The suitor identifies himself as an agnostic. He then describes how he was able to muster a vigorous show of faith. When the speaker falls in love, "tornó mi agnosticismo funcional" (my agnosticism came in handy). His courtship requires him to accept fare that is watered down or filled with extenders. Even as he professes faith in the restaurant's practices, he demonstrates his

continuing skepticism by providing more instances of sub-standard operations.

The line "tornó mi agnosticismo funcional" (my agnosticism came in
handy) raises suspicions about agnosticism, here implied to be an acceptance of the relativism of truths. In this poem, agnosticism reveals itself as
opportunism. The hero uses it to find the restaurant both adequate and
inadequate, basing himself alternatively on his love of the daughter and the
evidence of his senses. Amid its humorous turns, the poem does not support
the speaker's professed relativism. It makes the point that the restaurant is
dishonestly run and that the speaker knows this to be the case.

The poem echoes the ideals behind Jewish dietary laws, though without
direct reference to them. The restaurateur has not been caught selling
nonkosher items; he is violating standards common to all. The owner fails
to provide clean linen and adulterates the fare. These are offenses against
the principle, basic to *kashrut* regulations, that humans should have their
consumption of food elevated by protocols of purity. Here Tiempo does not
praise or advocate Jewish dietary laws but rather the universal concept that
motivates them.

The closing verse gives the speaker an opportunity to show that he is
really not as amoral or acritical as he has playfully claimed to be. He is
merely placating his future father-in-law and harbors plans to bring the
restaurant into line with standards of good practice. Though the joking
tone is maintained throughout, there is no doubt that the poem depicts
agnosticism as leading to an absence of moral bearings.

* * *

Several biographical poems assess the life and work of exemplary Jews.
The cases illustrate how certain public figures either manage or fail to
maintain the special legacy of Jewish civilization in the modern world. A
comparison of "Al Jolson" (105–6) and "Versos en la muerte de Larry
Semon" ("Verses on the Death of Larry Semon") (131–34) is useful. Each
concerns a Jewish performer in the worldly film industry, but the two
entertainers receive very different treatment. "Al Jolson," an open letter in
verse, reproaches Jolson for deteriorating from traditional Jewish song to
mere show business. "Larry Semon" is a eulogy, praising Semon's cartoon
art, film animation, and comic acting.[5]

"Al Jolson" may surprise readers of *Sabatión* who assume Tiempo's
stance to be unfailingly promodern. The case against Jolson appears to be
very like the complaint made against the character Jolson plays in *The Jazz*

Singer. The protagonist of this well-known film outrages his cantor father by turning from liturgical song to jazz. The poem, though, is not directed against the character but against the real-world Jolson; it uses biographical information about him and his original name, Iasha Yoelsen. The theme is Jolson's decline, emphasized through the reiteration of the phrase "No cantas como entonces" (You don't sing the way you did then) at the outset of each of the three stanzas. The past referred to is Jolson's youth, during which he sang traditional folk songs and cantored. The fourth stanza hints at a religious definition of Jewish duty:

Iasha Yóelsen: ahora tu voz tallada en llanto
sobre el cáliz del mundo vuelca en vano su son.
Jehová ya no preside la magia de tu canto
que es como un dulce rostro pero sin corazón.

(Iasha Yoelsen: now your voice carven in weeping
pours its sound out vainly over the chalice of the world.
Jehovah no longer rules over the magic of your song
that is like a sweet face but without any heart.)

Given the eclecticism of thought in the *Sabatión* poems, "Al Jolson" cannot be a condemnation of secularization and modernization as such. These features are not what makes Jolson's song "sweet but heartless." "Larry Semon" helps to clarify the problem. Semon also came from a ghetto background and made his name in Hollywood. But Semon's move to worldly sophistication appears as an enrichment, not a loss, for Jewish civilization. His career is eulogized: "Después a la pantalla / de un pro-digioso salto" (Then onto the screen / in a prodigious leap) and "En Hollywood se hizo / señor del lienzo pálido" (In Hollywood he became / lord of the pale screen). What virtue has Semon maintained and Jolson bartered away?

Tiempo emphasizes Semon's uninterrupted contact with the Jewish community. He was "fiel a su amor judío" (faithful to his Jewish love). The poem mutes Semon's reliance on impersonal, commercial media to make him a figure of the folk entertainer, "acróbata y payaso" (acrobat and clown). Semon's art is not directed to a Jewish audience and does not draw on any one tradition, but the poem attributes to it Jewish "magia" (magic) and "corazón" (heart). The implication is that these diffusely Jewish qualities may persist in art after specific ethnic traits disappear but only if the creator maintains a trace of Jewish spirit in work and life. The idea that modern, worldly endeavors may retain this element appears elsewhere in *Tiempo*, particularly in his tribute to Chaplin.[6]

"Equipaje" ("Baggage") (10) is plainly an urging to the creative person—who is directly addressed (perhaps the poet is speaking to himself)—to keep a certain cultural rootedness. Here a poet begins as an undifferentiated member of the poetic culture. His work has "monotonía como un reloj" (clockwork monotony) and an "opaco son" (opaque sound) until he listens to the everyday speech of ghetto dwellers. *Tiempo* tells this poet: "Pero halló [tu poesía] en la judería . . . música en su algarabía" (But [your poetry] found among the Jews . . . music in their patchwork of a language).

* * *

Noche hiemal en el ghetto

Tiritan las tres Marías
en su oscuro y vano lecho.

Atraviesan lentas sombras
la calle muerta de sueño.

El frío impacta en la piel
sus aguijones violentos.

La luna nieva y sus tenues
vellones cubren el ghetto.

En el metal de los gallos
la noche templa su celo.

Guiña un cartel luminoso
—*vox clamantis in deserto*—
sobre las turbias vidrieras
de los fondines hebreos.

Surcan los ríos de asfalto
los Lacrozes soñolientos.

Transgresores circuncisos
del séptimo mandamiento
naufragan en la luz fatua
de los zaguanes magnéticos.

La noche luce en Pasteur
zapatos de terciopelo.

Bocinas desesperadas
en la pleamar del silencio
rasgan su voz y se pierden
aullando en un túnel negro.

Un gato gime de amor
desde el alar de su imperio.

Jehová sonríe piadoso
bajo sus barbas de cielo.

(Winter Night in the Ghetto

The three Marys shiver
in their dark and fruitless bed.

Slow shadows cross
the street half-dead with sleep.

The cold strikes the skin
with its violent needles.

The moon is snowing and its tenuous
fleece spreads over the ghetto.

On the metal of the weathercocks
the night tempers its heat.

A neon sign winks
—*vox clamantis in deserto*—
over the murky windows
of the Hebrew eateries.

Sleepy Lacrozes furrow
the rivers of asphalt.

Circumcised transgressors
of the seventh commandment
flounder in the fool's light
of the magnetizing doorways.

On Pasteur the night
wears velvet shoes.

Desperate car horns
in the high tide of silence
shred their voices and are lost

howling down a black tunnel.

A cat moans with love
from the eaves of its empire.

Jehovah smiles compassionately
under his beard of sky.)

"Noche hiemal en el ghetto" (87–88) describes the Jewish district on a weekday night, not the numinous Sabbath to which Tiempo often refers. However, the night gains specialness from being called *hiemal;* Tiempo has passed over the common adjectival form *invernal* and the routine phrase *noche de invierno.* Just as the simple night in the shabby ghetto can merit such a noble adjective, the poem that describes that night can reach to all levels of speech for its lexicon. In this poem, it is possible to bring a term like *Lacroze,* the popular name for streetcars, together with the timeless, highly figurative *pleamar (high tide).*[7]

This eclecticism of wording corresponds to *Sabatión*'s view of modern urban existence, in which diverse possibilities coexist. The lexical variety makes the point that this pocket of Jewish culture is set inside a city that is not only predominantly Christian but also multicultural and that will necessarily make Jewish life more heterogeneous. Although the title sounds a Jewish note with *ghetto,* the first line contains a reminder that this area is not separate from its largely Christian surroundings. The lyrical *I* speaks from inside Jewish culture, as witnessed by his knowledge of the ghetto and his allusion to *Jehová.* Yet to refer to the stars, he uses a term of markedly Christian origin, "las tres Marías" (the three Marys). This allusion is seconded by a later citation from gospel narrative, transcribed in the Latin associated with Catholic liturgy. These clues show the speaker, for all his Jewish frame of reference, to have a mastery of the mainstream Christian culture.

Worthy of attention is Tiempo's use of *ghetto.* Though the term hardly has the surprise effect of *hiemal,* it is marked by its European quality. Consider, for example, that Bernardo Verbitsky's 1941 novel *Es difícil empezar a vivir (It's Hard to Start Living),* set in Jewish areas of the city, avoids *ghetto* and shows its hero disapproving of the term as a Europeanized affectation.[8]

Tiempo's rapid shifts in tone and register are clearly the result of a conscious set of choices. The poet draws attention to his eclecticism on many occasions. One poem, "Versos a un lexicón y a las corbatas" ("Verses to a Lexicon and the Neckties") (79–80) self-mockingly exaggerates the wild diversity of his lexical preferences. Poems often carry serious statements of the poet's right to mix and borrow (for example, the defense of Yiddish on page 54).

Tiempo chooses the lexicon of *Sabatión,* in all its diversity, to make certain statements. Some lexical choices celebrate the international speech of the cosmopolitan city. Tiempo favors terms that are by now widely internationalized, such as *vodka* and *jargon.* Elite loan words, though, are avoided in accord with the work's populist aesthetic. Technological additions to the lexicon, such as *asfalto,* are favored as a tribute to the modern era.

* * *

"Noche hiemal" displays a feature of Tiempo's writing much noted in his time: the inclusion of erotic references. Tiempo's referring in this vein to the Jewish population, which had been rigorously desexualized in Gerchunoff's treatment, lent an extra element of daring. This poem first hints of erotic desire in the figure of the cold stars, isolated not only in heatless space but also in their "vano lecho" (fruitless bed). The stars thus appear to be deprived of sexual, as well as physical, warmth. This metaphorical suggestion of desire is strengthened by the succeeding image of the night in heat pressing against the ghetto's weathervanes, which become the equivalent of live roosters. Before assuming the figure of a female in heat, the night has been strongly associated with the Jewish neighborhood it envelops. Now, with a dark, aroused female substance rubbing against it, the ghetto loses its innocent air.

The eighth stanza presents the strongest references to the excitation gripping the neighborhood. As notable as the boldness of the allusion is the poetic speaker's implied forgiveness of the brothel goers featured in this stanza. The lighthearted invocation of the Ten Commandments and the mock formality of "transgresores circuncisos" (circumcised transgressors) suggest that the sin in question, though indeed a sin, here is regarded with benign empathy for the ghetto dwellers and their human tendencies. This stanza makes the point that the men described are under Jewish law and for that reason can be characterized as transgressing it. The ghetto contains forces designed to both check and subdue human impulses and the errant urges that give rise to, and sometimes overcome, these controls. The biblical tradition of relating sexual misbehavior matter-of-factly—which Tiempo admired—here finds a modern correlative.

The final two stanzas confirm the benevolent character of the ghetto's collective eroticization. Directly after alluding to a cat's mating cries that fill the night air, the poem concludes: "Jehová sonríe piadoso / bajo sus barbas de cielo" (Jehovah smiles compassionately / under his beard of sky). By referring to God in such a markedly Jewish way, and with such assurance of divine tolerance for a degree of transgression, Tiempo promotes his version of Jewish conventions for the expression of sexuality and at the same time works to make this subject matter at home in Argentine literature. Like many of his generation, he sees relief from constraints of propriety as a means of literary revitalization.[9]

A survey of Tiempo's poetry quickly reveals the cultural sign with which he works most extensively: the Sabbath. The titles of his poetry collections—the 1930 *Libro para la pausa del sábado* (*Book for the Sabbath Pause*), winner of that year's Municipal Prize for Poetry; the 1933 *Sabatión argentino;* the 1938 *Sabadomingo* (*SabbathSunday,* also translatable as *SaturdaySunday*); and the 1955 *Sábado pleno* (*Full Sabbath*)—carry the term, as do the titles of individual poems. Moreover, in the poems frequent use is made of the word *sábado,* its adjectival form, and other terms referring to the Sabbath such as *pausa* (*pause*) and *descanso* (*rest*). In addition, following Tiempo's cross-cultural system, references to the Christian Sabbath second the ones signaling the Jewish Sabbath. The highlighting of the concept of the Sabbath is also accomplished by making the epigraph to *Sabatión argentino* a cryptic meditation on the meaning of this exceptional day and by subtitling the collection "Antiguas y nuevas donas para la pausa del sábado" ("New and Old Songs for the Sabbath Pause").

To see how Tiempo elaborates his modern, secular poetry around the essentially religious concept of the Sabbath, one may usefully start with Robert Alter's remarks on contemporary Jewish poetry in languages other than Hebrew and Yiddish. In Alter's analysis, the lack of an inherently Jewish medium can drive a poet to monotonous reliance on religious allusions, producing "a dense cluster of old rabbis, bearded Jews swaying in prayer shawls, flickering Sabbath candles, wailing walls, open Talmud folios, Torah scrolls, angular Hebrew letters floating through the air or tangled in burning bushes, a la Ben Shawn." The resulting narrow range of subject matter and imagery impresses Alter as an unfortunate deviation from the openness to secular experience of Hebrew poets who, by long tradition, "write of spring gardens, breasts that invite caresses, the pleasures of drinking, the misery of old whores, the evils of patronage, the squalor of prison, the boisterousness of common inns, claiming as their natural right of experience everything from humble cabbages to the grandeur of kings."[10]

Sabatión shows the same desire Alter here expresses: to maintain a wide scope of themes and images. The poetry of the volume does rely on references to religious ways. Sabbath observance, particularly, comes in for close attention, with Tiempo defending the idea of a period of limited activity. Yet there is also evidence of an effort to insure that worldly poetic elements—and readers of secular outlook—will be equally at home in these texts.

* * *

Sabatión porteño

Oleaje rubio. Vértigo. Folía.
Bajo el látigo azul de las auroras
bullen las calles de la judería.

Pasan lentas muchachas seductoras,
zumba la jerga de los trafagones
y entre la vibración de las sonoras

risas estallan las interjecciones
cuando los hijos de Israel realizan
con el agua solar sus abluciones.

Banderas de humo los tejados izan,
cunden las horas y la baraúnda,
mientras tus vanos sueños aterrizan

entre la grey aurívora que inunda
feria y zaguanes con su mercancía
pregonada con frase gemebunda.

En la humana pleamar padecería
—como yo entre morcones y buhoneros—
San Francisco de Asís: licantropía.

Pena de verse en todos los senderos
y en el espejo móvil de los ríos:
lobo de hermanos, lobo de corderos.

Pero llegan los sábados judíos,
misericordia y luz de las semanas
para tus sueños y los sueños míos.

Y abre el ghetto sus tímidas ventanas

por donde irrumpe generosamente
la lluvia celestial de las mañanas.

¡Sennacherib! ¡Sennacherib! la ardiente
voz de los muros imantó la espada
que trunca desde lo alto la corriente
del Sabatión. Y es nuestra la jornada.

(Great Buenos Aires Sabbath

Blond waves. Vertigo. Madness.
Under the blue whip of the dawns
the streets of the Jewish quarter bustle.

Slow, seductive girls pass by,
the jargon of street vendors buzzes
and amid the vibration of the sounding

laughter interjections explode
when the children of Israel perform
their ablutions with the water of the sun.

The rooftops raise banners of smoke,
the hours and the noisy crush spread out
as your useless dreams come down to earth

amid the gold-crazed herd that inundates
the market stalls and doorways with its merchandise
cried out in a moaning phrase.

In the human high tide, St. Francis
of Assisi—like me among the slobs
and hawkers—would suffer from lycanthropy.

The pain of seeing yourself down every pathway
and in the moving mirror of the rivers:
wolf to brothers, wolf to lambs.

But the Jewish Sabbaths come around,
mercy and light of the weeks
for your dreams and these dreams of mine.

And the ghetto opens its timid windows
into which there bursts, generously,
the heavenly rain of the mornings.

Sennecherib! Sennacherib! the burning
voice of the walls magnetically drew down the sword

that cuts off, from on high, the current
of the great Sabbath. And the day is ours.)

"Sabatión porteño" is, as the title correctly notes, a poem centered on the Sabbath. Yet to open up the possibilities of meaning he sees inherent in the term and concept, Tiempo assigns the greater part of the poem to that which is *not* the Sabbath. The poem is in three segments: seven tercets, two further but distinct tercets, and a concluding quatrain. Especially notable is Tiempo's reliance on conventions of *terza rima,* a form indissolubly linked to Christian tradition through its use in the *Divina Commedia.* The quatrain stands apart from the rest of the poem with its liturgical-scriptural language and high level of abstraction. The tercets, though, are similar in their form and relatively colloquial expression, so that the shift between the first seven and the last two tercets is entirely a function of the poem's praise of the Sabbath. The first seven stanzas describe what occurs in the absence of the Sabbath, whereas the last three show the privileged day itself.

The justification for this unequal distribution is twofold. As the poem points out, it is the overstimulation typical of weekdays that makes the Sabbath necessary and meaningful. On the other hand, the bustling street scenes provide livelier images than does the evocation of the Sabbath, dominated by the cessation of activity. It should be recalled that Tiempo had developed as one of his literary trademarks the lyrical vignette of busy street life.

The poem's opening line, a series of isolated nouns, appears to mimic the fragments of speech heard in the street. Only one of these units is extended by the addition of an adjective. The resemblance to staccato bursts of street sound is furthered by the periods that set full stops between the three elements. The words presented in this choppy series carry the meanings already expressed in the construction, alluding to the chaotic forces of the street and their effects on the human beings involved in the scene. Perhaps the most spectacular and innovative twist in the poem occurs in the sixth stanza, with its variant version of the legend of St. Francis. With his characteristic fondness for intersplicing cultural traditions, Tiempo mixes the saint's story with the werewolf lore.

This conjunction permits a playful turnabout. The poem does not contradict the traditional belief that Francis attained an exceptional tranquillity that he could impart to wild creatures. The conventional image of the saint fraternizing with wolves is assumed as a given. Tiempo adds a speculation, in the conditional mode, about how Francis might behave if immersed in the "humana pleamar" (human high tide) of the crowded ghetto. Overstimulated by the congested street, Francis retains his fabled closeness to wolves. But now, instead of communicating to the animals his peaceful holiness, he acquires their rapacity and turns to lycanthropy. Adding a further whimsical twist, the speaker in the poem claims himself to suffer from this improbable disorder. Lycanthropy here arises from immersion among street merchants, which suggests that it is a metaphor for the misanthropy and lack of charity provoked by seeing people in oppressive proximity and at their most aggressive.

This reversal provides the occasion for further surprising turns. The conventional epithet for Francis, "hermano de lobos" (brother to wolves) becomes "lobo de hermanos" (wolf to brothers), as the saint, his charity exhausted, now preys on his fellow men. The seventh stanza continues the subtly bitter series of jokes, employing the pastoral imagery of Francis legends (sheep, wolves, paths, and rivers) to complain of the urban horror of seeing other human beings ("seeing yourself," as the poem puts it) in constant closeness.

With the opening of the eighth stanza, the poem shifts away from the noisy street and from the playful experimentation it has so far displayed. The eighth and ninth verses convey the sobriety of the Sabbath in coherently arranged sentences, each occupying a complete stanza to itself. (Compare this order to the unexpected division of the sentence that runs from stanza two to three.) Enhancing this propriety is the lack of any eccentric metaphors that might tinge this ending with avant-gardism.

In his sudden restraint, the speaker in the poem parallels the individual who observes the Sabbath. Obviously, the parallel is not very literal, since the writing of secular poetry would have no place in a strictly observed Sabbath. But Sabbath restraint is poetically simulated by renouncing, for a given stretch of text, the pleasures, obviously dear to this poet, of describing urbanites amid their worldly pursuits and of creating a language full of jokes and whimsical metaphors.

The eighth and ninth stanzas are further marked as Sabbath by the biblical and liturgical shadings of the characterization of this special time as "misericordia y luz de las semanas" (mercy and light of the weeks). *Misericordia* can be counted on to evoke Catholic liturgical expression, virtually its only context in Spanish. The allusion to light draws on the metaphorical convention whereby humankind is sunken in darkness except when brought into the light through exertions of the spirit.

Despite the pious restraint of these stanzas, a return to the world is already under way. The first clue occurs when the poem divulges that ghetto residents actually enjoy a relaxed Sabbath observance. Rather than devote themselves entirely to religious concerns, they take advantage of the free time to allow their imaginations to flourish. With the line "para tus sueños y os sueños míos" (for your dreams and these dreams of mine), Tiempo moves irremediably toward a modern understanding of ritual time. Both *you* and *I* are benefiting from the exempt period to examine our own ideas and feelings.

The ninth stanza continues this tendency by returning to the street, now shown on the Sabbath. The previously frenetic residents now take no more vigorous action than opening a window to savor the fine weather. The figurative language remains modest, limited to a classical hypallage, "abre el ghetto sus tímidas ventanas" (the ghetto opens its timid windows), and to a trope in which rain and sunshine become interchangeable transforms of one another. The religious reference grows vaguely pantheistic, the weather containing or conveying the essence of the Sabbath: "lluvia celestial" (heavenly rain).

The last quatrain is the most liturgical. It begins with the public crying of a formula that separates the Sabbath from weekdays. In the poem's construction too, the cry effects this transition, bringing to an end Tiempo's poetic version of the Sabbath period.

Much of the novelty and interest of the concluding quatrain is in the crying out of a meaning-laden word, a typical resource in liturgical language. Tiempo gives a literary variant of this tradition of "calling out" in a language of biblical resonance. Here, in a complicated series of figures, the crying out of the name of the historical enemy of Jewish observance is performed by "la ardiente / voz de los muros" (the burning / voice of the walls), instead of merely echoing off the walls. The utterance then draws down a sword, cutting off the current that held together the heavens and the earth for the duration of the Sabbath.

This display of metaphors bears many traces of conventional religious discourse, particularly in the sword wielded "desde lo alto" (from on high) to alter life on earth. Yet in other ways, Tiempo moves away from religious thought. He avoids identifying the entity that wields the sword. "Lo alto" is one of his many diffuse and nonspecific terms that appear where a reference to the divinity might be expected. Moreover, the explanation of the Sabbath as a flow of current between this unspecified force and the observant Jews has a decidedly modern cast. A current that can be cut off (albeit with a sword from on high) and reconnected belongs to the era of technology. Whereas magnets are a long-standing part of human civilization, the idea of crying out as a magnetic force attracting the instrument of a higher will is also a mechanical, and therefore to some degree modern, notion. Tiempo, like other followers of avant-garde poetic thought, favored mechanical images as a way of making his verse strikingly contemporary.

The final stanza is, for these reasons, exemplary of Tiempo's efforts to unite the traditional with the modern, Jewish spirituality with some undifferentiated variety, and Jewish religious heritage with a secular, cosmopolitan conception of Jewishness. The stanza also achieves a balance within the poem itself, standing midway between the brash experimentalism of the first seven stanzas and the conservative, respectful tone of the following two. Although the conclusion displays touches of modernity in its allusions and its emphasis on innovative metaphor, it stops short of the earlier playful tampering with religious tradition.

Tiempo views the Sabbath, in essence, as do modernizers of Jewish thought who seek to retain meaning in ritual observances into the present era. His poetic presentation of the Sabbath resembles, for example, Abraham Joshua Heschel's interpretation, described as follows:

What is the Sabbath, Heschel asks. . . . Mankind, he suggests, lives in the realm of time. Man constantly fights the elements; he seeks to change the empirical world so that it will produce more goods for him. Beyond the realm of time, however, is the sphere of eternity. Eternity, for Heschel, symbolizes perfect reality. It lies above all our efforts in time and by the perfection of its vision it directs them. The Sabbath does, it is true, consist of laws and obligations. Sabbath observance includes the ritual activities of lighting candles, refraining from work, changing one's behavior pattern. . . . All that, however, is not essential. The essential power of the Sabbath lies in the glimpse it gives of a world beyond strife, of a period of peace and tranquility.[11]

* * *

Tiempo's Sabbath poetry represents an accommodation of diverse standards: those of the avant-garde, those of social poetry, and those Tiempo set for himself as a poet of Jewish tradition and as a defender of the modern transformations of Jewish life. It is necessarily a compromise between divergent criteria. The poetic language is far from the "new expression" advocated by the avant-garde. Its conservatism is not from any failure of imagination but from a desire to temper experimentation with both respect for tradition and concern for the portrayal of social realities. Tiempo's roles as a poet of Jewish tradition and an observer of ghetto life rule out any language so spectacularly innovative as to obscure the comment his poetry makes.

Though showing the ghetto dwellers in a worldly setting, the poems speak favorably of the maintenance of Jewish ways. Tiempo avoids any suggestion that Jews must choose between Jewish and Argentine ways; however, neither does he confront and challenge this widely held assumption, as later writers will do. He takes care to downplay the differences between Jewish ways and those of the long-established Argentine population. This edited vision offers an alternative to the popular argument that Jews must sacrifice ethnic and religious tradition to be good Argentines. Just as these two identities are compatible, so other supposed opposites prove complementary. High art harmonizes with popular culture, and religious concerns accord with worldly ones. Alternatively an avant-gardist, a realist, a neotraditionalist, and a modernizer, Tiempo celebrates the cosmopolitan environment as a space of new, hybrid cultural forms.

3 BERNARDO VERBITSKY

Toward a Critical Discussion of Jewish Argentine Issues

Bernardo Verbitsky (1907–1979) came to prominence with his 1941 novel *Es difícil empezar a vivir* (*It's Hard to Start Living*).[1] It is considered an important example of the realism that flourished in Argentina in the 1930s and 1940s. Criticism of the work has extolled its ability to bear witness to the social realities of its time. Juan Pinto, for example, lists it as one of the two works indispensable to an understanding of Argentina in the 1930s.[2]

This study examines the novel as an appeal for a more critical discussion of Jewish Argentine issues. The text offers itself as a starting point for such a discussion. At the same time the text shows, through the example of its hesitant protagonist, some of the difficulties that must be overcome to start up a critical dialogue. Verbitsky encourages, in particular, a revival of the Jewish tradition of examination and debate of social ethics. The novel makes the point that this heritage has become debilitated among Jewish Argentines. For historical reasons, this population has been reluctant to criticize society and, as is shown in the novel, has lost the skills needed to articulate such concerns. *Es difícil* also shows its protagonist learning how to overcome this inarticulate condition and acquire an ability to comment on events in society.

When Verbitsky's novel appeared, Jewish Argentine writing had still not moved far from its initial acritical mode. Gerchunoff had promoted a belief that Jewish Argentines should gratefully praise the nation, not subject it to critical questioning. Tiempo avoided some of the more objectionable features of Gerchunoff's approach, but Tiempo's celebratory lyricism did not offer much of a basis for questioning and evaluating social arrangements. Saúl Sosnowski has noted how difficult it was for such a model to emerge. In his analysis of the problem he shows that as late as the 1960s, the young playwright Germán Rozenmacher (1936–1971) still shied away from criticizing the social structure. Sosnowski suggests that to look at concerns within the Jewish family or community, as Rozenmacher attempted to do, the writer must be willing to examine and judge the entire national society. Verbitsky's novel began the move toward a society-wide analysis of Jewish issues in the light of social history.[3]

Es difícil has been pointed out as an example of Jewish subject matter in Kessel Schwartz's overview of Jewish Argentine writing. Nora Glickman raises the more analytical issue of how these themes are embedded in the overall novel.[4] The integration of Jewish concerns into a larger picture, a crucial matter in the novel, occurs through three basic procedures. The first is the use of symmetrical constructions. For example, episodes in the novel that are similar in structure and rhetorical function deal, in some cases, with Jewish issues and, in others, with problems of concern to any member of society. These parallel constructions make the point that Jewish issues are, in many cases, aspects of difficulties affecting the entire social structure.

Second, Verbitsky urges the reader to think about the possibilities for a revitalized Jewish discourse, beyond that established by tradition. The novel contains considerable discussion of the relevance or irrelevance of modern, secular imaginative writing, essays, and journalism. The protagonist, in his search for a better formulation of his inchoate ideas, turns to various forms of writing, both as author and as reader. The ways in which these modes frustrate him or bring him insight reveal what is most needed in future writing. In particular, Verbitsky makes a case for thoughtful discussion of such pressing Jewish issues as the maintenance of identity in a secular context. He stresses the point that a Jewish Argentine literature striving for official acceptability cannot meet the needs of reflective, questioning Jewish readers.[5]

Third, the novel is full of eloquent silences. It pulls back from making too definitive a statement about contemporary Jewish Argentines or their situation, identity, and needs. Major aspects of the plot remain unresolved or unclarified because any less equivocal treatment would implicitly constitute a form of editorializing commentary. The goal is not to deliver the last word on issues facing Argentine Jewry but to help begin what should be an extensive and lengthy discussion. To gain an idea of the novel's reticence, consider that over half the work has transpired before the Jewish subject matter for which it is so noted receives more than passing treatment.

* * *

Es difícil chronicles a confused period in the life of Pablo Levinson. Though Pablo is vaguely a medical student, a newsman, a writer, and a Jew, he finds it "difficult to start living" as any of these. In establishing parallels between Pablo's recovery of his Jewishness and his search for a meaningful occupation, the novel forges its structural unity. Uncertain of belonging in any of his possible roles, Pablo repeatedly puts himself through tests. The most notable such episodes are his resolutions to take his medical school examination and to observe Yom Kippur. The examination requires a fee and the risk of failure, both difficult for the poor and uneasy Pablo. However, it offers the chance to affirm himself as a student and future physician. The High Holy Days do not demand the same investment; Pablo makes this resolution without disclosing it. Yet it also provides a means to establish a currently imperiled aspect of himself, his Jewish identity.

Pablo fails both trials. The examiners call his name, but Pablo, who has been inattentive to his studies, remains seated instead of presenting himself for questioning. Pablo fails to observe Yom Kippur, forgetting that the Jewish day begins at sundown. Whether the issue is medical expertise or familiarity with Jewish tradition, the hero has neglected to acquire information he needs. The fact that the needed knowledge is easy to obtain—Pablo has the required textbooks and a pious friend—points to self-imposed defeat. Pablo cannot prepare himself for trials because he is too uncertain that he belongs in the very roles he seeks to master.

The portrayal of Pablo's insecure bonds to Jewishness and to society gains complexity through his friendship with Leo. Leo shares with Pablo the roles of medical student and contemporary urban Jew. However, for Leo neither is problematic; this stolid character is interesting only for the contrast he provides with Pablo and for the way he exemplifies, even with all his outward success, the failure of critical tradition. His unreflectively serene performance in completing his medical studies and in maintaining specifically Jewish behaviors contrasts with Pablo's floundering attempts. The interactions of the two bring to the fore Pablo's greater need and willingness to think about Jewishness and his lack of preparation for doing so; he does not know even the most common and banal terms of discussion. For example, he has never heard it suggested that the Jewish people have made a special contribution to the arts. Leo is almost monotonously correct in his knowledge of Jewish matters but seems to feel no drive to reflect on issues. He has acquired a Jewish education and now owns the resulting fund of knowledge like an inert possession.

The contrast between the two reaches an extreme during what is for Pablo the crisis of the holy days. Leo's observance is a matter of course; he knows what is required of him and gives it no further consideration. Pablo has precipitously taken up the unaccustomed holidays in response to a chance remark. He devotes vigorous, lengthy thought to the matter, his mind roiling with conflicting emotions, vague memories, and half-formed opinions; but he does not extend his efforts to the acquisition of knowledge.

When Pablo and Leo both study for the examination, the same contrast emerges. Pablo's thoughts during this period receive extensive coverage and in fact deserve such attention for their complexity and dynamic mutability. Observation of a clinical session sends him into a series of reflections (209–12). Indirect interior monologue reveals a mind fraught with doubts and conflicts. Pablo questions his own motivations in entering medicine, the concept of a medical priesthood, and the efficacy of current training practices. He succeeds in locating and exploring the most troubling areas of the medical profession, but in so doing, he ruins his concentration on the immediate subject matter (215–18). During the same period, Leo's intellectual and emotional response to the same stimuli is apparently not worth mentioning. The narrator sums up: "Leo rindió bien su examen. Intensificó su dedicación en las últimas semanas al enterarse . . . [del] puesto" (Leo did well on his examination. He intensified his dedication in the last weeks after he found out about . . . [the] opening) (215).

Leo is in some senses more positively presented than Pablo. He avoids the shameful failures that plague his friend. Leo's ingrained Jewish concern for knowledge and intellectually satisfying forms of livelihood stands him in good stead. Still, he is undeniably the lesser of the two, according to the criteria implicit in the novel. Leo seems to have mastered tradition, but the essential dynamic element is missing. He has failed to develop the spirit of analytical questioning that is historically part of Jewish thought.

Pablo, in contrast, has a restlessness of mind that makes him a good candidate to carry on Jewish traditions of evaluative analysis of and inquiry into society, although his present ignorance inhibits this ability. Because he is always in a process of development, as the title notes, he is at the beginning of his moral and intellectual life. He is potentially able to remedy his deficiencies, something that cannot be said of the already fully formed Leo. Moreover, Pablo understands the need for interpretation and debate. Leo sees no point in intellectual argument; he evades it even when Pablo goes to lengths to provoke him. The more adept and knowledgeable character cannot question the worth of the cultural legacy he appears to represent and for this reason is not a fitting representative. Leo's accepting placidity disqualifies him as an exemplary figure in a novel whose highest values—and the highest values it assigns to Jewish tradition—are critical awareness and discussion of society's ethics.

* * *

Reading, as a way to raise critical awareness, is a major topic in *Es difícil*. In hopes of clarifying his thought, Pablo reads a broad selection of materials. His progress as a self-taught reader of literature will be discussed shortly, but first one should note that Pablo is deeply affected by his nonliterary readings, and these sources receive close attention in the novel.

The nonliterary materials that so impress Pablo come to him unsought, in contrast to the literature he struggles to master. He must monitor news dispatches as part of his journalistic work, whereas political leaflets and manifestoes are pressed on him by student activists. When he reads newspapers, his mind is involuntarily drawn to advertisements for medical services, which fascinate him with their simultaneous euphemism and crudity. These readings, powerfully stimulating to Pablo's imagination, appear reproduced verbatim in the text of *Es difícil*. For example, news items from a wire service, bringing word of Hitler's rise, appear on pages 254–59, medical advertisements on pages 210–11, and the leaflets of student protesters on pages 282–85. The inclusion of these texts in their raw form carries the suggestion that a literary treatment of events, in which language is refined and themes are clarified, is inadequate to the task of conveying the harshness and confusion of many contemporary phenomena. This notion in turn helps to account for the form of *Es difícil*, at times vague, inconclusive, and full of gaps.

In this novel, which often gives little indication where it is leading, the scenes in which the hero reads literature offer a degree of guidance. Pablo makes an effort to become a critical reader of literature, though his background is scanty. His insights always appear to be essentially valid, but his ability to articulate them is weak. The reader of the novel is frequently the one to complete an observation that Pablo has left partially formulated.

A good instance is the scene (86–87) in which Pablo discovers, on his own, the realist aesthetic that is his literary ideal. Not too surprisingly, he favors the workmanly, specifically Argentine realism that Verbitsky recommended to the nation's writers. These ideas arise while Pablo examines and judges a small literary review. He carries out this evaluation while sitting among the journal's contributors, whose conversation also comes in for critical assessment. Like the famous library scene in *Don Quixote*, this episode contains novelistic clues to what is most needed in literature.

Pablo's severest judgment falls on an essay giving the author's ethereal impressions while listening to a piece by Chopin. Pablo first reacts with vague revulsion, thinking "todo lo vulgar y ramplón estaba" (it was as cheap and overdone as could be) (86), but soon develops his inchoate rejection into the beginnings of a realist aesthetic. The author's exaltation of the refinement of Chopin's work and his own responses to it has avoided the responsibilities Pablo sees as most incumbent on writers: observation (he doubts that any real listening occurred) and straightforward representa-

tion. These principles become clearer to Pablo, as to the reader, when he
next approves of an unaffected description of scenes of Jewish Argentine
life.

Pablo's only complaint about the latter essay is the too evident influence
its author has received from Israel Zangwill. Further pursuing the idea of
fidelity to the cultural setting in which the writer works, Pablo internally
objects to the writers around him using the term *ghetto* for Jewish neigh-
borhoods in Buenos Aires. To his mind, this lexical choice is a European
affectation that could distort the experience these writers aspire to express.
Verbitsky himself avoids the word *ghetto* throughout the novel, except in
the dialogue of the journal's writing staff, and seldom employs lexical
borrowings that would stand out from the plain Spanish of his text.

Although this scene makes the case for an Argentine literature faithful to
national realities, no doctrine of cultural nationalism is being propounded.
Indeed, Pablo obtains his self-guided education from a broad selection of
authors, Argentine and foreign, populists and practitioners of high art. The
pattern of his readings parallels Verbitsky's own set of preferences as a
reviewer and critic. Notably, Pablo finds it useful in establishing his own
personal identity and outlook to read modern, cosmopolitan Jewish writers. Verbitsky consistently promoted the best among such authors in his
literary criticism and wrote monographic studies on Stefan Zweig and
Arthur Miller (see the bibliography for a listing of Verbitsky's criticism). In
Pablo's literary experiences, as in Verbitsky's commentary, these writers
prove most interesting when they show Jewish characters engaged with the
secular, urban world and when they are themselves fully part of the literature of their respective countries.

* * *

Es difícil, with its relatively few narrative events, is a long novel. Its length
is in part a result of the narrator's practice of allowing the reader to observe
Pablo in the slow process of reaching his own conclusions. With his vague
and often acritical mind, the protagonist needs exposure to a variety of
experiences before he can draw a suitable generalization. The narrator is
under strict constraints in the information he can provide about Pablo.
Though he may reveal the protagonist's thoughts of the present moment,
the narrator cannot anticipate the future development of the young man's
ideas. Nor can he offer an analysis and interpretation of these half-formed
notions.

The past, which might illuminate Pablo's present state of mind, is closed to the reader unless the protagonist himself recalls it. *Es difícil* not only dispenses with the once conventional initial summary of the hero's relevant past experiences but also never interrupts the chronicle of his present confusion to supply background information. These rules of narration place the novel firmly in the here and now and give it its fragmentary construction.[6] The paucity of connecting and contextualizing material, and the narrator's reluctance to draw conclusions, help to account for the impression the novel makes on some readers. Carmelo M. Bonet gives characteristic expressions of this impression that the narrative does not coalesce into a novel: "More than a novel, it is the chronicle of a life"; "No story line is developed; there's no central conflict or dénouement."[7]

Perhaps the most outstanding example of the novel's reticence is its silence concerning the questions one would be most apt to ask about a young person confused over his Jewish identity. The reader may quite reasonably wonder how extensive Pablo's Jewish background has been. Typically vague is one of the few references to his childhood, when he suddenly remembers holidays:

Se entretenía en su visión, que de pronto entroncó con el recuerdo de muchos días de perdón que había pasado de chico en el campo. . . . Esa neblina blanca recordaba la sinagoga llena de hombres en una tarde calurosa de un día del perdón; faltaban pocas horas para el término del ayuno y allí seguían todos desde el comienzo de la mañana, con sus "tales" colgando desde los hombros. Ya era una escena marchita. Débiles, cansados, proseguían animosamente. Rostros amarillos transparentes de debilidad. . . . Por sobre los reunidos flotaba una neblina, un vaho pesado y agrio.

(He became absorbed in his vision, which suddenly came together with the memory of many Days of Repentance that he had spent as a child in the country. . . . That white mist was reminiscent of the synagogue full of men on the warm afternoon of a Day of Repentance; it was only a few hours till the end of the fast, and everyone had been going on since early morning, with his talit drooping down from his shoulders. It was already a withered scene. Weak, tired, they went on spiritedly. Yellow faces transparent with weakness. . . . Above the gathering there floated a mist, a heavy, bitter exhalation) (190–91).

This scene, hazy and befogged in Pablo's mind, veils his own degree of involvement in or understanding of these observances. Pablo's present family life affords even fewer indications. His sole family contact is an uncle so unforthcoming as to discourage inquiry. The family's past remains inaccessible; even its present is difficult to know about. Pablo himself is astonished by the scant flow of information. In one scene, his uncle tells him of his plans to move to the country only when arrangements are already under way. Pablo recognizes that his uncle's move would leave him "sin casa" (homeless) (231) but cannot inquire more closely into his part in the sketchily divulged plans. When the novel ends, Pablo still has no information on two important points: whether his exclusion from his family is permanent and why the separation is taking place.

Other indications signal the uninformative quality of talk within the family. His uncle and aunt are silent concerning Pablo's virtual abandonment of medical studies and his sudden surge of Jewishness. In their conversation, the shared past is not recalled; the reader can abstract from these exchanges very little information about family members. This pattern does not suggest that the characters are reserved but that they are inadequately bonded as a family. Since the family bears major responsibility for maintaining Jewish identity, together with imparting the knowledge required to continue tradition, Pablo is at a great disadvantage. He cannot obtain insight from a family unwilling to discuss either Jewish topics or its own unity.

Orphaned from the Jewish tradition of critical discussion, Pablo tries one measure after another to become part of such an exchange. He carries around in his mind an agenda of issues he desperately cares to argue over and analyze: Jewish immigration, the Radical government of the 1920s, the military coup of 1930, and university governance. Still, instead of worthwhile sessions of interpretive discussion, Pablo finds himself provoking aimless, acritical conversations. Samples of these frustrating exchanges appear throughout the novel, as when Pablo attempts to engage an old-line Radical party member in a polemical exchange:

—Yo—le dijo inesperadamente—, siempre fui radical . . .
—Sin saber por qué, por supuesto—le dijo Pablo buscando todavía el modo de pelearle.
—No, al contrario. Me siento muy cómodo en el radicalismo.
—¿Muy cómodo?
—Sí. Además, ¿qué otra cosa se puede ser sino radical? ¿Socialista?
—Por ejemplo.
—Pero es que el socialismo, a mi juicio, es demasiado dogmático.
El hombre tenía evidentemente sus ideas políticas o disponía por lo menos de términos que empleaba incurriendo en confusiones típicamente irigoyenistas y de antes de la revolución.

("I," he said unexpectedly, "was always a Radical . . .")

"Without knowing why, of course," said Pablo, still trying to get into a dispute with him.

"No, not that at all. I feel very comfortable with Radicalism."

"Very comfortable?"

"Right. Besides, what else is there to be besides a Radical? A Socialist?"

"Well, that, for one thing."

"But socialism, as far as I'm concerned, is too dogmatic."

The man evidently had his political ideas or at least a stock of phrases he used falling into the typical confusions of precoup Irigoyen followers) (163).

Notably, even after the old Radical's inadequacies are obvious, the exchange continues. The prolongation of the tedious discussion would be a tactless imposition on the reader's patience, except that it testifies to Pablo's desperate search for critical dialogue.

* * *

Pablo's difficulties as a slow beginner give the novel its characteristic form. The plan of *Es difícil* is to follow Pablo's faltering steps toward a knowledgeable articulation of his concerns. The narrator is not permitted to intervene and accelerate the exposition by explaining to the reader what Pablo perceived but was unable to bring into clear focus. Nor can summaries by the narrator be used to bridge those lengthy periods when Pablo makes little headway. These ground rules slow the novel's development; at times its pace is frustratingly sluggish. Yet this hesitant unfolding of the story works to convey the point that when the lively tradition of critical thought falls into disuse, it is indeed difficult to resuscitate.

4 DAVID VIÑAS

The Novelistics of Cultural Contradiction

David Viñas (1929–) is best known for his ambitious critical undertaking *Literatura argentina y realidad política* (*Argentine Literature and Political Reality*), designed to provide an analysis of the historical forces that have shaped Argentine literary culture.[1] At the same time, he has attracted critical attention for his dramatic and narrative writings.[2] Previous criticism has noted that Viñas's fiction conveys the same ideas expounded in his essays.[3] This circumstance is hardly surprising, and the work of identifying Viñas's social ideas in his fiction is too easy a task to require critical commentary. A more complex issue is the way in which Viñas's characters become interpreters of Argentine history and current political realities. Just as the audience for Viñas's writings (fiction or essay) either learns to understand his overall picture of Argentine society or fails to gain insight, his characters either learn to spot the cultural contradictions around them or absorb no new understanding. The failure to read and interpret Argentine political realities is most typically, in Viñas's writings, attributable to a mythified view consonant with ruling-class interests.

In Viñas's works, the myths that need to be unlearned and the historical realities that need to be learned are many. This study of his 1962 novel *Dar la cara* (*Making a Stand*) concentrates on one area in which the reader, and with him the characters, ought to acquire new insights.[4] This area is ethnicity, strongly associated with social class, and it includes the special ethnic issue of Jewishness. As Humberto Rasi has observed, "Viñas conceives of Argentine history as a continuum within which different classes in conflict compete successively to play the leading role in politics."[5] To look at any question of ethnicity, the student of society must first recognize that immigrant groups in Argentine society counted as a threat to the traditional elite formed during the 1880s.

Whereas the establishment group encouraged immigration to European- ize and "civilize" the country, particularly its interior, too much upward mobility on the part of immigrants or their children met with determined resistance. The ethnic person's understanding of his relation to society will be inaccurate unless this overall model of groups in conflict is basic in his mind. Yet, as analysis of the novel shows, the fundamental notion that the elite seeks to control the destinies and images of less prestigious groups is a difficult concept for Viñas's more myth-minded characters to grasp. The contradictions arising from a failure to learn the historical competition among groups create much of the matter of the narrative; in addition, they serve as a warning to the reader who may be liable to reject the conflict model.

Seconding this struggle between rising immigrants and entrenched old stock is a concept of the historical mission of the Jewish people. *Dar la cara* promotes an understanding of Jewish election or mission in which the designated task of the people is to take active responsibility for the just working of society. Viñas, basing himself substantially on certain of the traditional notions of Jewishness, extends the Jew's heightened responsibility to the community to include an obligatory dissident stance.[6] Whereas the idea of Jews as questioners and dissenters fits the notion of ethnicities in antagonism, the novel's two basic concepts about Jewishness also give rise to conflict. As immigrant latecomers competing for power, the Jewish characters may be misled by a dream of mainstream success that distracts them from their commitment to a just society.

In Viñas's *Dar la cara,* one basic feature of the novel's construction serves to present the many contradictions of the social and cultural situation. A character and his circumstance first appear as if they were not especially difficult to classify and comprehend. Most typical, a character makes his entrance in the novel behaving in a seemingly consistent, coherent fashion. Subsequent developments then uncover the disguised contradictions and incongruities of the matter, revealing a host of interrelated cultural problems and the myths that function to explain them away. What seems recognizable and easily assimilable proves more and more problematic and disquieting. As the complexity of the issue increases there is a corresponding accretion of information about the matter, some of it difficult to reconcile with other portions. The most desirable outcome of these novelistic procedures is to stimulate the reader to look beyond coherent appearances to see the interacting historical forces and long-standing cultural conflicts that shape society and individuals.

The following analysis focuses on two characters whose exposition follows this pattern of increasing complication. Each has a life filled with incongruities and contradictions strongly associated with a nonelite ethnic identity. The Syrian-Lebanese-Argentine Sabul is notable for his own inability to recognize the massive conflicts that influence his behavior and the responses of others to him. Bernardo Carman is the novel's most fully developed character. Unlike Sabul, he begins to examine his conflict-filled situation, just as the reader is expected to do. Bernardo begins to think through not only his outsider status as an immigrant family's son but also the special historical mission of the Jewish people with regard to social responsibility.

* * *

The inconspicuous ethnicity of Bernardo stands in contrast to the constantly visible Middle Eastern origin of his friend Sabul. Bernardo's appearance does not draw attention to his Jewishness; rather, those around him are reminded of his cultural identity only when his behavior coincides with the Jewish stereotype. Sabul, though, finds his markedly nonstandard features a target of frequent commentary. He is often addressed as *turco* or *turquito,* terms that in popular Argentine usage cover a host of vaguely related ethnicities. Moreover, the type of attention his ethnic identity elicits is of a remarkably unintelligent nature. On one occasion, an interlocutor breaks off an unrelated conversation to inquire whether Sabul is *turco,* then discards Sabul's reply that he is *siriolibanés* by telling him the distinction is of no importance. Even the protagonist, Bernardo, who attempts to think in an independent fashion, frequently finds stereotypical associations running through his mind at the sight of Sabul. For instance, Sabul often reminds Bernardo of an exotic prophet (140).

Sabul, like other characters and phenomena in the novel, initially presents a more coherent image than his subsequent thoughts and acts reveal. The characteristics he first displays are youthful impetuosity and a fondness for highly abstract social criticism. He celebrates his army discharge by aiming a seltzer-water siphon at both things and people; in a more restrained mood, he pronounces sententiously on the Argentine national character. This early evidence tends to establish Sabul as an uncomplicated individual—rash, not always well considered in his remarks, and disdainful of standard notions of propriety. Though this preliminary picture of Sabul fits well with his self-definition, it does not account for information later revealed about him. The romantic-spontaneous myth of Sabul covers a host of contradictions. The reader gradually learns to see in the young man and his theories the illusory reconciliation of antiestablishment feelings with adoring reverence toward the elite.

The first clue to Sabul's gravely askew mode of thought is the persistence with which he denies the materialist basis of various social arrangements. This tendency results in, for example, his statement that prostitutes are not interested in earning money from their activities: "son aeconómicas" (they are noneconomic) (138). Although such improbable statements may at first seem a young man's ploy to startle his listeners, the repetition of this antimaterialist note soon shows that Sabul is genuinely obsessed with a spiritualized myth of society.

A secondary set of disparities arises from Sabul's efforts to explain his own relation to the elite. His theories prevent him from seeing society as a scenario of various groups warring for prestige and power, relying on such considerations as class and ethnicity to disparage competing groups. Instead, he seeks to understand his career frustrations through a romantic rhetoric of "angry young men" versus noninnovative established writers. An example is his visit to the offices of a prestigious magazine. Although the circumstances of his encounters with the staff strongly hint that his problem is his outsider status, Sabul continues to think of himself as intellectually too daring for the staid review. The fact that his social status prevents his ideas from even obtaining a hearing is obscured by this rhetoric of romantic rebellion. The narrator conveys Sabul's thoughts: "El los utilizaba, los utilizaría: eran ellos quienes quedaban por debajo de él, de sus proyectos inalterablemente lúcidos . . . los viejos afrancesados" (He was using them, he would use them; they were the ones below him, below his unswervingly lucid projects . . . those old Frenchified guys) (195).

Sabul's ethnic markedness allows for one of the book's most vivid incongruities. This young man, in his person, is a constant reminder of the "avalanche" of immigration that Argentina received from the 1880s onward. The reactions Sabul elicits demonstrate the widespread awareness of who is and who is not of immigrant stock, with associated stratification.

If Sabul were aware of the complexities of immigrant-group status in Argentina, including the troubled, contradictory history of official policy, his own experiences could provide him with many insights into the phenomenon. Consider Sabul's efforts to secure entry into establishment publishing. As an outsider, the young man stands scarcely a chance of entering a circle limited to an elite of individuals of long-standing "good" family. A staff member expertly destroys his pretensions to upward social mobility: "la condescencia del Secretario le resultaba desvergonzada y se sentía una muchachita que tenía que quitarse la ropa" (the condescending attitude of the Secretary seemed shameless to him, and he felt like a girl who had to take her clothes off) (212). Yet, only the reader is allowed to learn from Sabul's experiences. The young man himself remains resolutely closed to any accurate understanding of his situation as the product of an outsider immigrant group or any understanding of the historical forces that have produced that situation. Sabul adheres to a dangerously mythified view of Argentina. His theories on national character closely resemble those of the real-life social critic Julio Mafud and ignore uncomfortable historical forces.

The notion of rootedness is central to Sabul's social thought. To his way of thinking, Argentines are not properly in touch with their cultural heritage. He sees the construction of a uniform cultural patrimony for all Argentines, regardless of class or other social grouping; Argentines descend from the gauchos who lived nomadically on the unfenced pampas before the drive toward Europeanization.

Here Viñas has found the opportunity to expose, through his narrative of contradictions, a myth he has also attacked in his critical essays. In Viñas's analysis, the image of the gaucho has been reformulated to fit the needs of the dominant class. During the intense drive to "civilize" the pampas, the gaucho was a figure of barbarity, inferior to the hard-working and literate immigrants who were to populate the interior. However, once the real-world gaucho was displaced and European immigrants were rising in society, the balance shifted. Now the gaucho received a higher value for such traits as purity, nobility of spirit, independence, and non-European qualities: "Lo que desde 1854 había sido una explícita apelación al inmigrante como reemplazo del gaucho, hacia 1902 es puesto al revés; eliminado el gaucho, su mitificación se inaugura" (What since 1854 had been an explicit designation of the immigrant as the replacement for the gaucho, around 1902 becomes reversed; now that the gaucho has been eliminated, his mythification begins).[7] The point of this new myth is to deprive the immigrant of status and to curb his rise to a higher social position, hence the absurdity of the gaucho-pampas myth being so vigorously expounded by an ambitious son of immigrants.

The narrator, when not representing Sabul's thoughts through some form of interior monologue, maintains a deadpan sobriety of language in referring to this character. For example, he describes in objective terms Sabul's continuing difficulties in obtaining an interview: "Tendría que esperar al empleado. Esperar, porque ésa era la cuarta vez que había subido a *La Revista*" (He would have to wait for the clerk. Wait, since that was the fourth time he had gone up to *The Review*) (195). In contrast to this plain statement is the romantic language that is the natural medium for Sabul's myth. Sabul tries to find Argentine social reality in "las esencias . . . [e]so que se siente cuando uno camina por Corrientes y mira hacia arriba . . . algo que viene desde abajo . . . desde lo primario . . . [e]sas fuerzas imponderables que predeterminan al argentino . . . al hombre raigal que siente el tango" (the essences . . . [w]hat you feel when you walk down Corrientes and look up . . . something that comes up from below . . . from the primordial depths . . . [t]hose imponderable forces that make the Argentine what he is . . . the man of roots who feels the tango) (141). Sabul's profound incongruity is not simply the disparity between his beliefs and the existing social reality; the dramatic irony of his outsider status is seconded by the inappropriateness of the language he utilizes.

He uses this romantic rhetoric to account for his rejection by the elite despite such signs as the open disdain a *La Revista* staff member shows toward his obscure and foreign-sounding family name (210). Indeed, all three staff members with whom Sabul interacts allude to his undistinguished origins and single out his last name for emphasis.

As Sabul fumes at the editorial staff for reiterated delays in receiving him, he views them as "Viejos sin sensibilidad para el país" (Old guys with no feeling for the country) (195). The narrator cuts into Sabul's romanticizing of his situation with a reminder of the cruder underlying realities. Noting Sabul's "pelo de africano" (hair like an African's) (195), the narrator reintroduces the factors of ethnicity, associated class status, and lack of elite affiliation. These are factors that the young man himself persistently denies through his rhapsodic notions and rhetoric.

The plot line concerned with Sabul also allows Viñas to insert into the novel a critique of certain bourgeois notions of writing.[8] As noted, Sabul believes that he writes in a way contrary to established tendencies and that his writing is capable of disturbing stodgy readers and writers; this belief does not, however, prevent him from greatly exerting himself to enter the most sedate of magazines. He can be found variously awed by the names on its roster (211) and "casi agradecido" (almost grateful) for any attention from its staff (213). The suspicion that Sabul is no threat to entrenched interests is fully confirmed when the reader receives an opportunity to observe him actually engaged in the work of writing.

Viñas's narrator describes Sabul at work before the reader has any opportunity to penetrate the young man's thoughts. The narrator emphasizes that writing is work, in line with the Marxist imperative not to disguise the labor involved in all production, no matter how intellectual or creative: "colocó la hoja en la máquina, tecleó un poco, se frotó la frente" (he placed the sheet of paper in the machine, he tapped on the keys a bit, he rubbed his forehead) (367). Sabul, though, has an exalted notion of the act of writing, and particularly of himself as inspired writer. He describes his work to himself in ludicrously inflated terms: "estaba haciendo otra cosa: antes como poeta, ahora como periodista; allí como voz individual, unívoca" (he was doing something else: before as a poet, now as a journalist; there as an individual, single voice) (370). Amid all these high-flown thoughts about the nature of his mission and his voice, Sabul avoids the fact he is working hard to make his writing fit a certain standard.

The comicality of this scene resides in the standard that Sabul strives to attain. His model is obviously the elaborate rhetoric used by genteel Latin American journalists. The reader will be properly horrified and amused by Sabul's fondness for hackneyed, high-flown speech: "Repasó *magistral* y se quedó conforme, tachó *sendos* que siempre se emplea mal. *Pristino* lo entusiasmaba, pero no había forma de colocarlo. Ya había usado *coruscante* que era una de sus preferidas*" (He went back to *masterly* and felt satisfied with it, he scratched out *of each,* which is always used wrong. He especially liked *pristine,* but there was no place for it to go. He had already used *shimmering,* one of his favorites) (370). Sabul's fondness for the self-consciously Latinizing *coruscante,* particularly, shows his adherence to a fetishistically puristic ideal of Spanish. As well as favoring pretentious word choices, Sabul has a fussy, pedantic horror of stylistic "sins": "Y se descubrió haciendo una mueca: un *que* afrancesado" (And he found himself making a face: a Frenchified superfluous *que*) (370).⁹

The final incongruity to the story of Sabul is his inability to discern that this hypergenteel concept of language is as establishment as the Frenchified expression he denounces. The reader is clearly expected to find humor in Sabul's sense of linguistic superiority. Sabul, though, makes his picayune purism into a sign of his supposed rebellion. Excising the offending *que* from his writing, he claims a victory over the establishment: "Y a los viejos afrancesados había que liquidarlos. Sobre todo después de lo de *La Revista*" (And those old Frenchified guys had got to go. Especially after what happened at *The Review*) (370). His personal myth of rootedness and revolt versus Europeanized conservatism allows him to dismiss the greatest contradictions in his own ideas and form of expression.

After the reader finds Sabul perpetuating a pretentious rhetoric, the character has no further role to play in the novel. The implication is that just as Sabul cannot learn, he cannot teach. Sabul's vague suspicion that he is fundamentally favorable to the elite (for example, see page 199) has not led to insights into the nature of this attraction or into its relation to his myth of Argentine history. Sabul and his ideas are static, unable to change. The narrator gives a sign of this dead end by refusing to allow Sabul to continue in the story.

* * *

Whereas Sabul is a determined misreader of social realities, Bernardo appears as a nonreader, or superficial reader, of matters that require interpretation. In consequence, he is not a figure of ridicule, as Sabul increasingly comes to be through his successive misinterpretations of events.

Rather, Bernardo figures as an individual essentially like the reader of the novel in that he is expected to see the larger historical pattern in social issues. However, his initial frivolity, ambition, and near acceptance by the elite group impede development of an historical consciousness, retarding the growth of his understanding. The process of his gaining insight into his situation—that of himself as immigrant-stock outsider and the Jews as bearers of social-ethical responsibility—takes from the beginning of the novel to its ending nearly six hundred pages later.

As do other figures and phenomena in the novel, Bernardo first presents a more coherent image than fits his state of development. He appears as a responsible member and leader of the community—in this case a multi-ethnic community comprised of an army outfit just then being discharged. Bernardo initially gives signs of possessing several virtues that contribute to the overall ideal of a socially aware and responsible community member. In this sense, he seems to be complying with the Jewish notion of ethics, in which there is a recognized need to be alert to what is happening in society and to seek to steer the community on the right course. Bernardo's seemingly positive characteristics include his ability to establish himself as a leader, his history of involvement in student affairs, his capacity to converse on social and political themes, and his apparent altruism.

However, the reader, judging Bernardo against the ideal of responsible community involvement, learns to question the worth of these qualities and the assumption that the character is morally responsible for others. The rescue of a friend, Mariano, from his fellow conscripts gives a first impression of altruism, since Bernardo must risk social disapproval to stop the hazing. But as the novel presents more scenes involving Mariano and Bernardo, it becomes evident that their relation is a highly ritualized one in which Bernardo is continually succoring his wealthy, dependent friend. The idiosyncratic nature of their bond becomes more apparent in a scene in which Bernardo urges Mariano to confess his personal problems, repeatedly incites him to weep, and then comforts him (187–93). There are persistent hints at a homosexual link between the two young men and at an entrapment in the stereotyped roles of sufferer and altruist. Mariano, unmarked by ethnicity, suggests the theatrical nature of their interaction when he accuses Bernardo of creating occasions to play "el Judío Virtuoso" (the Virtuous Jew) (192). This reproof is of interest not only because Mariano uses reference to Bernardo's less prestigious ethnicity to compensate for his own loss of face but also because, however crudely formulated, Mariano's jibe does point accurately to Bernardo's superficial mastery of his role as moral leader.

Following the opening scene, Bernardo's persona as a moral leader again comes in for questioning as the narrator presents information far less favorable to the character. On his release from the army, Bernardo spends a good deal of time carousing with his fellow recent dischargees. In brief scenes, he appears wandering the streets with his friends, playing childish pranks, urging a young man to approach a young woman, and in general falling into a pattern of youthful frivolity with *machista* overtones. During this portion of the novel, there are only occasional reminders that Bernardo may harbor a special moral sense. At one point he does pause to reflect that he is unlike his companions in his occasional disgust at their mindless pursuit of easy women (138). Such flashes of incipient insight are quickly extinguished; Bernardo concludes that his reluctance to pursue unknown women is an advantage because it masks his lack of social skills (138).

Particularly interesting are Bernardo's sporadic attempts to defend women's entitlement to be considered thinking beings. Bernardo is able to appreciate the intelligence and independence of Mariano's girlfriend, Pelusa, and to recognize that women are penalized for displaying these qualities. However, he expresses his empathy with her deviance only when he can count on an assenting audience, that is, Pelusa and Mariano. When with his other friends, he appears willing to accept a standard *machista* view of women.

As Bernardo moves away from the euphoric first days of his discharge, a new set of clues emerges, promising new revelations about his troubled relation to society. This promise seems especially strong when the young man resumes his contact with student politics. As before, Bernardo makes a strong initial impression. He has spent time in the student movement and is able to win the ear of his contemporaries. Though his ardor for political action seems low, there is an apparently complete explanation for this reluctance. The narrator provides a transcription of Bernardo's thoughts on the issue, including phrases the young man has heard from others. These comments indicate that Bernardo is simply suffering from the widespread disappointment over the presidency of Arturo Frondizi but should not be counted out as a political person because of this temporary blow (50–51). It also appears that his inability to support a current student strike is rooted in a belief that this action is ill-conceived. Despite his disillusionment, Bernardo is able to maintain an interest in discussing political events of the immediate post-Peronist period.

This image of a politically aware individual gradually fragments as more and more shortcomings appear in Bernardo's grasp of society and his relation to it. The most fundamental of these is his inability to take an interest in history. Proficient as the man may seem at analyzing the politics of the day, he does not inform himself about the antecedents of current affairs.

History, with its forces in conflict, is available to Bernardo in a fragmentary text that he refuses to read. The "text" consists not only of historical analyses but also of the historical testimony of people who could further the young man's understanding. Bernardo's landlord is an exiled Spanish Republican; his father, an offspring of the Jewish colonies of the interior and a longtime devotee of Juan B. Justo, is a leader of Argentine socialism. The hero's lack of interest in these witnesses to history is not the result of any well-considered doubts about the value of their political experiences or testimony. He is prepared to listen to lengthy, trivial discussions of present-day matters. But Bernardo considers the past to be no concern of his. This attitude is summed up in his rejection of David Viñas. The narrator relays Bernardo's thoughts on seeing the name on a theater advertisement. After some childish jibes at Viñas's "bigotes excesivos, un poco ridículos" (overgrown moustache, a bit ridiculous) (99) and his ambiguous ethnic identity, Bernardo reveals his disaffection with the older man's continual efforts to promote a historical consciousness:

Viñas, sí, siguió Bernardo, uno de esos veteranos que siempre daban la lata con lo del 1945 esto y lo del 1945 aquello. Bueno, hicieron lo suyo . . . diez años inflándolo a un Mayor que escribía sobre filosofía y a una colección de viejos liberales que creían en la República Española, el poeta Alberti y Haya de la Torre. "Pobres."

("Oh yeah, Viñas," Bernardo went on, "one of those guys who go way back and are always going on about how in 1945 this and in 1945 that. Well, they did their bit . . . for ten years now they've been inflating a leader who wrote about philosophy and a collection of old liberals who believed in the Spanish Republic, the poet Alberti and Haya de la Torre. 'Poor old guys'") (100).

Throughout this inconclusive section of the novel, including Bernardo's post-army celebrations and his gradual reentry into student affairs, Jewish matters receive the same treatment as Argentine history. The hero lives surrounded by signs that could constitute a text about the Jewish heritage and Argentine Jewry. He subjects these potential clues to the same nonreading he accords history, leaving them as isolated items. For example, he recalls some passionate Zionist rhetoric he has heard from a family of his friends, but without interest (48–49). The friends' statements raise complex questions, for they are supporting the idea of an incompatibility between Jewish and Argentine identity. Rather than question the validity of this presupposition, Bernardo expresses indifference: "yo no siento ni medio de todo eso" (I don't feel even half of all that) (48–49). His unwillingness to engage in analysis of the problem is frustrating to the reader of the novel because Bernardo gives indications of undeveloped and unarticulated insights. His brief formulation of his position as an Argentine Jew is full of interesting implications that he declines to think through: "Irse, no; pero tampoco disfrazarse" (Leave, no; but not disguise yourself, either) (49).

The novel hints that Bernardo is not merely slothful in his thinking about Jewish issues but that he has no model for critical discussion of them. An example of this inadequacy is the romantic rhetoric with which his Zionist friends seek to interest him in Judaica: "Kinsky se exaltaba hablándole de la tradición hebrea. Los macabeos, Varsovia, el Aleph y los asombrados ojos de una muchacha sefardí" (Kinsky got all excited telling him about the Hebrew tradition. The Maccabees, Warsaw, the Aleph, and the wide-with-wonder eyes of a Sephardic girl) (49). This emotional harping on the glories of the Jewish people is meaningless to the analytical-minded Bernardo.

Bernardo's father's remarks on Jewishness offer another type of inadequacy. The father, caught up in the land-of-opportunity notion, is fascinated by Jewish penetration of high circles. His son remembers with apparent derision his father's talk of the glories of the Jewish intellectual tradition, in which appear the names of Albert Einstein, Alberto Gerchunoff, and León Dujovne. The series of names sounds ridiculous and incongruous because of the disparity of importance among the attainments of those listed. Viñas has pointed out, in his essays, that Gerchunoff and Dujovne won their places in the world of high culture by their skill at pleasing and soothing the nonimmigrant establishment.[10] The father's admiration for them, as well as his entrepreneurial rise to ownership of a drugstore named El Progreso, suggests that the man deserves attention as an exemplary case of the great myths of the liberal era. His son, though, grants no importance to his father's words, on the general supposition that older people and Jewish topics lack meaning for him.[11]

The height of the student strike forces the contradictions in Bernardo's thought and character to manifest themselves. The full incongruity of his ideas and actions is conveyed by the narrator's thorough reporting of the young man's consciousness, which proves to be filled with thoughts he must hide from his contemporaries. In his role as principled leader, Bernardo attempts to halt the students' strike (207–9). His thoughts, revealed during an antistrike speech, are notably far from the issues involved. Bernardo focuses on the response he obtains: the face of Mariano "que lo adoraba con devoción" (who was worshiping him devotedly) (208), and the other listeners whose esteem he hopes to win. In Bernardo's mind his oratorical voice is like the clarinet of a performer; he judges its qualities independent of the message it might seek to convey: "su clarinete comenzaba . . . a soltar ese chirrido agudo y estupendo" (his clarinet began . . . to let out that sharp, stupendous wail) (208). By following the student action through Bernardo's eyes, the reader is able to obtain a good deal of information about the hero's standing among his contemporaries and about the amount of respect and attention he can still claim. Yet it is impossible to form an image of the strike as a political phenomenon because the social issues at stake have no place in Bernardo's mind.

The silence surrounding the strikers' issues cannot reasonably stem from reticence on the part of the narrator. Indeed, Viñas's novelistic narrators have drawn complaints for their excessively detailed revelation of all that happens to the characters. The inference of this silence, then, is that the strike means little to Bernardo except as a public performance event.

The scenes of student unrest also serve to bring to a crisis the novel's previously planted theme of immigrant ambition. This question was left unresolved when Bernardo sneered at his father's lionizing of Jews in the Argentine establishment. Because Bernardo would not think through the historical basis of his father's confusion between merit and social acceptance, the entire problem comes back to disorient him. The strike now appears to him as a danger to the completion of his law studies and subsequent placement.

As the conflict between dissent and career advancement becomes acute, Bernardo reveals his profound inability to recognize social-ethical problems. Driven by forces he declines to analyze, he throws himself into frenzied and incoherent behavior. First he tries to stop the strike, then he petitions to take examinations during the strike, and finally in the midst of his petitioning he leaps up, runs outside, delivers a prostrike speech, and is physically attacked by a self-styled fascist.

The pell-mell succession of disparate actions, with little connecting or explanatory material provided by the narrator, may well create uncertainty as to Bernardo's state of beliefs. The narrative aggravates this lack of clarity by dropping Bernardo for some time following the fascist's attack. Another significant silence arises, pointing again to something missing in Bernardo's relation with social issues. When the silence surrounding Bernardo's subsequent involvement in the strike is broken, any doubts the reader may have had about the hero's melodramatic conversion receive confirmation. "¿Qué pasó con la huelga?" (What happened to the strike?) (478), Bernardo is suddenly heard to inquire, revealing that his swift surge of commitment to dissent was fleeting indeed.

Though the lightning regeneration of the hero's political engagement proves superficial, the narrative of the student strike provides the beginnings of his eventual enlightenment. Embedded in the frenetic events of the strike are moments that guide Bernardo toward his neglected social-ethical mission. During his period of greatest conservatism and conformity, Bernardo allows a friend to disparage Jews as troublemakers: "Claro, mi viejo, vos sos distinto, pero cuando yo te hablo de judíos, me refiero a los que no saben qué es el país ni lo sienten" (Of course, good buddy, you're different, but when I talk to you about Jews, I mean the ones who don't know what the country is and they don't feel it) (221). The student fascist who attacks Bernardo also equates Jews with political subversion; the latter scene, filled with violent action, allows Bernardo no opportunity to react to this notion.

The question of Jewishness as a call to social action disappears from the novel after the student strike, only to reemerge with greater force at the novel's end. The ending is, in a sense, a second chance for Bernardo to make the commitment he earlier botched. Whereas the first conversion scene takes place in the public space of the university on strike, with protestors attending to Bernardo's words and actions as a student leader, the second allows him no appreciative audience. And whereas the hero's thought was previously distorted by his antihistorical worship of youth and novelty, the final conversion scene takes place before the Spanish Republican exile who represents the continuing history of dissent.

Most significant, Bernardo's second conversion takes into account the contradictions and incongruities inherent in his cultural situation. His new consciousness arises from an antagonistic stimulus, the fascist's equation of Bernardo's Jewishness with his involvement in dissent. The hero is able to recognize this anti-Jewish slur as, paradoxically, a correct guide to an orienting definition of Jewishness. Looking at his graffito-smeared wall, he thinks:

Judío andate. No era algo especial con él, pensó Bernardo; no decía *Carman judío andate,* sino simplemente *Judío andate . . . Judío andate.* Los judíos molestaban, por eso: era natural; los judíos hedían y nadie los tragaba. ¿O para eso: judíos eran *todos* los demás, menos ellos? —Ustedes son judíos, váyanse. Judíos disolventes, judíos lieros, judíos que siempre andan planteando cuestiones. Judíos, ustedes no creen en lo que hay que creer. Váyanse.

("'Jew get out.' It didn't have anything to do with him in particular, thought Bernardo; it didn't say 'Jew Carman get out,' just 'Jew get out . . . Jew get out.' Jews were a nuisance, that was it: it was natural; Jews stank and nobody could stand them. Or maybe the thing was this: Jews were *everybody* else, except them? 'You're Jews, get out. Divisive Jews, troublemaking Jews, Jews always going around raising questions. Jews, you don't believe in the things you're supposed to. Get out'") (585).

The ending carries through the novel's overall plan of bringing both reader and hero to recognize and learn from the grotesque contradictions of an ill-structured society. It is a fitting ending because it does not provide a uniform resolution of conflict, as Bernardo's earlier conversion scene initially appeared to do. Bernardo's new awareness does not provide him with a course of action or a role to play—indeed, role playing has hindered the development of his consciousness. By leaving Bernardo at a moment of heightened consciousness, rather than showing any prescribed or ideal route for carrying that consciousness into action, the novel strongly suggests that the young man still has a great deal to work out in finding a conscientious response to the surrounding society whose full scope of contradictions he has only begun to perceive.

5 JOSÉ RABINOVICH

A Poetics of Disputation

It is a safe conjecture that the polemical realism of José Rabinovich (1903–1978) has discouraged inquiry into the literary procedures that carry his statements about society.[1] In poetry, particularly, realism has proven difficult for critics to appreciate and analyze.[2] Rabinovich's work increases the difficulty by emphasizing the ungainliness that realistic traits can impart to poetry.

This chapter considers the ways in which Rabinovich's realistic techniques, which at times give his poems a seemingly ragged artlessness, promote statements about religion, ethnic identity, and ethics in society. The poems analyzed are from his 1970 collection *El violinista bajo el tejado* (*The Fiddler Under the Roof*), containing texts written over a considerable period of time.[3] This work especially lends itself to commentary because it expresses two of the author's ideals: to achieve a plain, unsentimental vision of recent Jewish history and present-day Jewish issues and to evaluate problems of social organization by moral standards. It also is a good example of Rabinovich's effort to give his poetry a grounding in Jewish, especially biblical, stylistic traditions and to distance it from high art. In its proletarian populism *Violinista* reveals the extent of the author's debt to Eastern European cultural thought and especially in the realist tendencies that thrived within the early-twentieth-century avant-garde.

This examination starts with a description of general traits, both stylistic and ideological, of Rabinovich's writing and continues with a detailed consideration of a single poem, "Responso" ("Response") (158–62). Explication of the prominent ideas in this poem permits analysis of how Rabinovich's distinct formal features further the poem's argument. The conclusion takes up the evaluative question of how worthwhile Rabinovich's texts are when considered as poetry.

* * *

Perhaps the most fundamental of Rabinovich's distinguishing characteristics is the methodical delimitation of his subject matter. Although it is accurate to call him a poet of Jewish life, his choice of sectors of reality discourages the fascination with folkways and tradition that the characterization suggests. The life of Eastern European Jewry has claimed the attention of literary artists who have commemorated its uniqueness. Authors have been fascinated with the virtually all-Jewish environment in which these unemancipated Jews maintain an intense concentration of religious piety as well as traditions and folkways. Possibilities for rhapsodizing over this rich and quintessentially Jewish culture evoke the lyrical paintings of Marc Chagall.

In the starkest contrast to Chagall's magical vision of *shtetl* life is Rabinovich's stringently ascetic approach. He renounces the use of those elements of Eastern European Jewish life that would seem the most likely candidates for successful poetic treatment. The title *El violinista bajo el tejado* extends a warning to the reader. It is, of course, a reworking of the phrase from Sholem Aleichem describing the situation of Russian Jewry in czarist times and popularized as the title of a musical stage and movie version of that author's Tevye stories. The inversion is an unusual one because whereas verbal turnabouts typically make a phrase more arresting, Rabinovich's title turns a striking image into an ordinary one. The title's abrupt veer toward the mundane suggests a swerve away from the presentation of Jewish life as folkloric, away from the musical's sentimental treatment of *shtetl* existence. Indeed, the need to perceive Jewish ways and religion in their workaday, routine aspects is stressed in Rabinovich's collection. It becomes a central argument of, for example, "Raíces" ("Roots") (202–6), which argues that Jewish identity is natural and commonplace rather than exotic. More broadly, the shift toward the pedestrian hints at a concern with persistent Jewish issues that will require hard work and thought to solve.

Any general characterization of *Violinista* should contain an admission that its plain speech may prove disagreeable to readers who favor subtle and complex ambiguities in poetry. Rabinovich's poetry is clearly written in such a way that it may be declaimed. Especially melodramatic are the monologues spoken by an individual in the toils of some crisis, filled with outrage and grief over the state of the world. This theatricality tends to tinge Rabinovich's work with *kitsch* associations.

As well as this low-status link with poetry declamation, the collection has a more honorable tie, one to biblical exhortation. From the biblical tradition, Rabinovich adopts the contentious exchange with God, most famously present in the Book of Job, and the polemic exemplified in the prophets' urgings to repentance. "Excomulgado" ("Excommunicated") (145–49) consists entirely of the angry lamentations of a disgruntled sufferer who, following a time-honored practice, addresses the problems of theodicy by declaring himself at odds with divinity. Traditional too is his contention that in questioning God's trustworthiness, he at the same time sets himself apart from the community of trusting believers.

"Excomulgado," together with other poems concerning human-divine conflict and arbitration, utilizes long-standing stylistic conventions for the treatment of theological problems. What is more interesting here is the fact that Rabinovich's reader need not know the stylistic forms used in theological writing. In the case of "Excomulgado," a cursory knowledge of the Book of Job would be sufficient to connect the ordinary reader with the conventions that Rabinovich is here renewing. Indeed, the poem prompts the reader to recognize the Job form by stressing the bodily indignities inflicted on the speaker's person. Hemorrhoids, among these ignoble plagues, are a recurring topic throughout *Violinista*.

Current events discussed in prosaic language occupy a surprisingly prominent place in Rabinovich's poems. This undisguised factuality is apparent in the several poems devoted to criticizing the Catholic hierarchy. "Una vacante" ("A Job Opening") (154–57), a poem resembling an editorial open letter, illustrates this tendency. The speaker expresses a wish for a post at the Vatican from which to exercise a benevolent influence on that institution. Among other defects that the would-be reformer perceives in the church is its loss or neglect of the salutary tradition of striking covenants and agreements with God, bargaining and entering into exchanges beneficial to both divine and human interests. The pope in this poem is specified as Paul VI and is accused in some detail of neglecting his pastoral function. He is seen as cut off especially from the fruitful old ways of Judeo-Christian religious culture. The speaker asks:

¿Cómo quiere negociar un pacto
con el Hacedor
o un convenio con el Señor
un tratado de paz
un tratado incondicional
mientras sus tropas
se exterminan con balas de odio
con piedras, con gases,
con uñas y con saña?

(How to negotiate a pact
with the Maker
or a treaty with the Lord
a peace treaty

an unconditional treaty
while his troops
exterminate each other with bullets of hate
with stones, with gases,
with fingernails and fury?)

(156)

The use of symbolism, potentially capable of moving a text into the category of artistic writing, in "Una vacante" contributes to the blunt, newspaper-editorial effect. With disregard for subtlety, the speaker comments on Vatican architecture: "Al Vaticano le gusta las columnas, / una columna es un símbolo / de héroes, de poder, de mando" (The Vatican likes columns, / a column is a symbol / of heroes, of power, of command) (157). Similar observations could be made about "La devolución" ("The Return") (58–61), a denunciation of the practice of giving Jewish children a Catholic upbringing while sheltering them from the Nazis.

An extreme of factual content is reached in "El Papa" ("The Pope") (62–65), which gives the current estimate of the number of the pope's followers, the specifications of the pope's garb, and descriptions of certain ceremonial acts carried out by the pope and other Vatican dignitaries. In addition to these factual matters given in detail, others are hinted at. Persistent allusions to the Vatican's poor record in the defense of European Jewry suggest that the pontiff under discussion is Pius XII.

Overt statements of opinion give the same starkly direct, corrective-realism effect. "El Papa" supplements its many items of information about Vatican affairs with a negative critique of the higher clergy. The speaker asserts that true confession and reconciliation with God takes place "no en el confesionario . . . sino con el pan en la mano / con un cubo de agua en la mano / hasta con una escoba en la mano / pero principalmente / con el corazón en la mano" (not in the confessional . . . but with bread in the hand / with a bucket of water in the hand / but mainly / with the heart in the hand) (62). The principle of "every man his own priest" is reaffirmed with such artlessly plain sentences as "No le es necesario concurrir / al Papa" (He doesn't need to go / see the Pope) (62). Such bald setting-forth of opinions makes "El Papa" seem to belong only partly to the realm of poetry. This disputatious text points to Rabinovich's two models: modern manifesto editorial writing, and the Bible with its many forms of polemic, invective, and exhortation.[4]

Many of Rabinovich's lines derive their blunt quality from lexical choices that at first seem too modern, jargonistic, and banal for the subject matter at hand. For example, the speaker in "Eclipse," in a discussion of theological problems, announces "Estaría dispuesto a firmar / un pacto de no agresión / con el Señor" (I would be inclined to sign / a nonaggression pact / with the Lord) (151). The harsh critic in "Una vacante" wonders if he can find a place on the pope's balcony "Donde la zona espacial / no está violada / por ningún ave de presa" (Where the air space / is not violated / by any bird of prey) (156) and reutilizes the peace negotiators' "nonaggression pact." Whereas these two examples involve the jargon of international relations, technological terms also surface unexpectedly, as in the suggestion of a procedure for producing "una fotocopia de Dios" (a photocopy of God) (199) in "Amén."

In the case of these unusual lexical options, the initial effect is of irreverence; yet Rabinovich is treating serious matters with due respect. Modern-day terms of warfare and political aggression, such as treaty terms and talk of "air space," sound more appropriate for news reports than for metaphysical considerations. Yet it should be remembered that biblical language is full of contemporary terms alluding to war and to military and diplomatic relations between groups. The difference is not in the fundamental referent, which in both cases is armed conflict and the questions surrounding it, but in the modernity of Rabinovich's terms of reference. Because of its archaic ring, talk of "swords into plowshares" is easier for today's reader to accept as part of a discussion of loftily solemn matters. Nonetheless, it makes as much sense to speak of human beings' quarrels and covenants with God and with one another in modern terms as in biblical ones. Rabinovich is following the biblical precedent of discussing these tension-filled situations using the terminology of conflict suitable to his time.

The curious allusion to photocopying God follows the same type of logic. Certainly the Bible tells of attempts to gain an image of, or access to, God by various means. For example, the Tower of Babel narrative, like Rabinovich's remark about photocopying God, speaks of technical devices meant to perform a feat that can be accomplished only spiritually. The comment on a human tendency is essentially the same, but again the use of the terminology of the present moment seems jarring. The contrast between the apparent frivolity of these references and their justifiability is in itself a commentary. Rabinovich draws attention to the widespread habit of mind that consists of venerating the antique, alien nature of biblical expression rather than the biblical content, a habit reflected in the horrified reaction of certain groups to any attempt to modernize liturgical language.

Rabinovich's value-laden realism has certain other set, formal procedures that are easy to identify from collection to collection. The convention of stanzas has been virtually abandoned. The poems are all fairly long by present-day standards, four pages being the usual length. Invariably, single spacing is used. Variation in line length creates a jagged, erose right edge. The poet makes frequent use of the period for purposes other than ending a sentence. Often a phrase is set off from the surrounding text by being punctuated as if it were a complete sentence. "Eclipse" has "Luz de cre-púsculo." (Twilight.) (151) and, even more oddly, the isolated dependent clause "Cuando me identifico." (When I identify myself.) (150). At the same time, some complete sentences are left without any ending mark.

Stranger yet, to the educated reader's eyes, is the use of periods within a sentence, as in "Fuera de la medida" ("Outsize") (91–96). Here one finds "hasta donde llega / la pluma que lleva el viento. / Para el concurso del cielo" (as far as / the feather goes, borne on the wind. / For the contest of the heavens) (95). Even when a period seems to end a conventionally acceptable sentence, the sentence in question may not remain ended. The continuation of the utterance after the period then starts without a capital letter: "y con una carcajada / satánica / me dio la bienvenida. / quise prenderle fuego" (and with a Satanic / laugh / he welcomed me. / i tried to set him on fire), from the poem "Culpable" ("Guilty") (171). As one might expect, these striking violations of grammatical rules occur alongside less disturbing ones. The run-on sentence, for example, is hardly a daring exercise of poetic license, yet in Rabinovich's work it furthers his anarchistic statement by offending the purist's sense of what constitutes a correct sentence.

The resulting texts do not look entirely like poems. Rabinovich, by trade a typesetter, was undoubtedly aware that his preferred format made his poetry resemble less prestigious genres, such as broadsides and leaflets. The similarity to nonart forms corresponds to an antielitist ideal whose sources in Eastern European aesthetic thought will be discussed in the conclusion of this chapter. The layout of the poems in *Violinista* sustains the proposition that poetry is written for the hard work of making assertions, and at the same time the layout masks the fact that the poetic form in itself has required attention, care, and deliberate choices to assume such a definitive character.

* * *

An example of Rabinovich's ruggedly antisentimental depiction of Jewish life is "Responso" (158–62). Like many of the poems of *Violinista*, "Responso" is a dramatic, polemical monologue. The speaker in this text is the grandson of its protagonist, an altruistic Jewish blacksmith. Reminiscing about his grandfather's virtuous behavior, the speaker defends an ideal of natural, unritualized religiosity, the contrary of which—the prescription of exercises of piety—is denounced through unfavorable comparison with the free-form, heartfelt worship of the smith. The formalistic side of Christianity, especially Catholicism with its officials, titles, and other apparatus, comes in for Rabinovich's usual sarcastic dismissal, as does the Jewish Orthodox insistence on the exact observance of ritual commandments. "Responso" bears the same essential message as "El Papa." Just as the Christian in "El Papa" can reconcile himself with God while going about his everyday work, the Jew in "Responso" need not follow a clerically dictated ritual or artificially separate labor from communion with God.

What first claims the reader's attention is the juxtaposition of Christian language with the description of the life of a Jewish blacksmith. From its very title, "Responso" provokes curiosity by its appropriation of language typical of Christian worship. A puzzle is set forth in the title and the poem's opening with the speaker's announced intention to describe his grandfather. How can a poetic evocation of a thoroughly Jewish individual be classified as a "response," a characteristically Christian liturgical form? The reader is led toward an unraveling of this unexpected tie between the grandfather and Christian tradition.

The first clue to the correspondence between title and text comes in the opening sentence. The blacksmith was, according to his grandson, widely renowned as a holy individual. The lexical choice is not inherently Christian as opposed to Jewish, for holy and saintly people, and even saints, exist in Judaism as well as Christianity. The difference in the two traditions' concept of saintliness, though, becomes a significant point. Whereas Catholicism features highly formalized definitions of sainthood, epitomized by canonization proceedings, the great Jewish saints and holy men are recognized by general acclamation, by a widespread perception of their piety and altruism. The blacksmith of the poem is clearly in this latter tradition of saintliness, for the opening lines celebrate the far-reaching fame of this holy man.

The contrast between Catholic formalism and Jewish reliance on community consensus becomes an issue in the text that follows. The principle that human saintliness manifests itself in concrete behavior is part of Rabinovich's poetic statement. This here-and-now concept of saintliness is always imperiled by officially imposed (especially Catholic) ones. To assign praise and blame, "Responso" adopts features of the biblical formula of blessing and curse. At the same time, in urging the reader to feel free of purely ritual requirements and to attend to the meaning of religious acts, the poem draws on the stylistic conventions of exhortation.[5]

With "Su herrería era una capilla judía" (His smithy was a Jewish chapel) (158), the text resumes its play of oppositions. The disparity that most quickly strikes the eye is between the Christian term *capilla* and its immediately adjoining modifier, *judía*. Beyond this readily apparent contrast of noun and modifying adjective, an unusual equivalence is established between *herrería* and *capilla*. Though here linked in a relation of interchangeability, the two terms in real-world use are almost always confined to their respective realms, the secular and the religious. The secular/religious dichotomy and the speaker's presumable desire to challenge its value are by no means Jewish vs. Christian problems. The following line brings this point home by substituting for *capilla* the closest Jewish term, *templo*. As well as calling the smithy/chapel "quizá un templo" (perhaps a temple), this next line violates the secular/religious boundary in another way. The activity found in the temple is *tempering* (literal and figurative): "un templo donde se templaba" (a temple for tempering). The consecrated temple is linked by similarity of form to workaday tempering. Jewish laws pertaining to worship, though, make the occasions on which one would go to temple the very times when labor is proscribed. The poem has begun to develop a challenge to the ritual commandments of Judaism, since these place work on a lower level than study and worship, excluding useful labor from the realm of piety.

The intermingling of realms next surprises the reader by blurring a division normally maintained between human beings and other animals. The blacksmith deserves the respect conventionally due members of the clergy. He is a *párroco* (*parish priest*) charged with the care of a congregation, but the congregants whose spiritual life he directs are all horses. These are, by common reckoning, beyond the reach of religious ministry, "profanados hijos del Señor" (profaned children of the Lord) (158), and are further diminished in dignity by their rough treatment as workhorses. The blacksmith's achievement is, through the respect and empathy he gives these devalued creatures, to encourage whatever spark of spirituality they may unknowingly harbor. In measuring his success, the grandson claims the blacksmith could both transmit divinely inspired messages to his flock (he is a nuncio) and receive messages from them concerning their spiritual condition (he hears confessions), the two great communicative tasks reserved for well-recognized religious spokesmen and most typically for clergy.

Rabinovich's treatment usually entails a renunciation of the potential for lyricizing the subject matter. This poem does not cleave, however, to the plodding realism Rabinovich frequently employs to fully realize the stating of opinion. The boundary that must be crossed to minister spiritually to horses has led the blacksmith to violate an even stronger category division. Animated by the smith's powerful empathy, his tools acquire understanding and agree not to hurt the horses. The main rhetorical point is not that the objects managed to bargain but that the smith vitalized them with consciousness. This extraordinary feat is proof of the saintly and priestly quality the poem has been attributing to him. The blacksmith's eagerness to care for fellow creatures and his spiritualization of his craft have put him so at peace with the world that he can negotiate pacts with portions of that world, crossing the divisions between human and lower beings and between animate and inanimate items.

"Responso" displays no nostalgic urge to celebrate such unique sectors of Jewish culture as the irreparably lost world of the *shtetl*.[6] Instead, it concentrates on those aspects of the blacksmith's behavior that can be duplicated by any virtuous and conscientious worker. When the grandson says that the blacksmith could not think of his tools as pieces of metal because he prayed together with them, he establishes a principle applicable to all forms of human labor. The picture projected in "Responso" must remain free of any culture-specific clutter in order to draw attention to the human issues that are at the core of the poem. *Chamuscado* (*singed*), the typical epithet repeatedly assigned the grandfather, alludes to a universally encountered characteristic of metalworkers. The blacksmith's work is noble not because of his ethnicity, or because his task is rural, old-fashioned, or physically strenuous, but entirely because of his holistic attitude toward labor.[7]

The blacksmith's artless gift for communing with nature and manufactured objects gives, in turn, a clue to Rabinovich's persistent use of terms derived from institutional Christianity. The formalized manifestations of piety, such as chapel attendance, confessions, and the famously elaborate bell system of Notre Dame Cathedral, all stand for unnecessary institutionalization of the religious impulse. The poem mentions them to reveal their needlessness. The argument against them is the example of the blacksmith, who accomplishes all the supposed goals of a tightly organized religious life without any reliance on its structuring conventions. The rhetorical result is to cast the terms *chapel, nuncio, confessional,* as well as their referents in real-world religion, into disrepute.

The most marked formal characteristics of "Responso," such as the avoidance of stanzaic organization, originate in the same set of ideas that provide the content of the poem. The lack of stanzaic division certainly follows the antiformalist imperative of the poem. Just as the blacksmith need not interrupt his labors, begun before dawn, to pray in strictly ritual style, the poem need not break for conventional spacing. The smith's everyday worship is a totality. The continuous flow of text follows a like principle.

"Responso" also shows Rabinovich's idiosyncratic definition of the sentence. Two independent clauses appear end to end without either transitional matter or a capital to indicate a fresh start. The end of the second clause would seem to be the end of the sentence because of a period. Yet, the next line adds a third independent clause parallel in construction to the first two, without a capitalized first letter to signal a new sentence. In his disregard for the rules that produce educated-sounding discourse, Rabinovich resembles early-twentieth-century Soviet graphic artists from the realist faction of the avant-garde, who predicted "the destruction of everything connected with classical style, orthography, syntax and verse construction" and claimed "proportion and composition of type . . . are not independent of the substance being conveyed."[8]

* * *

An entire book could be devoted to specifying and tracing the substratum of ideas from which Rabinovich texts have arisen. It is likely that they reflect the utopian current of Eastern European intellectual life of the late nineteenth and early twentieth centuries. To cite a celebrated instance, one may point to the late religious-social thought of Leo Tolstoy. The novelist's ideal of manual labor combined with unreflective, unritualized piety is certainly embodied in the smith of "Responso." Tolstoy found religious spirit in the careful craftsmanship of simple people. Just so, the speaker in "Responso" justifies the smith's habit of praying at work by saying "Orando, el puño se pone piadoso" (In prayer, the fist becomes pious) (159) and by stating that the smith and his equipment prayed together.

In the Russian-Jewish milieu, closer to Rabinovich's experience, it is easy to identify examples of antiauthoritarian and antiformalist thought, particularly in strong anarchist tendencies with their reliance on inherent human capacities of self-governance. In the artistic realm, the poetry of Saul Tchernihowsky may be cited for its frequent attacks on the ritualistic commandments so tightly enforced in Orthodox practice.[9] Consider one of Tchernihowsky's most frequent targets: the set of prescribed procedures surrounding Jewish men's prayer. A recurring image is the once observant individual bursting free of his phylacteries on perceiving them as an instrument of bondage. Tchernihowsky's recommendation for transcending the limitations of ritualism is a drastic one involving a revival of "paganism," whereas Rabinovich more moderately praises such homemade modifications of observance as the smith's fusion of prayer and work. Yet both show parallel signs of a desire to abandon hierarchically determined forms.

The special circumstances of Rabinovich's writing should give any evaluator pause. The poetry at issue is clearly not designed to meet certain criteria commonly used in judging poetry. It would not be reasonable to apply a criterion of subtlety to Rabinovich's writing. The most hortatory stylistic forms, from the denunciatory broadside to the prophetic call to repentance, provide the organizing conventions for many Rabinovich poems. When he turns away from established models of grammar, he has the backing of the utilitarian-minded Russian precursors of social realism. It would be fair to judge his work by saying it has dual citizenship, belonging foremost to a category of writings with a directly pragmatic purpose. Rabinovich's texts belong both to poetry and to the tradition of polemical discourse running from biblical curse and invective to modern proclamations.

6 JOSÉ ISAACSON

An Open Letter to Spinoza

Rather than a sampling of poems, the 1977 *Cuaderno Spinoza* (*Spinoza Notebook*) by the well-established Argentine poet José Isaacson (1922–) is a single, if complex, communicative act.[1] The work's unity is manifest above all in its overriding preoccupation. The modern-day poet Isaacson (his poetic persona, as it appears in the work, will be designated as Isaacson) seeks rapport with the seventeenth-century philosopher Benedict de [Baruch] Spinoza. The effort to reach out across the centuries is more than a theme running through the poems. This quest for connection with Spinoza determines the construction of the book and supplies its reason to exist. It also gives rise to two problematic, but highly dynamic, features of the collection. These two troubling points will be the focus of the following analysis of *Cuaderno Spinoza*.

The first difficult question *Cuaderno Spinoza* poses is that of its status as an act of speech, as speaking to a hearer or interlocutor. The poems are the linguistic means of turning to Spinoza and developing an imaginative link with him. The most obvious sign of this communicative situation is the large number of poems directly addressed to Spinoza, as are several entitled "A Baruch Spinoza" ("To Baruch Spinoza"), and the frequent practice of calling out to Spinoza by name. Moreover, poems not linguistically cast in the Isaacson-to-Spinoza mode still form part of Isaacson's overall address to Spinoza. For example, when Isaacson poetically rewrites Spinoza's correspondence, the focus is still Isaacson's attempt to attune himself and the reader to Spinoza's mind and thus to enter into communion with him, to "quebrar el silencio" (break the silence) (156).

However accurate it is to call *Cuaderno Spinoza* a communication from Isaacson to Spinoza, such an account of the work is incomplete. The fact of the book's publication places it in a category unlike the private journal its title suggests. *Cuaderno Spinoza* is like one of those texts that make the reader a concerned third party examining correspondence not addressed to him. Yet this third party is no spy, for the material exists to provide him with insights. The exemplary case of this arrangement, and a useful model to which to compare *Cuaderno Spinoza,* is the open letter. The open letter has a putative addressee (who may or may not ever notice it) but, to be successful, must speak to its most likely public of readers.[2]

In this analysis of *Cuaderno Spinoza,* the entire collection, whatever the format of individual poems, will be considered as an open letter to Spinoza. Under this definition, the work must be "open" enough to allow diverse readers to find meanings in it. Though the messages in *Cuaderno Spinoza*—letters, soliloquies, and prayers—may look private, they must prove worthwhile to a reader who is unlike either Isaacson or Spinoza and may not care intensely about Isaacson's relations with his forebear. Otherwise, Isaacson would be taking advantage of a public forum to air personal concerns. In effect, Leonardo Senkman has complained that *Cuaderno Spinoza* is so written as to confer upon the descendant of Iberian Jews a sense of "legitimación."[3]

A second problematic area is the relation between Isaacson's poetry and Spinoza's writings. It might seem simplest to see *Cuaderno Spinoza* as reflecting, in poetic form, Spinoza's philosophy. But *Cuaderno Spinoza,* on examination, proves to be too divergent from Spinoza's work to count as a verse setting of the philosophy. Isaacson very freely suggests that Spinoza's philosophical assertions are not to be taken seriously. He frequently raises doubts about the philosopher's aspirations to pure rationality, and he expresses, through a perversely mystical reading, appreciation for Spinoza's less rational aspects.

Philosophical ideas are not *Cuaderno Spinoza*'s main attraction. Rather, *Cuaderno Spinoza* draws attention to emotionally significant features of its subject's life and work. As will become apparent in the study of particular poems, Isaacson turns to Spinoza as a figure of the great Sephardic civilization that, after its Golden Age in Moorish Spain, continued to sustain itself in Diasporic communities throughout Europe. The troubled career of the philosopher and his enormous difficulty in remaining within any community provide material for Isaacson's poetry.

Isaacson draws further away from Spinoza's philosophy as such by questioning the value of the form in which it is couched. The philosopher designed a form of discourse so rigorous as to resemble geometrical proofs. This innovation is often regarded as a misstep. Mortimer J. Adler gives the negative consensus concerning Spinoza's pseudogeometrical exposition: "His *Ethics* is written in strict mathematical form, with propositions, proofs, corollaries, lemmas, scholia, and the like. However, the subject matter of metaphysics and of morals is not very satisfactorily handled in this manner, which is more appropriate for geometry and other mathematical subjects than for philosophical ones. . . . Spinoza . . . failed to some extent to communicate . . . and it seems likely that the form . . . was a major reason for failure."[4] Isaacson, who as a poet represents and favors a

language without aspirations to scientific rigor, appreciates Spinoza's experiment only paradoxically as the symptom of an ardent desire for perfect
knowledge.

After examination of these two areas of difficulty, it will be possible to
evaluate *Cuaderno Spinoza*'s resolution of them. Two questions then arise:
Does *Cuaderno Spinoza* draw the reader into communication with Spinoza,
or does the reader often remain excluded from Isaacson's address to the
philosopher? How worthwhile was Isaacson's against-the-grain appreciation of Spinoza, in which the philosopher's most strenuously asserted rigor
is devalued and his emotional or quasimystical significance, suppressed in
his writings, is elevated?

* * *

To see how Isaacson deals with the first of these issues, the need to open
the open letter, one should examine "Benito de Sefarad" (91–94). This text
has the format predominant in the collection, that of an intimate letter from
Isaacson to Spinoza pleading for a greater closeness. The terms used in this
plea determine whether or not the reader can duly share in the work of
reaching out to Spinoza and in the sought-after empathetic bond with the
philosopher.

"Benito de Sefarad" is typical of those poems in which Isaacson utilizes
one of his personal characteristics as a possible key to contacting Spinoza,
in this case, that of his Sephardic ancestry. He argues that a shared ancestral
experience, that of expulsion and exile from the great Judeo-Spanish civilization of the medieval period, provides common ground between him and
his addressee. He lays a claim of near-kinship on his fellow Sephard:

Baruj,
quizá en Orense o en Burgos,
alguna vez
nuestros abuelos cruzaron
sus exilios,
y yo,
junto a este nuevo Jordán
de antiguos mapas
contigo me encuentro.

(Baruch,
perhaps in Orense or in Burgos,
once

our grandfathers' exiles
crossed,
and I,
by that new Jordan
of ancient maps
find myself with you.)

Although it would be possible to study the poet's relation to his Sephardic ancestry, it is more interesting to consider what value such references may have for Isaacson's readers. After all, *Cuaderno Spinoza* only feigns the form its title suggests, that of a private journal or personal notebook undertaken for the author's benefit. Readers other than Isaacson must derive some advantage from the devices he employs in approaching Spinoza; otherwise, they really would be in the role of outsiders perusing a stranger's personal papers.

How likely is it that readers will be part of the special community Isaacson is establishing through Sephardic allusions? Taken in its most literal sense, the question could be rephrased: How likely are readers to have Sephardic ancestry? Senkman, in his negative evaluation of the collection, seems to see this as the question at stake. He criticizes Isaacson for exalting the exceptional quality of Sephardic lineage.[5] If he is right, then Isaacson is guilty not only of elitism but also of excluding a large segment of his readership from full appreciation of the dynamic at work in "Sefarad." Consider that a Jewish Argentine reader, who might well feel drawn to Isaacson's work on Jewish themes, is most likely of Eastern European origin. Those Argentines of Spanish peninsular ancestry may well have Sephardic forebears, but they are not apt to be fully aware of the heritage or to have maintained Hispano-Judaic cultural traits. These conditions apply to the entire Spanish-speaking world.

The link with Sepharad and with the Sephardic exile must be broadly construed to allow non-Sephardic readers to enjoy a connection with the legendary Jewish civilization that flourished in Spain. Such a link is possible because the poem makes the Sephardim representative of larger human groups—so many and such broad groups that the reader cannot fail to be included.

In the logic of the poem, all readers have a special conduit to the Spanish-Jewish experience because they are users of the Spanish language and conversant with the culture associated with that language. The opening lines of "Sefarad"—"Cuando España fue / Sefarad" (When Spain was / Sepharad)—are a useful overstatement. Although *Sepharad* is undeniably the Hebrew word for *Spain,* in practice *Sepharad* and *Sephardim* can never be coterminous with *Spain* and *Spaniards.* *Spain* is *Sefarad* only to those who thought of it as such, that is, to those with a Jewish frame of reference. Moreover, the terms cannot be interchangeable because the phenomena to which they allude are unlike. *Spain* may refer to the political entity, the geographical territory, and the civilization of that name. *Sepharad,* though, can refer only to the civilization that arose among the Jews of Spain and continued, to diverse degrees, in their subsequent exile. Yet, Isaacson has chosen to make the two seemingly equivalent rather than turn to such accurate, if flat, lexical choices as "When Spain contained Sefarad."[6]

What is gained by the equivalence of the two terms? It draws attention to the fact, long neglected in the discussion of Spanish culture, that the Spanish Jewish Golden Age was as much a high point in Spanish as in Jewish history. Josef Hayim Yerushalmi, certainly a major figure in the recovery of Sephardic history, has stressed that until the expulsion, neither individuals nor cultural achievements had to belong either to Spanish or to Jewish civilization. Only later did it occur that when a creative person assumed a fully Jewish identity, "the Peninsula now lost another son . . . reclaimed by the Jewish people. In a bygone age, both might have claimed him equally."[7] The principle that the Jewish and Spanish cultures are inextricably conjoined benefits readers of *Cuaderno Spinoza.* (One should note that "Sefarad" duly reflects the blurring of the distinction between Spanish and Portuguese identity, especially typical of the contemporary Jewish community, subsuming both under the terms *Spanish* and *Spain.*[8]) The poem does not presuppose a reader with an explicit and well-articulated knowledge of Sephardic culture, but it makes the point that a reader of Spanish is an heir of Iberian and hence of Sephardic civilization.

The first stanza gives added importance to the Spanish language and to the Spanish reader's special advantage in understanding Spinoza's Sephardic exile experience. The Sephardim are credited as "forjadores . . . de las palabras / más viejas / que en español se pronunciaron" (smiths . . . of the / most ancient words / ever uttered in Spanish). They were, that is, shapers of the very language through which Isaacson and the reader hope to contact them now.

Up to this point, "Sefarad" might seem merely to extol the virtues of the Sephardim (for example, their excellence as silversmiths). But the second and third stanzas reveal that the non-Sephardic reader has a point of entry into this privileged culture. It is his sensitive and nuanced grasp of Spanish and Iberian culture that allows him to appreciate the variants of Spinoza's name. Only one of the names is entirely within the domain of Judaica: the

Hebrew name Baruch. Another, the Latinate Benedictus de Spinoza, is outside Iberia; stripped of its national markings, it reflects Spinoza's assimilation into general Western European intellectual life. All the other names, though, are Iberian: Espinoza de los Monteros, Benito orensano (a term that requires a recognition of Spanish place-name adjectives), Benito, and Bento Despiñoza. The reader is encouraged to see that his awareness of the values of these variants is a beginning toward understanding the seemingly exotic Spinoza. The same appeal recurs in the poem's closing aphorism: "Hasta los nombres / tienen su exilio" (Even names / have their exile).

Moreover, the second stanza offers a peculiarly linguistic clue into the mystery of Spinoza. A pun on his name brings to the fore his prickly personality and thorny system of thought. Although this comment involves a Jewish reference (the burning bush), it is worth noting that the allusion is a familiar part of Christian culture. The use of a pun to approach a difficult issue may well lead the reader unaware into a traditionally Jewish turn of thought. The idea that there are powerfully magic meanings hidden in the supposed accidents of language is central to the Kabbalistic notion of hermeneutics. A reliance on the secret significances of words, and especially of names, is especially well suited to the period in which Spinoza developed. It was an era characterized by mystical extravagances: "A generation filled with the east wind of mystical ravings hungered after signs and wonders, and signs and wonders came without stint."[9]

* * *

As well as these linguistic connections, a second factor binds the Argentine, New World, and human groups to the phenomenon of Spinoza and the exile he incarnates. In the above-cited stanzas, directly following his most specific reference to Sephardic Spain, "Baruch / perhaps in Orense or Burgos," Isaacson rapidly shifts his reference to his own time and place, where his encounter with Spinoza occurs.

The "new Jordán" by which he now stands is the Río de la Plata, an identification reinforced later in the poem by a physical description of the Plata: "te llevo a mi Jordán / mi barroso río" (I take you to my Jordan / my muddy river). What right does the Plata have to figure as a new Jordan? The clue is in the phrase "ancient maps." Isaacson supplies a facsimile of a 1507 map displaying the very feature that concerns him. In his gloss to the reproduction, he notes that the river labeled as the Jordan is, in fact, the Río de la Plata.

The Plata as a figure of the Jordan suggests several propositions. The Jordan is, of course, the river to cross to transform exile into redemption.

Early cartography, in placing the Jordan in the New World, expressed the pervasive, if confused, conviction that the new continent would fulfill the sweeping promises of Bible and of legend—in this case, the recovery of the promised land. A longing for such a return indicates a feeling that one is wandering in exile. The condition of exile then becomes the common factor uniting all those implicated in the Jordan-Plata figure. The early explorers were displaced Europeans (including, no doubt, many Sephardim) wandering in a strange land. As contemporary Argentine essayists have asserted (for example, Héctor A. Murena and Ezequiel Martínez Estrada), the disorientation and alienation of these early settlers may well have left a legacy of estrangement that persists to the present day.[10] In this sense, Argentina itself is a locus both of exile and of a drive, sometimes bizarre in its manifestations, for return and redemption.

Spinoza can best be understood by fellow exiles because he is the quintessential figure of expulsion and displacement. He represents in his own person the *galut* of the Jewish people, the Sephardic expulsion from the Iberian peninsula, and finally the excommunication from the Diasporic Sephardic community of Amsterdam. Isaacson mediates between the two spheres of exile, for he is a historical emissary from the Sephardic experience and a sharer in the exile that is inherent in the New World.

Beyond these specifiable cases of exile, with their roots in historical circumstances, the poem evokes a more diffuse form of rootlessness. Isaacson continues, throughout the collection, to vary and extend the meaning of the terms of exile and redemption. For example, in "Recorrí tus textos" ("I Pored Over Your Texts") (154–56), the treatment of the alienating vastness of the Argentine South places Isaacson again in the tradition of the above-cited essayists. Less emphatically, though, a subtheme is insinuated, or the reader is permitted to insinuate it: that the accumulation of social injustices is tantamount to a form of exile. Such a proposition appears, mutedly, in the following stanza:

Dolorido Sur
mi patria maltratada,
entre tantos más
soy un afligido.

(Wounded South
my ill-used homeland,
along with so many others,
I am in pain.)

      (156)

The collection does not proceed far into this thematic area.

More clearly brought out is the most ample conception of exile possible. Once the poems have raised the notion of an existential exile, such as that experienced by the uprooted inhabitants of the New World or the southerners contemplating vast, empty expanses, the notion obviously must apply to all readers by virtue of their human existence. In effect, the poems recognize this necessary possibility of an element of exile in all human lives. By page 196, Isaacson has sufficiently opened and amplified the terms in question that he can assert: "Al cabo de la historia, / todos los ríos son el Jordán / y santas / todas las tierras / que el hombre padece y fructifica" (At the end of history, / every river is the Jordan / and every land / is holy / that man suffers with and causes to bear crops).

To sum up, "Sefarad" is characterized by its appeal to widening and overlapping sets of possible readers. These sets eventually include every person who could conceivably read the text. At first reading, "Sefarad" may seem flawed by its specific emphasis on an ancestral connection readers may not share. Yet Isaacson generalizes the Sephardic legacy until all Spanish-language readers enjoy the benefit it confers: a route of access into the mystery of Spinoza, and hence into perennial puzzles of human identity. The meaning of exile is similarly expanded from the Jewish Diaspora or the post-Expulsion Sephardic dispersion to give the term meaning for the New World, for the vast expanses of Argentina, for the victims of social wrongs, and finally for all human beings.

* * *

Beginning on page 177, shifts in the collection's structure increase the reader's involvement with Spinoza and what he represents. Previously, *Cuaderno Spinoza* was dominated by the poetic persona of Isaacson. The voice of Isaacson was heard calling out to Spinoza and pronouncing soliloquies and prayers reflecting on his efforts to reach the philosopher. Now the collection breaks away from the Isaacson-to-Spinoza format.

Between page 177 and page 229, interspersed with other types of text, one finds a poetic recreation of selections from Spinoza's famous correspondence.[11] Twenty-six of these have Spinoza as putative author, albeit a much poeticized Spinoza as a look at the real-world philosopher's considerably drier correspondence makes clear. The seven remaining pseudoletters are from Spinoza's correspondents, who draw him out on matters he has previously discussed.

The principal reason to recreate Spinoza's correspondence is, of course, to bring out aspects of his personality that Isaacson finds to be repressed. The reconstituted Spinoza allows—often between the lines—glimpses of a highly emotional nature. A second justification, though, is to provide relief from the Isaacson-to-Spinoza arrangement. The latter always risks making readers mere onlookers at Isaacson's spectacular struggles to reach Spinoza and Sepharad. The letters eliminate the mediating figure of Isaacson, with his importunings, expressions of doubt, and meditations. His removal from the scene allows an unimpeded view of Spinoza's own expression and of the book's least personal topics: reason and its potential, the nature of being and change, and the obtaining of knowledge of ultimate matters. Even though it is true, outside the poems' frame of reference, that the real-world poet Isaacson controls Spinoza's voice, within the world of *Cuaderno Spinoza* the reader is able to contemplate Spinoza without any intermediary.

The appearance of the letters ushers in a further change in the structure of *Cuaderno Spinoza*. In the section dedicated to correspondence, two texts anticipate the next segment and the innovation that will define it: poems in Spinoza's voice without a human correspondent. Two of the letters from Spinoza give rise to such new texts. Spinoza's letter to G. van Blyenbergh (193–94) gives rise to "Descartes y yo" ("Descartes and I") (194–95). Unlike the letters, this text is not derived from the real-life Spinoza's correspondence; it appears to be a self-addressed reverie elicited by the epistolary poem preceding it. The sequence and conceptual relation of the two texts suggest that after completing the letter to Blyenbergh, Spinoza developed further thoughts that he voiced only to himself (with the reader eavesdropping).

Such a soliloquy-type scenario is further implied by the difference between "Descartes y yo," presumably not addressed to anyone, and Spinoza's earlier comments on his philosophical predecessors, directed to Hendrik Oldenburg ("Bacon y Descartes," "Bacon," 179–80). In the semipublic commentary, Spinoza responds to Oldenburg's request to hear more of his comments on the two philosophers. Spinoza answers as a contentious, competitive professional colleague. He finds fault with Bacon's method of exposition—"Describe / y casi nada demuestra" (He describes / and hardly demonstrates anything)—and choice of subject matter. In short, he provides a professional evaluation.

"Descartes y yo" answers no question and appears to arise from Spinoza's own thought processes. The emphasis shifts from Descartes's work to his and Spinoza's common motivation. Spinoza abandons the strenuous effort toward objectivity that, if one accepts *Cuaderno Spinoza*'s analysis, has always masked an emotional outcry. His comment on his similarity to Descartes is the very one Isaacson might have made: "aunque no podamos /

dibujar el sentido, / el amor / nos presta las alas / y el vuelo es posible"
(even though we can't / trace out the meaning, / love / lends us wings / and
flight is possible) (194). With its unguarded talk of the emotional drives
behind philosophical inquiry, this text gives the closest look at Spinoza so
far in the collection.

The penultimate letter brings in its wake another startlingly unmediated
view of Spinoza. "Oración entre dos luces" ("Prayer Between Two Lights")
is an overheard prayer. Spinoza, formerly self-assured to the point of
arrogance, now admits himself to be overwhelmed by the task at hand and
in need of divine assistance. Moving away from his ultra-rationalist's stance,
he appeals: "Si como el barro / en las manos del alfarero / estoy, /
háblame, Señor" (If I am like clay / in the hands / of the potter, / speak to
me, Lord) (227).

After one more letter, the collection becomes dominated by Spinoza's
voice. The texts in the remaining segment (229–81) include prayers, reveries,
and private reflections on Spinoza's public statements. The reader enjoys
the greatest possible freedom to explore Spinoza's private self and thoughts.

Though Isaacson's addresses to Spinoza continue to appear sporadically
after page 177, their status is now changed. The Isaacson-Spinoza connection is no longer the only one open to readers eager to understand the
philosopher and the mysteries associated with him. Isaacson becomes only
one of the seekers after Spinoza's essence, since all readers of the book can
now examine Spinoza's correspondence, prayers and soliloquies. The implication is that Isaacson's vigorous efforts to summon or conjure Spinoza's
spirit were initially necessary. Once the contact is established, the reader is
more and more on his own in broadening the communicative link with the
philosopher. The poetic persona of Isaacson does not fade away but loses its
privileged character as the reader enjoys direct access to Spinoza.

* * *

Isaacson is quick to draw attention to the paradoxical relation between
Cuaderno Spinoza and the philosopher's writings. "De algún modo / tus
textos le trasmiten / un sentido a mi escritura" (Somehow / your texts
transmit / a meaning to my writing), he tells Spinoza in an account of his
idiosyncratic reading of the treatises, "Recorrí tus textos" ("I Pored Over
Your Texts") (154–56). Isaacson is least concerned with the aspects of Spinoza's thought that the philosopher most worked to display. Even when the
poet turns for material to the treatises, especially the *Ethics,* it is to reveal a
mercurial, impassioned Spinoza behind the would-be strict rationalist.

One indicator of the reinvention of Spinoza is that it is not very productive to compare the thematic content of Isaacson's *Cuaderno Spinoza* with that of, for example, the *Ethics*. A detailed comparison can only confirm what is immediately evident: Isaacson cares for the hidden subtext he discerns in the philosophy and not for the statements that are manifest for all to see and analyze. Another sign of his specialized preoccupation with Spinoza is his relative lack of interest in commentaries on and explications of the treatises. In the prefatory "Advertencia" ("Warning") (9–10) Isaacson accounts for his background in Spinoza. Among the commentators, writers of a more romantic and impressionistic turn (such as Israel Zangwill in his *Dreamers of the Ghetto*) are favored over scholarly explicators. More value, though, is given to Novalis's phrase for Spinoza, *drunk with God,* a characterization confirming Isaacson's own reading of the philosopher. Finally, Isaacson's feelings about the entire matter of Spinoza gain precedence over any type of mediating commentary.

If the content of *Cuaderno Spinoza* and that of the *Ethics* seems almost too easy to characterize, that relation between the formats of the two works restores the needed element of complexity. *Cuaderno Spinoza* has paid, in its layout, a curious homage to Spinoza's unusual ways of organizing philosophical discourse supposedly to achieve maximal rigor. The collection of poems undeniably mimics certain features of the *Ethics* and adds other features in the same pseudogeometrical mode.[12] To begin with, the poems of the collection are not spaced in the manner conventional for poetry, that is, designed to call attention to the uniqueness of each poem. In *Cuaderno Spinoza,* the beginning of a poem only sometimes coincides with the beginning of a new page. Titles are not placed above the text but rather are level with the opening line and to the left of it, running up to the left margin. The result is that the textual layout more closely resembles that of a continuous treatise with subheadings. Such a characterization also describes the *Ethics,* though the two works are by no means identical in layout.

In other cases, Isaacson has been more geometrical in form than Spinoza himself. This is particularly evident in the case of the correspondence. Consider Spinoza's "Carta II, a Enrique Oldenburg" ("Letter II, to Hendrik Oldenburg") (177–79). The *Cuaderno Spinoza* version shows Spinoza able to pare down complex trains of thought to their barest elements:

Toda sustancia
es
infinita.

Sólo una
es
la sustancia existente.

(Every substance
is
infinite.

Only one
is
the existing substance.)
                    (178)

   The above, though, has been distilled out of a letter that displays no such
severe economy but is bulky with conventionally polite turns of phrase and
transitional or explicatory matter.[13] *Cuaderno Spinoza* pares the original
letter down to its most geometrical form and at the same time adds elements. Subtitles, which the real-life letter does not use, appear in its poetic
counterpart, again suggesting austere rigor. The stanza cited above beginning "Only one . . ." is compatible with Spinoza's pantheism and could,
with an elegantly cryptic conceptual twist, have been fitted into the original
letter. However, Spinoza did not make this final turn of thought and phrase;
Cuaderno Spinoza made it on his behalf, as if salvaging a missed opportunity. In its minimalistic form and parsimony of means, its treatise-like
subheadings and nimble inclusion of cosmic unity in the discussion, the
poetic version of the letter is more Spinoza-like than Spinoza's own work, in
the sense of pursuing a geometrical severity.
   It would be easy to say of *Cuaderno Spinoza*'s quasigeometrical form that
the poems parody Spinoza's longing for rigor, or subvert it. Yet such a
characterization is too simple to account for Isaacson's imitation of Spinoza. The nature of the relation, whose importance is suggested by the
prevalence of pseudogeometrical features in *Cuaderno Spinoza,* is further
illuminated by the work's thematic statements about Spinoza and his extreme notions of rigor.

* * *

   Isaacson's judgment on Spinoza's experiment is easy to discern. Like
Adler, cited in the introduction to this study, Isaacson finds proofs, scholia,
and lemmas unsuitable for the transmission of insights. In Isaacson's expressed view, Spinoza deluded himself as to the efficacy of rigor: "tu amor /

por las líneas rectas / solía desviarte / de las ideas claras y distintas / que tanto amabas" (your love / for straight lines / was apt to lead you astray / from the clear, distinct ideas / that you loved so much) (148). Yet Spinoza's mistaken effort has virtues other than the intended transmission of logically acquired knowledge. The philosopher has left a testimony to his ardent longing to know God: "Las formas geométricas / fueron / el poema de tu razón enamorada" (Geometrical forms / were / the poem of your reason in love) (126). By reading this inadvertent testimony to Spinoza's spiritual and emotional experience, Isaacson does not learn philosophy but rather learns about ardor and exile, the complications of human identity and the temptations of unbounded rationalism.

Cuaderno Spinoza abounds in poems casting doubt on Spinoza's pretensions to strict reliance on reason. "En los márgenes de tus teoremas" ("In the Margins of Your Theorems") (114-18), a characteristic example, shows Isaacson confronting Spinoza and challenging the philosopher on this very point. Turning around Spinoza's "Este tratado exige / lectores / libres / de la superstición / y el miedo" (This treatise requires / readers / free / of superstition / and fear), Isaacson subjects him to questioning: "¿Pudiste / acaso, Baruj, / librarte / de la superstición y el miedo?" (Were you, perhaps / able, Baruch, / to free yourself / from superstition and fear?) and answers the question negatively. From this direct challenge in the opening lines, the poem goes on to present counterarguments to Spinoza's denial of the supernatural or mystical element in human understanding.

* * *

More complex than the oppositional stance typified by "En los márgenes de tus teoremas" is the striving toward a harmonious reconciliation. The poem "Amo los helechos" ("I Love Ferns") (106-9), an unusual text in *Cuaderno Spinoza,* offers just such an attempt to find a middle ground between Isaacson's and Spinoza's projects. The first three stanzas of "Amo los helechos" appear to be anomalous material within the collection of poems. Whereas the texts of *Cuaderno Spinoza* are tightly linked to one another and to the problem at hand, that of connecting with Spinoza, the beginning of "Amo los helechos" is that of an autonomous, meditative ode. The poet seems to turn away from his project to admire the striking form of the fern. Yet it is unreasonable to suppose that the poem is truly an independent ode or reverie, for such goes against the entire tendency of the collection.

The first three stanzas, then, form one segment of the poem not only because of their common first line but also because they constitute a puzzle. The function of this section, with its detailed admiration of the fern, is to raise the question of why it belongs in *Cuaderno Spinoza*.

With the fourth stanza, the appearance of the familiar-looking terms *sustancia* (*substance*), *forma* (*form*), and *seres* (*beings*) marks a return to the book's normal subject matter. These are the terms Isaacson has been using as he cites, paraphrases, and comments on Spinoza's writings. Isaacson has now reentered Spinoza's lexicon and, in effect, the philosopher's conceptual realm. His concern in the fourth and fifth stanzas is philosophical and Spinozian: a pantheistic vital substance shared between all beings and deriving from an original, divine source. But the route by which he comes back to Spinoza's terms and concepts is unlike any so far utilized in the collection. Previously, Isaacson contemplated Spinoza's life and writings. Now he has left Spinoza aside for the space of three stanzas and has arrived at consideration of his philosophical concerns through the experience of beings themselves, as emblematized by the fern.

Here is an implied statement that the issues Spinoza considered are questions that naturally arise in the human mind. The experience of the world stimulates an inquiry into the nature of being. Isaacson makes the point that Adler summarized by calling philosophical questions "child-like."[14] If Spinoza's preoccupations are altogether understandable, what then of Isaacson's contention that Spinoza's efforts were wrongheaded? Clearly, the poem "Amo los helechos" shows that it is natural to take up Spinoza's favored philosophical problems and to reason about them using the philosopher's terms. What is misguided is the effort to ban from this undertaking all irrational elements. "El milagro / excluiste de tus teoremas" (You left no room for miracles / in your theorems) (116) is a typical complaint. "Amo los helechos" offers itself as a demonstration of how Spinozian problems may be entertained without the severe rationalistic constraints the philosopher imposed.

The poem approaches the problem of being from an experiential and imaginative entry point. Isaacson arrives at the issues set forth in the fourth and fifth stanzas by savoring the impression made on him by the agreeable contemplation of the fern (stanzas 1–3). By an imaginative exercise, and one pleasurable to the mind, he arrives at the notion of a substance shared between all beings (stanza 4). The next stanza continues to utilize terms seemingly derived from a philosophical treatise, but a fresh irrational element has worked its way in. With its talk of naming as a magical act of bringing into being, the fifth stanza is markedly Kabbalistic. The question of the mature Spinoza's degree of involvement with this form of Jewish mysticism has long been debated, both by intellectual historians and by such lay enthusiasts as Jorge Luis Borges.[15] Isaacson here offers no solution to the historical question but rather illustrates the compatibility between Spinoza's concerns and those of the Kabbalists.

Following the third and fourth stanzas, with their close resemblance to philosophical discourse, a segment of three stanzas breaks away from reasoned discourse. Isaacson here does not abandon his philosophical subject matter but subjects it to a resolutely irrationalistic treatment. The language becomes antilogical in the way of surrealistic or avant-garde poetic language.[16] It violates commonsense semantic boundaries and creates logically impossible juxtapositions. This strategy reaches its extreme in the highly metaphorical eighth stanza. Here the ambiguity surrounding the poet is characterized in a series of logically inconceivable figures, such as a "duro anillo / de neblina" (hard ring / of mist).

Having made this definitive break with strict rationality, the poem brings back the treatise-like language that first appeared in the third and fourth stanzas. The terms are again common to Isaacson's and Spinoza's writing. Yet Isaacson resolutely maintains the right to irrationality that he has just established with his wild metaphors. However soberly philosophical the bulk of the terms may be—*finitud* (*finitude*), *eternidad* (*eternity*), *formas* (*forms*), *Ser* (*Being*)—the stanzas can be read and made sense of only by bringing in a considerable element of the subjective and experiential. For example, the figure of finitude taking solace in infinity has no meaning when the two terms remain as abstractions. Both must be not only personified through the poetic figure but also vivified with personal perception. Once finitude comes to mean a human experience of finitude and infinity to mean the individual's contemplation of the infinite, to use a perhaps crude paraphrase, sense is restored to the stanza. The combined illogic of such a statement, together with the fact that it makes sense when a subjective element is added, suggests a proposition about philosophy in general. Isaacson is demonstrating that philosophy can be successful communication even when the features Spinoza most feared as contaminating influences are admitted into the discussion.

Though Spinoza is not addressed or referred to directly in the poem, "Amo los helechos" is one of Isaacson's most positive statements about, and one of his strongest expressions of warmth toward, the philosopher. Whereas many poems rebuke Spinoza for an excessive pursuit of rigor, "Amo los helechos" demonstrates a willingness to share his ideas and, to some extent, his sparely logical terminology. The issue in this poem is not to question what Spinoza has done but rather to supplement it with the components the philosopher misguidedly edited out of his own discourse. The emphasis on love, dominating the four closing stanzas, harks back to *Cuaderno Spinoza*'s contention that Spinoza's work was really based on a fervent, not a logical, desire to know. Following this logic, "Amo los helechos" offers a form of discourse more truly Spinozian than Spinoza's own repressed writings—and in doing so, makes Spinoza one of the poets.

* * *

The above commentary can serve as a guide in formulating answers to the evaluative questions posed at the outset of this study. First, how valid is the complaint that the book is designed to satisfy the needs of Isaacson, who self-servingly seeks "legitimación" (Senkman's term) through his Sephardic ancestry and special relation with Spinoza? As the analysis of the collection's organization makes clear, the exclusivity of the Isaacson-Spinoza communication is not consistently problematic through all sections of the book. It is primarily in the first section, up to page 177, that the poetic persona of Isaacson plays so prominent a role, with his letters or appeals to Spinoza and his prayers and meditations concerned with reaching the philosopher. Senkman seems chiefly interested in the Isaacson-to-Spinoza communications, for he speaks of the work as Isaacson's "imaginario intercambio epistolar con Spinoza" (imaginary exchange of letters with Spinoza), "cartas que Isaacson escribe a Spinoza" (letters that Isaacson writes to Spinoza), and he several times refers to a dialogue between Isaacson and Spinoza.[17] The portions of the work that are most accurately described by such phrases are vulnerable to such complaints, since they risk making the reader an ignored spectator at the dramatic working-out of Isaacson's individual problems. The fact that Isaacson is here a poetic representation and not the real-life author of the volume can hardly be a consolation to the virtually excluded reader.

However, the Isaacson-to-Spinoza communications do contain material efficacious in reincluding the reader. Foremost is a range of cultural allusions that establishes commonalities for a group that is not Sephardic or even Jewish but that uses the Spanish language. In some cases, the group referred to is defined as the totality of Argentines, Latin Americans, or the human race. With the coming of the correspondence, beginning on page 177, the dominance of the Spinoza-Isaacson bond is broken and never reestablished. From this point on, the reader has ample access to the phenomenon of Spinoza, as ample as does anyone, including "Isaacson."

Although it would be unfair to criticize the entire book as being too dominated by the poetic person of Isaacson, such a comment could well apply to the first section, in which the reader must approach Spinoza through Isaacson's mediating efforts. Negative criticism could most justly center on the great length of this opening section and the long wait the reader must endure for reassurance that the book is for all readers.

The question of Isaacson's work in relation to Spinoza's philosophical writings is easily answered using Isaacson's many challenges to the philosopher and his unusually harmonious approach to his writings in "Amo los helechos." Isaacson's interest in Spinoza is clearly very far from a philosopher's. He does not see Spinoza's reasoning as successful in leading readers to well-established truths and, in effect, is not concerned with such truths: "No tengo / respuestas que ofrecer" (I have no / answers to offer) (108). He is willing to accept certain aspects of Spinoza's writings: the basic curiosity about ultimate questions, the desire to think through issues of metaphysics, and even some of the basic terminology of the philosopher. However, the discourse Isaacson constructs with these elements, adding the emotive and mystical notes he detects suppressed in the philosopher's writings, is radically unlike a philosophical statement of any type. Emotional and experiential matters are always given priority over reasoning; rational exertions are often seen as essentially symptoms of great passions, such as love of God. The synthesis Isaacson achieves between Spinoza's contribution and his own is sometimes a dynamically conflict-filled one and sometimes a successful unification. In either case, though, the result is hardly part of the philosophical enterprise and is altogether part of the poetic one.

7 MARCOS RICARDO BARNATÁN

The New Novel as Access to Kabbalah

El laberinto de Sión (*The Labyrinth of Zion*), the 1971 novel by Marcos Ricardo Barnatán (1946–), is recognizably in the manner of the Latin American new novel. It presents diverse fragments for which the reader must construct a unity.[1] This study of the work considers it as the signs of the narrator-hero's effort to recover for himself and the reader the riches of Sephardic culture, particularly its mystical side. The protagonist seeks to present this culture so that it will have meaning for a modern Spanish-language reader attuned to contemporary literature, not to the specifics of cultural history. Deeming Kabbalah the essential contribution of Sephardic civilization, the hero chooses a form for his book that is markedly influenced by this variety of mysticism.

As Frank Kermode has observed, texts purporting to reveal hidden wisdom typically make themselves difficult to construe. The hermetic text demands an exercise of interpretive imagination from those who would benefit from it. Only by making sense of the writing, sometimes quite arduously, does the reader become entitled to enjoy the insights the text sets out to display.[2] However, to see the novel as organized like an esoteric commentary and to identify it as Kabbalistic do not resolve the problems *Laberinto* raises. Such a characterization of the work calls attention to its problematic relation to the already existing body of Kabbalistic texts and commentaries.

Kabbalistic writing, which began as commentary directly on Torah, came to have its own canonical texts and centuries' worth of additional works reelaborating its central ideas. Given this accumulation, one needs daring imagination to make a fresh statement. One must somehow discover a task left undone. Harold Bloom, in his 1975 *Kabbalah and Criticism,* remarks, "Kabbalah is essentially a *vision of belatedness.*" He observes that even Gershom G. Scholem, the great modern scholar of Kabbalah, could make a worthwhile new contribution only by first overcoming the problem of his late arrival on the Kabbalistic scene. He imaginatively "transformed his own belatedness, in regard to the necessary anteriority of his subject, into a surprising earliness."[3]

If Scholem, for all his scholarship, faced such a struggle in justifying his entry into the field, what hope can there be for the hero of *Laberinto*? He is neither pious nor truly scholarly; his preceptors are a withdrawn aunt and a "professor" who appears to live by amusing wealthy friends with his knowledge. Moreover, the 192 pages of *Laberinto* contain much material seemingly remote from Kabbalistic concerns: society gossip, childhood memories, and literary commentary.

This study views the hero's much-flaunted dilettantism as a dynamic feature of the novel. The hero emphasizes his casual grasp of Kabbalism and his love of worldly matters because they point to the originality of his Kabbalistic design. By fitting these disturbing elements into its system, the novel makes its bid to be a unique addition to Kabbalistic writing and hence one worth creating.

To examine the hero's Kabbalism and his effort to present it in an original way, one should consider separately three contributions to his system. The first is what the hero obtains from his Tía Luna, who develops in him a Kabbalist's understanding of language. The inchoate notions of Luna are then supplemented by the fully articulated teachings of Professor Max, who leads the hero through sacred and profane knowledge. Finally, there is the hero's own addition, which takes Kabbalah into the realm of literary writing.[4]

Tracing the specifically Kabbalistic elements requires reference to known standards of Kabbalah. For this purpose, I will refer to two much-noted modern works, one a reliable presentation of the development of Kabbalah and the other, like *Laberinto* itself, a deviant utilization of Kabbalistic thought. The first is Scholem's 1941 *Major Trends in Jewish Mysticism;* the second is Bloom's *Kabbalah and Criticism.*[5]

Consideration of the novel's mixture of Kabbalism with surprising new elements leads to two evaluative questions. The first is the degree to which this lightweight treatment of Kabbalah can be considered part of Kabbalistic commentary as such. The second is whether *Laberinto* has succeeded in justifying its existence by saying something or textually doing something not previously said or done or expectable. The question of the novel's usefulness as a commentary on the social identity and situation of contemporary Jewry has already been posed by Leonardo Senkman, who found the work "frivolous," an assessment that could hardly be refuted.[6]

* * *

The first segments of *Laberinto* offer scant indication of how to understand the work's organization. Transcriptions of personal reflections and letters succeed each other, united only by their common esoteric and Sephardic themes. With the appearance of Tía Luna, however, the reader gains a hold on the text. The narrator-hero, in speaking of his aunt and her meaning for him, adopts a familiar pattern: autobiographical reminiscence. It is fitting that Tía Luna should provide the earliest opportunity to glimpse the novel's order and sense, for she serves a like function as the hero's first guide to the world's significance. Moreover, the tenets she inculcates in him have a strong correspondence with the concepts that motivate the overall organization of *Laberinto*.

Why is Tía Luna such a source of meaning? At the most literal level, she is the adult most willing to spend time with the child-hero. The neurasthenic, sickly child and the eccentric, ethereal woman are thrown together because of their shared withdrawal from the sparkling social life that absorbs the rest of their family. Tía Luna, though, has a far less banal explanation for their closeness. She believes herself to be drawn to the hero with the mission of pointing out to him, and to those around him, his elect status. This exceptional birthright consists, more overtly, of the inheritance of the finest Sephardic ancestry and, in a more hidden sense, of an entitlement to penetrate the mysteries. Here is how the hero recapitulates the understanding of his specialness that Tía Luna promotes:

A TIA LUNA LE GUSTA DECIR A MIS AMIGOS QUE YO ESTOY DOBLEMENTE ENTRONCADO CON EL LEGENDARIO APELLIDO QUE ELLA MANTIENE CELOSAMENTE. ES IMPORTANTE SER HIJO DE LA HERMANA ELEGIDA POR EL DESTINO PARA UNIRSE A UN HOMBRE QUE OSTENTA ENTRE LOS SUYOS AQUEL MITICO NOMBRE QUE APRENDIO A PRONUNCIAR CON RELIGIOSA VENERACION. . . . PARA TIA LUNA YO SOY DOBLEMENTE PARTE DE . . . ESA SEMPITERNA PUREZA . . . CON SUS RITOS Y SUS ALTARES, CON TODOS SUS FABULOSOS SIGNOS Y SENALES SECRETAS DESDE EL INSTANTE EN QUE ABANDONO EL PARAISO PENINSULAR DE SEFARAD.

(TIA LUNA LIKES TO TELL MY FRIENDS THAT I'M DOUBLY RELATED TO THE LEGENDARY FAMILY NAME SHE JEALOUSLY MAINTAINS. IT'S IMPORTANT TO BE THE CHILD OF THE SISTER CHOSEN BY DESTINY TO BE UNITED WITH A MAN WHO PROUDLY BEARS AMONG HIS NAMES THAT MYTHIC NAME HE LEARNED TO UTTER WITH RELIGIOUS VENERATION. . . . FOR TIA LUNA I AM DOUBLY PART OF . . . THAT ETERNAL PURITY . . . WITH ITS RITUALS AND ITS ALTARS, WITH ALL ITS FABULOUS SIGNS AND SECRET SIGNALS FROM THE INSTANT IT ABANDONED THE PENINSULAR PARADISE OF SEPHARAD) (60).

This summation includes the two most prominent notes in Tía Luna's idea of the hero's chosenness. First is the emphasis on the powerful magic of names, letters, and language in general, a typically Kabbalistic tendency. Second is the conviction that the hero has gifts of understanding independent of any effort he may make to acquire an education.

Luna does not emphasize the hero's Sephardic bloodlines but rather his names as the means of transmission of his exceptionality. This insistence on linguistically contained powers bespeaks a Kabbalist's confidence in the word, which Luna imparts to the hero. She confers on him, to use Bloom's phrase, "the advantage of a magical theory of language, a theory most strong poets have shared, secretly, with all Kabbalists" (76). The two frequently join in activities best described as rendering homage to the written word. Although reading forms part of this tribute to the text, it is not a necessary component, since the forces that move through letters and words can be appreciated without the assignment of specific meaning to those signs. This principle is at work in the hero's vivid secret encounters, under Luna's aegis, with his grandfather's Hebrew Bible. Neither can read the text, but Luna deems it important for the hero to experience the privileged Word:

Me resultaba difícil sostener el libro. Creo recordar sus gruesas pastas azules estampadas en oro. . . . Era el gran libro del abuelo, en el que todos ponían los sumos cuidados, el libro que ocultaba ese secreto que daba luz al rostro de los que sufrían. Entonces era tan sólo un catálogo de letras desconocidas, páginas de extraños signos contorsionados. . . . Los miraba uno a uno, maravillado en aquel laberinto indescifrable pero sin embargo profundamente amado. . . . Algo me decía ya que era el Gran Libro, el mítico receptáculo de todos los libros.

(It was hard for me to hold the book. I think I remember its thick blue covers with gold embossing. . . . It was grandfather's great book, which everyone treated with the utmost care, the book that hid that secret that shed light on the faces of those who suffered. Then, it was only a catalogue of unknown letters, pages of strange contorted signs. . . . I looked at them one by one, in a state of wonder at that indecipherable, but still deeply beloved, labyrinth. . . . Something already told me it was the Great Book, the mythical receptacle of all books) (57).

The manifestations of piety discussed so far involve accepted notions of mainstream Judaism: devotion to Torah and respect for the Hebrew language and its very characters. Luna and her nephew simply take these principles to heart with a fervor that is mystic. In other rituals, Luna and the hero go beyond the norms to venerate reading even when the texts are profane. With Luna as guiding presence, always at his side as he reads, the child has intensely vivid reading experiences with secular periodicals (58) and novels (59). The encounter with these works becomes transmuted into *"una parsimoniosa ceremonia, un rito"* (*a parsimonious ceremony, a ritual*) (59), *"aquel paraíso . . . donde comencé a temer y a amar lo desconocido"* (*that paradise . . . where I began to fear and to love the unknown*) (59).

The extension of traditional reverence for canonical Scripture and Hebrew to include texts on worldly topics and in nonholy tongues is a determining principle in *Laberinto*. By the time Luna appears in the novel, the reader must already have remarked the curious care and attention that the hero lavishes on certain pieces of writing. For example, he presents the complete text of the exhibit labels in the Musée Grevin, leaving them couched in their original French as if not to lose any shade of meaning. Such reverential solicitude over the text's integrity seems out of proportion with the content, focused on the public lives of French celebrities. If one accepts the notion, associated with Luna, that the most mundane texts may serve in a magic ritual of extracting meaning, the inclusion of the exhibit labels becomes potentially justifiable. As eventually becomes more evident, the Musée Grevin legends do belong to one of the hero's idiosyncratic canons, the text formed by the legendary high life of European, and especially Jewish-European, society. Throughout *Laberinto,* other seemingly trivial or gossipy fragments of text will prove to have a place in the select collection of writings from which the hero derives mythical significance. The discussion of Professor Max's influence on the hero will address the question of why certain texts, rather than all discourse, enter into the hero's expanded Scripture.

* * *

As well as convincing the hero he has inborn powers of decipherment and the ability to make reading canonical, Luna gives him a confidence in the knowledge he possesses without study. According to her understanding of his birthright, the hero already possesses access to hidden lore and insights independent of outwardly applied education. She is horrified, for example, that the child's father would hold him to worldly standards of reading ability (58) and, in her absorption with the child, shields him from the standardizing effects of both lessons and upbringing. Her procedure is to allow the child to explore and expand what is already in his mind, however eccentric his intellectual formation may grow.

At a literal level, Luna may seem to be binding the child to her in a shared imaginative world. More productive for the comprehension of *Laberinto,* she may be seen as espousing a view of knowledge well rooted in Kabbalistic tradition. Although principled study of Torah and commentaries is the chief route to illumination, certain individuals may bypass rigorous scholarship yet intuitively attain Kabbalistic knowledge. This tenet accounts for the tolerance with which Scholem treats certain amateurs of Kabbalah. Though his own erudition is great, Scholem welcomes the contributions occasionally made by ill-educated colleagues. He observes that "real insight into the world of Kabbalism" came from "Christian scholars of a mystic bent." Lacking a "critical sense as to historical and philological data in this field, [but with a] fine philosophical intuition and natural grasp," these casual scholars could make insightful statements except in "problems bearing on the facts" (2).

Such an intuitive contribution is the only one the oddly educated hero can hope to make. Luna's insistence that the hero's inner bent determine his learning helps to explain the startlingly dilettantish air of *Laberinto*. The text is supposedly the hero's chosen means of exhibiting his esoteric understanding. Yet, in it, he makes himself appear to be a most haphazard student of Kabbalah. The scholarly Kabbalist should rivet his mind on Hebrew Scripture and characters; in Scholem's words: "Hebrew, according to the Kabbalists, reflects the fundamental spiritual nature of the world; in other words, it has a mystical value" (17). *Laberinto* avoids the primary material of Kabbalah. Hebrew script appears nowhere in the text, and transcriptions of Hebrew into Roman script occur rarely. French is the language that supplements the novel's basic Spanish, with occasional examples of Ladino. The Bible and its most closely associated commentaries are seldom alluded to. Nor is the scholarship on Kabbalah cited in any reassuring way.[7] Though the real-world author has dedicated his novel to Scholem, the narrator-hero seems to avoid respected authorities in his field. The Kabbalistic commentaries he cites are typically whatever readings his friends and family may bring to his attention. He cites an "extrañísima antología" (very strange anthology) of writings on "Science et réligion dans Carthage" (science and religion in Carthage) (89); "*un pequeño libro de tapas de cartón negras, 'El Universo de Mathurin Régnier', de O. W. Herber*" (*a small book bound in black cardboard, "The Universe of Mathurin Régnier," by O. W. Herber*), a sometime friend of the hero's mentor (171); the private journals of his grandfather, a visionary (146); and "un fragmento del Idra Suta, el enigmático comentario del Siphra Dzenniutta de Schimeón Ben Jochai" (a fragment of the Idra Suta, the enigmatic commentary on the Siphra Dzenniutta of Shimon Ben Hochai) (189), to give characteristic examples. These allusions reveal the hero's aleatory study of Kabbalah, based on an assurance that his inherent chosenness will attract to him the material he needs to know. The belief that systematic organization of knowledge is necessary contaminates the structure of *Laberinto*. The reader's inquiry into the hero's private esoterism cannot be linearly progressive but must follow the same wandering and, as the title hints, mazelike pattern as the protagonist's quest.

* * *

As the hero grows and becomes able to interest adults, he gains a new guide, Professor Max. The inarticulate Luna has always been, to the hero, more of a luminous presence than an actor in human society. He sees her as "un personaje fabuloso" (a fabulous character) (37), "MARAVILLOSA-MENTE INOCENTE Y SEPARADA DEL RESTO DE LOS HUMAN-OS" (MARVELOUSLY INNOCENT AND SET APART FROM OTHER HUMANS) (60). Max's Kabbalism, though, is part of his sociability. His occupation seems to be that of houseguest or parlor entertainer to distinguished exiled Sephardim. He has ingratiated himself with the hero's mother, to whom he is "un auténtico genio, un verdadero dios" (an authentic genius, a true god) (31). Numerous references build an image of Max as a troubling combination of entertainer and esoteric searcher. The hero devotes considerable space to documenting Max's convoluted thought and practice, apparently because the professor's eclecticism gives the pattern and clue to his own.

The first question Max's behavior raises is whether he does not belong more to the realm of glamour than to that of spiritual quest. Max is well versed in society and celebrity gossip and is skilled at exalting the fabled style and sophistication of the great Sephardic families. However, a magical note persists in his showmanly services to his patrons. For example, when the rise of the parvenue Madame Marcamp disturbs the women of the hero's family, Max soothes them with damaging information about her. The possession of this knowledge requires him to have somehow witnessed Marcamp's obscure, provincial girlhood (33). The common phrase "been everywhere and known everyone" takes on supernatural overtones when applied to Max. Consider his personal knowledge of the great figures of European Jewry: "*Max me hablaba de la pequeña sala de consultas de Freud en Viena como si hubiera concurrido a ella desde siempre y con la frecuencia de un amigo íntimo o de un paciente crónico*" (*Max spoke to me of Freud's little office in Vienna as if he had always gone there and as often as an intimate friend or a chronic patient*) (125); Max refers to "mi querido pariente Karl Marx" (my dear relative Karl Marx) (126). He claims to know the inner life of Walter Benjamin (27) and to have personal experience of the most rare or hidden works of esoteric teachings. Clearly, Max is no common name-dropper; the fact that he can produce knowledge obtained from his preternaturally extensive connections suggests, rather, that he has occult ways of experiencing and learning.

The role Max plays could be described as that of an occult teacher disguised as an amusing guest. Though the family may applaud Max as simply a "hombre de verdadero mundo" (man who has really seen the world) (31), the erudition and gossip with which he regales them has a hidden, tendentious current. On one occasion, Max is left to amuse the child-hero while the family is traveling. He distracts the boy by encouraging him to play with a Spanish deck of playing cards. The Spanish deck is, of course, the occultist's Tarot without the Major Arcana and may be easily used by Tarotists. Looking back on the episode, the now-adult narrator spots the secret lesson in the toy and notes that Max had written a study of the esoteric uses of the Spanish deck (89). In another anecdote, Max salvages a rained-out vacation by reading aloud passages from the *Encyclopedia Britannica;* his topics are not only Sephardic (of immediate interest to the family) but also mystical and occult. Whereas it could be said that Max's erudition is designed to amuse, a more important observation is that his entertaining patter is fashioned to keep alive the occult and mystical traditions that might otherwise die out among worldly Sephardic families. This subtle pedagogy is continued by the hero, whose text strives to fascinate and gossip with the reader while steadily making certain points about the mystical culture it presents.

* * *

What is the hidden knowledge that Max seeks to communicate through sociable strategies? Max is a Kabbalist, but one who utilizes certain tenets of Kabbalah to expand its range. He takes full advantage of the Kabbalistic tolerance for syncretism; for substitutions in which, as Bloom notes, "meaning wanders" (82); and for a ritualistic, cultic approach to Judaism. He exercises these liberties not out of mere eccentric showmanship but to bring Kabbalah to people who are as modern and secularized as is the hero of *Laberinto* and, presumably, as are its readers. It should be noted that even when the hero is a Kabbalistic apprentice, Max does not require of him pious observance, close study of Torah, or any renunciation of twentieth-century cosmopolitan culture.

"Extraordinary eclecticism," according to Bloom, is so much a part of Kabbalistic tradition that "a reader versed deeply in the interpenetrations of Kabbalah with [other occult] strains learns to be very tolerant" of syncretisms (16–17). Max's Kabbalah is, to begin with, very much in the tradition of syncretistic occultism based on the supposed magic correspondences between all systems of hidden knowledge.[8] From allusions scattered throughout the work, it is clear that Max, and the hero after him, have turned to the works of alchemists and necromancers. In addition, such unusual extensions as the Gilgamesh epic (119), handreading (130), and the secrets cultivated in a Masonic Lodge (117) become material for the occultist's search as construed by Max and his disciples. At the most lurid extremes, vampire lore (132) and Eliphas Lévi (149), the Kabbalistic charlatan rejected even by the generally tolerant Scholem, find their places in the system.

Originality, though, cannot lie in the contamination of Kabbalism with the magician's arts. Scholem laments the inevitability of such admixtures (35–36). More novel is that knowledge about the visible world is transformed into hidden wisdom. To effect this turnabout, Max exploits a tendency that Bloom has summarized: "Like poets, the Kabbalists richly confused rhetorical substitution with magic" (71). Bloom observes that the saying of one statement for another and the replacement of one meaning with another proceed with great license among Kabbalists. In the extreme case of Gematria, in which numerologically equivalent phrases become interchangeable, Bloom finds "interpretive freedom gone mad . . . [as] any text may be made to mean anything" (71). Though Kabbalah rests on the assumption that meaning in Torah is absolute, Bloom finds it often indistinguishable from, for example, the critical thought of Jacques Derrida, in which meaning is indeterminate (52–53). In Max's set of substitutions, the concept of hidden becomes flexible indeed. To know about the Divinity may still be the object of the search, but other bodies of occult information also have a place of privilege. The lives and deeds of the great figures of European Jewry, secularized as well as pious, are held to contain mysteries worthy of arduous penetration.

An example of the extension of mystical hermeneutics is Max's commentary on the death of the critic Walter Benjamin. To a literal mind, Benjamin's attempt to enter Spain was a practical response to the persecution of Jews in Nazi-occupied France and the degree of protection Franco had then extended to them. Max's version omits all recent history. In his highly interpretive rendering, Benjamin was seeking to end the Sephardic exile. As a disciple paraphrases Max's reading: "Cruel destino el suyo, morir en el desierto sediento frente a las puertas del oasis prohibido" (What a cruel fate befell him, to die in the thirsting desert at the gates of the forbidden oasis) (27). A classically mythic pattern of Exile and Redemption replaces the accidents of twentieth-century political history.

The magical reading of Benjamin gives further clues to Max's procedure. The choice of Benjamin is telling, for this exemplar of the modern Jew's engagement with secular culture also studied Kabbalah and grew close to Scholem.[9] These characteristics make him a proof of the proposition, central to Max's project, that Kabbalism may thrive in the absence of traditional piety. Moreover, the interpretation of Benjamin is from a work entitled *La Poésie de Sepharad*. References to this text indicate that its title refers not to Sephardic balladry but to a mysterious, spiritually poetic essence that Max perceives as informing all matters connected with Jewish Spain. Such a magic current occurs as much in apparently here-and-now phenomena as in those sanctified by time and religious tradition.

By such displacements and extensions of conventional mystical and occult terms, Max is able to include within his Kabbalistic program his this-worldly specialties, society gossip and the avant-garde. Whereas Max may be said to earn his keep with his intimate wisdom concerning great families and individuals, it would also be fair to say that he is the keeper of a cult that venerates the history of European and especially Sephardic Jews and that strives to venerate them by investing them with the greatest glamour. As noted, his knowledge of these figures is not obtained entirely through daylight means but requires hidden arts. The treatment he gives to them also forces these personages beyond the realm of gossip into that of myth and archetype, endlessly susceptible to such interpretations as imagination may provide. Such a conviction accounts for Max's study and worship of such celebrities as the actress Cécile Sorel. Max exalts the "única, insupera-ble" (unique, insuperable) Sorel in an ecstatic outpouring that leaves him "*casi muerto*" (*almost dead*) (68). He is outraged when a listener profanes Sorel's legend with a mention of Rita Hayworth, a figure who cannot be substituted into the realm of privileged knowledge.

* * *

A further characteristic of Max's system is its persistent emphasis on the elements that have been most suppressed in the development of mainstream normative Judaism: magical ritual and cultic worship. To show his eccentricity in this regard, Max appears in contrast to the stodgy Rabbi Khaen, who continually reminds the family of their transgressions of Law. Despite his priestly-caste name, the rabbi avoids the cultic-celebratory side of religion and is only once seen in fervor—but even then the occasion is his daughter's compliance with the norm of procreation (85–86).

Far from this insistence on right behavior, Max's chief recommendation to disciples is to approach their endeavors as if performing a rite. He praises the growth of the hero's Kabbalism—"Adivino que su interés ha sido exclusivamente litúrgico. Tan sólo el hechizo, el encantamiento de lo ritual" (I gather that your interest has been exclusively liturgical. Sheerly the enchantment, the spell cast by ritual) (126)—and he disparages the rabbi's Halakhic urgings as an effort to "quemarnos una verruga que nunca nos molestó" (burn away a wart that never gave us any trouble) (125–26). The hero continues the theme by appreciating his own advancement from "*buscar el rostro de Dios*" (*seeking the face of God*) to "*buscar las ceremonias de Dios*" (*seeking the ceremonies of God*) (94).

Scholem observes, with distaste, how quick Kabbalists have been to return to the discarded portions of Judaism that link it with "*mystery* in the sense in which the term was used by the Ancients" (30). In Scholem's assessment, "this revival of myth right in the heart of Judaism" is certainly justifiable when it "raised the Halakhah to a position of incomparable importance for the mystic, and strengthened its hold over the people" (30).[10] Such a vindication of magic rite cannot extend to Max, who never includes, among the many encouragements he gives the hero, an exhortation to observe Law. The return to secret sacrament would fall, rather, into the category of Kabbalism that illustrates "the dangers which myth and magic present to the religious consciousness" (35). Indeed, Scholem's summary of the problem could serve as a gloss on *Laberinto*'s title: "Kabbalism, which set out to preserve Him, to blaze a new and glorious trail to Him, encountered mythology on its way and was tempted to lose itself in its labyrinth" (36).

The effort to recover the magical forms of worship discarded by monotheistic and ethically centered Judaism takes Max's system into the area of goddess cultism. Such a deviation appears in the hero's reminiscences of Luna, written after his apprenticeship with Max. Using information Max has supplied him, he identifies Luna with a recurring figure of mythical royalty (37). As he recalls his rapturous reading, or text-worshipping, sessions with Luna, he emphasizes the "LUZ QUE YO HABIA NOTADO EN ELLA . . . EL LUMINOSO HAZ" (LIGHT I HAD PERCEIVED IN HER . . . THE GATHERED LUMINOSITY) (60), illuminating his first moments of secret understanding. These comments and other similar ones do not identify Luna closely with any one female deity but allow her to fill several such roles. Her conceivable personae range from the Shekhina or Divine Presence, who holds a legitimate place in the development of mainstream Judaism, to such proscribed divinities as Astarte and other moon goddesses.[11]

A polytheistic and goddess-worshipping tendency seems common to Max's entire circle. Allusions of this type appear in writings attributed to Max, his disciples, the hero, and the hero's grandfather, particularly in ecstatic accounts of their mystical experiences. For example, in an unattributed visionary narrative are Hecate (97), a vestal virgin in a tunic (96), and Juno with her peacock (98). Another such text makes of Mary Shelley a modern incarnation of the *"hija del Erebo y de la noche, hermana del Sueño"* (*daughter of the Erebus and of the night, sister of Dreaming*) (131) and refers in vague terms to a *"mujer de oro"* (*woman of gold*) (132) who, profaned and wounded by flashbulb-popping newsmen, finds present-day New York an unsuitable realm. Perhaps the most extreme of these references are those appearing in "Esposa de las tinieblas" ("Wife of Darkness") (146–48), supposedly an excerpt from the grandfather's journals but perhaps altered by passing through Max's hands. Here the goddess of death receives a privileged status indeed. Her power to subsume within herself all manifestations of death is daringly compared to Torah's capacity to sum up and complete all great writings (148). This by some lights sacrilegious analogy impresses on the reader how far Max's associates have gone in their recovery of the pagan cultic strains that were suppressed to form modern Judaism.

* * *

By the time he composes his text, the hero-narrator has already received two strong influences. Luna has given him a belief in the magic powers of language and confidence in his own innate mystical wisdom. Max's legacy includes a magus role for the Kabbalist, the inclusion of high-society lore in Jewish mysticism (his original contribution), and a reversion to the proscribed element of pagan rite in Judaism. What then, if anything, is left for the hero to add to this modern, freely construed Kabbalism?

As Bloom's essays emphasize, the recipient of influence finds it not only painful but life-threatening to be the mere transmitter of a predecessor's original attainments. However grateful the recipient may be for the guidance he has received, he must find something lacking in his heritage that he can now supply, thus justifying his work.[12] So, although much of the hero's writing seems indistinguishable from Max's, he manages to introduce an unprecedented element into his own Kabbalistic mixture. His specialty is the intensely literary coloration he gives to *Laberinto*. This literariness involves two components. First, the hero is a commentator on European Jewish literature and its great innovators. Second, his text is a showily artful one, relying on an aesthetic of self-display and a spectacular disregard for real-world usefulness.

As Max turns to the legends of Jewish life in Europe, so does the hero, but his search has a distinctively literary focus. The narrator's meditations on the fabled Jewish writers become an attempt at intuitive compenetration with, and hence a recovery of, certain writers representative of European Jewry. There is a tendency to favor those authors who, uncertain or troubled in their Jewish identity, most require an effort of reclamation. The most evident sign of this search through the literary past is *Laberinto*'s undisguised mimicry of Marcel Proust's lifework and persona. Like Proust and like the protagonist of *A la recherche du temps perdu,* the hero is a sickly, hypersensitive child, overwhelmed by his dazzling mother. He grows up in a household that is less like the home described in *Recherche* than like the adult Proust's circles, full of artists, famous society hostesses, and entertaining guests.

Although more Proustian repetitions could be cited, what is more noteworthy is that *Laberinto* performs certain functions that Proust's work cannot. Because it arose in a post-Proustian cultural ambience, *Laberinto* provides a look at Proust that could be obtained only after the master's work had become widely known. The characters in *Laberinto,* with their fetishistic admiration for the *belle époque,* are aware of Proust's accomplishment. This consciousness is revealed in, for example, the remark that Proust's "vil patraña" (scurrilous nonsense) (69) has blighted the name of the true Swans, "con una sola ene" (with just one n). But overt allusions are only part of the novel's "belatedness" relative to Proust, to use Bloom's (17) term. The hero cannot himself remember the period Proust's *oeuvre* reflects. His literary evocation of it must be an artful reconstruction, from some forty years' remove. He hears of its protagonists, from salon-goers to performers, as the fascinating, remote objects of his family's nostalgic conversation. To form a visual image, he must rely on the Musée Grevin, which enshrines the turn of the century. His insistence on revealing the mechanisms by which he regenerates an image of the Proustian era makes it especially clear that he is creating an artificial tribute to that time.

In another sense too, the novel is set apart from, and comments on, Proust. The hero of *Laberinto* and the text he organizes are as overt in their Jewish identity as Proust and his writing are "in the closet." By combining a thoroughly Jewish outlook with textual echoes of Proust, *Laberinto* offers itself as a possible answer to a long-standing question in the critical consideration of Proust: whether, and if so how, to include him among Jewish writers. Charles Lehrmann seems to emblematize the problem when he declares that "Proust does not belong to Jewish literature" yet must allude to him in his study *Jewish Influences on European Thought*.[13] *Laberinto*'s response to this issue is to give a glimpse of what Proust's novelistic world might have been had it included a Jewish cultural component.

Whereas the Proust allusions are the most frequent by far, other figures, such as Heinrich Heine with his difficult relation to Judaism, have a place in the system of references. Poets of the Judeo-Hispanic Golden Age and the anonymous Sephardic balladeers also appear. Although these latter writings are certainly not lost to Jewish tradition, they are in need of reclamation and emphasis as part of the cultural legacy of Spanish-speakers. It is, after all, to a Spanish-reading public, with its typical cultural background, that *Laberinto* seems most clearly addressed, an audience whose knowledge of Spanish culture is probably most deficient in the non-Catholic areas.

Barnatán is the only one of the eight authors examined who focuses on Jewish elites—here, a leisure-class family and its intimates and legendary members of the entertainment world. These stylish characters live the high life even when their social standing and means of support are shaky. Seemingly remote from the concerns of livelihood and from the struggle to find a place in Argentine society, they could be said to make Barnatán and his work unrepresentative of Jewish Argentine writing. Yet they broaden the scope of this literature by providing intricate variants on crucial preoccupations. Distanced from the Argentine scene, the family members have only increased the anomaly and unease of their situation. They are now New World creatures trying to maintain their bearings in the Old while still striving to come to terms with their previous history of exile and displacement. By elegantly masking issues of class and social prestige, they set themselves further adrift; their circle consists in great part of persons difficult to situate in society's hierarchies. It is amid this scenario of ambiguity and disguise that the protagonist's Kabbalistic quest, simultaneously a search for connection with Jewish Spain, unfolds.

* * *

In making his text a literary piece, the hero assumes a self-revelatory, individualistic stance. Such a position makes him a familiar and understandable type to readers accustomed to the self-display characteristic of artists since romanticism. At the same time, he breaks with the tradition summarized by Scholem: "The Kabbalists . . . are no friends of mystical autobiography. They aim at describing the realm of Divinity and the other objects of their contemplation in an impersonal way. . . . They glory in objective description and are deeply averse to letting their personalities intrude into the picture" (16). The hero of *Laberinto* entertains the reader with revelations about his unusual circle of friends, rapturous secret reading sessions with his otherworldly aunt, quasi-idolatrous cult of the great Jewish personages, and mastery of gossip. His dilettantism, neurasthenia, and passivity are all on display. Moreover, he includes personal accounts of mystical visions; as Scholem notes (16), such visionary narratives, though common among Christian mystics, are suppressed in Kabbalism.

* * *

The evaluative questions now arise: Does *Laberinto* make an addition to Kabbalistic commentary as such, and can it make some other claim to originality? The first of these questions can now be answered. *Laberinto* is too deviant to belong even to the more luridly occultist fringe of Kabbalistic study and commentary. It leads away from the preoccupations that join Kabbalah to mainstream Judaism: concern for Law, study of Torah and its commentaries, and attention to the Hebrew language. With his incursions into neopaganism and his worship of exceptional personalities, the hero often appears to be an idolatrous cultist. Moreover, his continual spotlighting of his own unique experiences places him outside Kabbalistic tradition.

However, in its efforts to be vivid and impressive to readers who might pass by more conscientious presentations of Kabbalah, the work ventures into unexplored areas. Professor Max is innovative, as well as bizarre, in making celebrity gossip part of Kabbalism. The hero's obsessive relation with figures of literary Jewishness, whom he seeks to bring more fully into Jewish literature, provides an additional area of newness.

If *Laberinto* cannot count as a commentary on Kabbalah, in what relation does it stand to that mystical system? The work belongs, clearly, to modern writing, to the new novel. It is designed for a reader who understands the experimentalist's techniques, who can assemble a fragmented text and accept a fundamental instability of time and place. The reader is not, however, expected to bring to *Laberinto* any knowledge of Hebrew, the Bible and its commentaries, or Sephardic culture. The hero supplies all needed information.

These circumstances suggest that *Laberinto* uses the experimental new novel to bring an appreciation of Kabbalah to readers remote from the topic. It takes advantage of a fact noted by Frank Kermode in his 1979 *The Genesis of Secrecy:* Readers of innovative twentieth-century novels have much in common with readers of the hermetic wisdom books of earlier times.[14] Because the modern reader has the experience of searching for hidden correspondences and unities, he is prepared for the search for a vague, occult meaning. *Laberinto* takes him on such a quest, not offering any reliable set of information about Kabbalah but instead offering, as the novel's hidden knowledge, a consciousness of the special worth of the mystical awareness developed in the high Judeo-Hispanic culture of the Middle Ages.

8 MARIO SZICHMAN

A Questioning Eye on Jewish Argentine History

This chapter examines an insolent novelistic challenge to prevailing versions of Jewish immigration to Argentina—a challenge given in the 1971 novel *Los judíos del Mar Dulce* (*The Jews of the Fresh-Water Sea*) by Mario Szichman (1945–). To obtain a view of the officialized history Szichman rebuts, one can counterpose his work to the 1910 novel *Los gauchos judíos* by Gerchunoff.[1] As Edna Aizenberg points out in "Parricide on the Pampa: Deconstructing Gerchunoff and His Jewish Gauchos," Szichman's work provides an accurate summary of the struggle later writers have carried on against the overwhelming presence of the elder figure of Jewish Argentine letters.[2]

In making this comparison, I am not stating that Szichman wrote his brash novel expressly to counter *Los gauchos judíos*. The notions that *Mar Dulce* seeks to refute may certainly be found in texts other than Gerchunoff's. However, *Los gauchos judíos* provides a useful compendium of officially approved propositions concerning Jewish Argentine immigration and settlement. By virtue of its fame and its canonical stature in Argentine literature, it necessarily exercises an effect on subsequent efforts to render novelistically the Jewish Argentine experience. Written for the Argentine centennial, *Los gauchos judíos* continues to be by far the best-known work of Jewish Argentine literature, despite critical objections and mockery.[3]

Szichman's novel disparages the official version Gerchunoff promulgates, through two related strategies. The first is the undoing of the lyrical smoothness and coherence by which Gerchunoff presents a convincing, but untrue, account of Jewish immigration to Argentina. Szichman utilizes the repertory of innovative techniques typical of twentieth-century novelistic experimentation to unmask the ideology of stylistic perfection.

Szichman's second procedure is the casting of doubt on the trustworthiness of historical accounts. His novel reveals a massive network of distrust: characters do not believe each other's stories, the reader cannot believe characters or narrator, and the narrator is a thoroughgoing skeptic. Yet the novel does not urge despair over the difficulty of grasping history. Indeed, it urges readers toward a more rigorous examination of history with due attention to the class interests of its chroniclers.

* * *

It is conventional for authors to seek to avoid a slapdash effect in their writing and to demonstrate their control of language and textual organization. This ideal is behind the much-noted lyrical smoothness of *Los gauchos judíos*.4 *Mar Dulce,* in jarring contrast, stands out for its disregard for balance and unity. The latter novel rejects the time-honored goal of elegance in favor of abruptness and irregularity.

Because of its consistency, *Los gauchos judíos* offers readers a stable indication of the types of truths it presents. It never claims to be faithful to events by realistic documentation. From the outset, the rendering announces itself as an artful, stylized one, in which the narrator sings of happenings: "He ahí, hermanos de la colonia y de las ciudades, que la República celebra sus grandes fiestas, las fiestas pascuales de su liberación . . . digamos el cántico de los cánticos, que comienza así: 'Oíd mortales . . .'" (Behold, brothers in the settlements and the cities, the Republic now celebrates its great holidays, the Passover holidays of its deliverance . . . let us say the canticle of canticles, which begins thus: "Hear ye mortals . . .") (11).

Whereas *Los gauchos judíos* disavows the intent to transcribe raw realities, it claims the power to convey essential truths. The implication is that the unseemly, accidental, and low have been suppressed to bring forth the significant aspects of immigrant experience. An example is the treatment of characters' speech. Gerchunoff's Jewish characters are able to communicate in a Spanish that is not only standard but also often elevated and archaic: "El cielo entrerriano es protector y suave. Hallándose solo, por ejemplo, en medio del campo, el espíritu no sufre sugestiones de miedo; su luz es benigna" (The heavens over Entre Ríos are sheltering and gentle. Finding itself alone, for example, in the middle of the countryside, the spirit feels no hint of fear; its light is benign) (89). This stylization smoothes over a real-life linguistic diversity that surely gave rise to confusion and awkwardness. Yiddish-speaking Jews had to deal with speakers of both standard Argentine Spanish and gaucho dialect. In the novel, Yiddish and imperfectly mastered Spanish do not figure. To betoken their origin, the narrator and Jewish characters use occasional words and phrases in the high language, Hebrew. They have no difficulty communicating with gauchos, though the latter speak dialect: "¡Trai la guitarra, Juan! Entuavía sé algo" (Bring the guitar, Juan! I still know a little something) (54). The "low" aspects of Argentine Spanish permitted to the rustic characters (such as the use of the *voseo* page 57) never affect the speech of the Jews. This departure from verisimilitude corresponds to the idea that immigrants are to raise the level of culture of the pampas areas.

Though the perfect language of *Los gauchos judíos* has drawn Viñas's fire,[5] it is consonant with Gerchunoff's smoothing over of irregular realities. Its internal consistency and congruence with the plan of the novel inspire confidence that Gerchunoff is following a well-thought-out procedure in presenting only what he deems worthy. The novel is reassuring and convincing according to the principle of believability summarized by Eric S. Rabkin:

In narratives, different sorts of events may be reported. . . . Such tales fit . . . into the social fabric of believability. The tale might be better or worse told. Narratives that are the least susceptible to physical test must be judged most by their well-madeness.[6]

As well as presenting a seamless narrative, *Los gauchos judíos* claims a trustworthy and believable character by affiliating itself with canonical writings. Critics have often noted Gerchunoff's persistent biblical and talmudic touches, both in stylistic mannerisms designed to recall these writings and in abundant quotations and allusions, as well as in his naming certain chapters of his novel after books of the Bible. Though the narrator is supposed to be a Jewish settler, sections of the work seem narrated by an omniscient, God's-eye commentator.[7] Finally, Gerchunoff's novel not only alludes to the history of the Jewish people as recorded in canonical texts but also itself appears as a continuation of the line of writings that codify and give meaning to that history. Argentine immigration is presented as the fulfillment of God's historical promise for "Judíos errantes, desgarrados por viejas torturas" (wandering Jews, torn by ancient tortures) now "cautivos redimidos" (redeemed captives) (11) in a South American Zion.[8] In the face of Gerchunoff's effort to present a smoothly persuasive version, modern-day critics have hastened to disparage his account as unreliable. Sosnowski and Viñas have pointed out in special detail the omission of issues unflattering to the Argentine government, such as the pro-European racial theories that lay behind immigration policy.[9]

* * *

Szichman's novelistic retort to the official account of history centers on a particular objection. From the point of view implicit in *Mar Dulce,* a presentation such as *Los gauchos judíos* is blameworthy, above all, for disguising the fact that it is nothing but a human version of events. *Los gauchos judíos* offers its lyricization of history as if the treatment were simply suitable to the subject matter, called for by events themselves and not by self-serving human interests. As Szichman breaks away from this confident mode, he works to destroy the assumption that any rendering of events can simply and innocently be the one most suitable.

The first step in revealing the unreliability of versions is to make accounts of events look manifestly questionable. Szichman is like Gerchunoff in utilizing the above-discussed assumption that an elegantly polished, uniform chronicle wins readers' confidence. His procedure, though, is to discourage trust with an irregular narrative.

To begin to see Szichman's rewriting of Gerchunoff, consider again the issue of characters' speech. Szichman dwells on the linguistic awkwardness of immigrants and on the indecorous and confusing situations this produces. In a characteristic passage, the novel's narrator ridicules the faulty Spanish of the protagonists, the Pechof family, as "el lenguaje de los argentinos, empastado de palabras en jeringonza, lleno de ademanes forzados que suplían palabras olvidadas, y tergiversado por un libérrimo empleo de los tiempos verbales que hizo fallar a los Pechof en la predicción de cosas del futuro que ya habían sucedido" (the language of Argentines, held together with bits of jargon and argot, with a lot of strained gesturing filling in for forgotten words, and reduced to a jumble by a very free use of verb tenses that made the Pechofs fall into the prediction of future things that had already happened) (108).

Lack of uniformity makes a patchwork of the characters' speech. Among the Pechofs, Salmen has a foreign accent, Itzik has a speech defect and sometimes lapses into baby talk, and Dora swiftly shifts to suit her language to her varying identities. The Indians the Pechofs meet may speak standard Spanish (179) or comic-book "savage" talk: "tú poner en círculo la carreta" (you put wagon in circle) (105). The irregularity of the linguistic situation is matched by its lack of decorum, with numerous vulgar expressions in Spanish and Yiddish. Dated catchphrases give the language a historicity far from the atemporality of Gerchunoff's expression.

* * *

Another issue muted by Gerchunoff and emphasized by Szichman is the official version of Jewish Argentine history. *Los gauchos judíos* embodies this account but never admits that it exists. Szichman's work includes brief examples of the government version in order to ridicule its contrived self-interest. Here *Mar Dulce* mocks the Argentine Zionism and patriotic fervor typical of Gerchunoff:

En el país que habían preparado para engañar a la gilada inmigrante, no había ni indios, ni flechas envenenadas, ni . . . miserables, petisos, gordos, pajeros o anti-semitas . . . los inmigrantes se hacían domadores extraordinarios, ante los ojos primero burlones y luego asombrados de los criollos.

(In the country they had set up to fool the immigrant dupes, there were no Indians, no poison arrows, . . . nobody down and out, short, fat, no wankers, no anti-Semites . . . the immigrants became great bronco busters, with the *criollos* looking on, the mockery in their eyes turning to wonder) (77).

The passage burlesques Gerchunoff's perfect language, Promised Land topic, and avoidance of unpleasant matters. But beyond its value as pastiche, it shows Szichman's insistence on labeling all versions as such. This particular account constitutes a film within the novel, a government propaganda piece entitled "Argentina, tierra de promisión" ("Argentina, Land of Promise"), echoing Gerchunoff's 1952 *Argentina, país del advenimiento* (*Argentina, Land of Things to Come*).

Such explicit framing devices are rare. Yet other narrative accounts become more subtly framed and tainted with suspicion. Such contamination occurs when evidence arises that events are tailored to fit some preconceived pattern. An example of this implicit framing is the story of Itzik Pechof's dismissal from his job, told by the narrator (28). The principal reason not to trust this anecdote is that it too perfectly resembles a burlesque-type comedy routine. Because one can identify the original model, the suspicion follows that the use of the conventional joking format has overridden considerations of veracity. The fact that the novel's central narrator would make use of such a standard piece, undercutting his own credibility, shows the novel's vigorous attempt to put readers on guard against all chronicles, including its own.

The narrator often discredits characters' remarks by pointing out that their supposedly direct expressions are far from original. For example, when Jewish characters discuss Israel, the narrator betrays to the reader that they are repeating the editorial opinions of the *Di Yidische Tzaitung* (221), placing the conversation as a conventionalized set piece. Rebellious young people try to reject this model by equating Zionism with imperialism, but the narrator reveals that they are all parroting the same catchphrase.

Framing and labeling devices are only the most apparent of Szichman's strategies for casting doubt on accounts. The novel constantly challenges the versions propounded by respected figures. Indeed, the idea of the authority inherent in a speaker receives a brashly satirical treatment.

As noted, Gerchunoff grants his characters the presumption of veracity. When one of them makes statements, his word is good. The more eminent the character, the more extreme statements he may make on personal authority alone. Consider the opening scene of *Los gauchos judíos*. Here a wise rabbi persuades a congregation to leave pogrom-ridden Russia for Argentina. The audience knows nothing of Argentina except for the rabbi's assurances:

—¡Ya veréis, ya veréis! Es una tierra donde todos trabajan y donde el cristiano no nos odiará, porque allí el cielo es distinto, y en su alma habitan la piedad y la justicia.

("You'll see, you'll see! It's a land where everyone works and where the Christians won't hate us, because there the heavens are different, and in their souls abide piety and justice") (15).

The shtetl-dwellers might, realistically, wonder about these assertions, which run counter to their experience of Christian-Jewish relations and the traditional hope for a Palestine Zion. Yet their response is unquestioning: "Los israelitas sumidos en éxtasis, balbucearon: —¡Amén!" (The Israelites, plunged into ecstasy, babbled: "Amen!") (15).

The rabbi is a charismatic speaker. In addition, he is able to impress the rural audience with his authoritative citations.[10] Yet, his personal qualities are not the only reason to accept his assertions. His promises about the new land are, within the novel, true. The characters are not disappointed on arrival in Argentina. They interpret their experiences to fit the pattern of redemption the rabbi has foretold.

A startling example of this belief in fulfillment occurs in the chapter "La muerte del Rabí Abraham" ("The Death of Rabbi Abraham") (60–63). The group's leader is killed by a drunken gaucho. The immigrants do not allow themselves to doubt that they are living amid "piety and justice" or to express unease over their situation. The narrator shows them to be composed and efficient in handling the matter: "Sacaron a Rabí Abraham del corral y lo dejaron tendido en el suelo, en el centro del rancho. Lo cubrieron con un lienzo blanco . . . parecía Nuestro Señor Jesucristo" (They took Rabbi Abraham out of the corral and they laid him on the ground, in the center of the ranch. They covered him with white linen . . . he looked like

Our Lord Jesus Christ) (63).[11] The analogy the narrator makes adds a note of piety transcending religious distinctions, reinforcing the interfaith harmony that the episode might otherwise have placed in doubt.

Other chapters prove equally lacking in substantive signs of skepticism. The chapter "La revolución" (147–55), the only one dealing with dissent, simply concerns a disagreement over minor administrative questions. Its inclusion seems to assert that such was the extent of dissenters' protests.

The undoubtable solidity of the rabbi's remarks, and their subsequent confirmation by events, involve issues that critical readers may find highly questionable. These are propositions about the special meaning of Jewish peoplehood. The more general one is that God meant the Jews to practice farming. Applied, this principle implies that urban Jewish civilization, as exemplified by the Judeo Spanish Golden Age, represents a wrong turn in Jewish history:

Fué en España donde los judíos dejaron de cultivar la tierra y cuidar sus ganados. No olvide usted . . . lo que se dice en el Zeroim, el primer libro del Talmud, al hablar de la vida del campo: Es la única saludable y digna de la gracia de Dios.

(It was in Spain that the Jews ceased to work the earth and raise their livestock. Don't forget . . . what it says in the Zeroim, the first book of the Talmud, when it speaks of country life: It is the only way that is healthy and worthy of the grace of God) (16).

It is hinted that the expulsion of the Jews and the Inquisition represented divine displeasure over the urbane sophistication of Spanish Jewry.[12]

Such propositions are, outside the novel, bizarre. As the term shows, the Judeo Hispanic Golden Age is well esteemed. Charles C. Lehrmann sums up the common understanding: "The Spanish era is considered . . . the greatest accomplishment of the Jewish genius and the Semitic spirit since Biblical times."[13] The rabbi's ability to make absolute truths of these shaky assertions is an index of Gerchunoff's attempt to establish the novel as the proper rendering of events.[14]

* * *

On the other hand, an acute awareness of the unreliability of accounts is dominant in *Mar Dulce*.[15] To appreciate the emphasis on dissent, consider the attempts of Dora and Berele Pechof to establish a history of the family and of the Jewish Argentine experience. Each resembles the above-cited rabbi because each tries to present a certain version of matters to the community addressed. The rabbi never elicits a challenge, but Dora and

Berele are constantly subjected to querulous objections. Whereas Dora's versions are clearly self-seeking ones, Berele is trying to establish a reliable family history by compiling a semidocumentary film. With no respect for Berele's efforts to make accurate statements, his family disrupts the showing of the film, loudly disputing the accuracy of events and the significance given various aspects of their history.

Dora and Berele are easy to dismiss as faulty historians. Dora is discernibly eager to shame her relatives with damaging stories. Berele must rely for information on his self-serving elders and is ingenious about his ability to capture history. More-skilled fabricators of history show how manipulation succeeds. Exemplary in this respect is El Gordo Bevilacqua. Layout editor of a paper, Bevilacqua savors the stage management inherent in presenting news. He has on hand materials for a lengthy illustrated obituary of Eva Perón. Awaiting her death, he amuses himself and his colleagues by rearranging the materials to produce different effects.[16]

Bevilacqua is, of course, reacting to the Peróns' insistence on spreading a highly manipulated, official version of Eva's life. But even lacking this stimulus, the editor discovers that news events lend themselves to multiple and varied presentations. Meditating on this, he shows Natalio Pechof how the record contained in seemingly truthful news snapshots reveals unexpected instability. Moreover, the raw, uninterpreted compilation of photographs is meaningless:

Bevilacqua quiso mostrar que en los momentos en que estaban sacadas esas fotos, la historia era indecisa, y cualquiera podía llegar a ser importante. Entonces formó mazos de gabinetes con peronistas y exiliados, y todos eran igualmente probables. La foto de Evita surgía entre esas figuras, y carecía de dramatismo, a menos que se rodeara su cabeza con un círculo de tinta y se le colocara encima una flecha.

(Bevilacqua wanted to show that at the moment those pictures were taken, history was undecided, and anyone could become important. Then he put together cabinets made up of Peronists and anti-Peronist exiles, and they were all equally probable. The picture of Evita turned up among those images, and there was nothing dramatic about it, unless her head had a circle inked around it, and above, an arrow pointing to it) (30).

The newsman is constantly fascinated that documentation does not spontaneously provide an account but that sequence and meaning come from a chronicler's intervention. He collects inadmissible documents, such as photographs of Evita before she has mastered the ability to play up to the camera.

Whereas Bevilacqua resents Eva's control of her image and personal chronicle, Dora envies and emulates it. In her efforts to win advantage over relatives, Dora would like to enjoy such mastery over her role and persona. In her vision, Argentine society is made up of groups vying for status. She seeks to assimilate herself into the highest prestige group to which she can aspire at any given moment, so

camuflará su cuerpo para que coincida con los decorados por donde transite; una mancha marrón en el mentón, una naricita respingada, una voz finita, y un lenguaje de solterona cursi y sentimental cuando trabaje de oficinista; el pelo estirado para atrás, los perfumes con olor a polvo facial y la voz de arrabalera cuando sea la dueña del quilombo.

(she will camouflage her body to make it coincide with the scenarios she passes through; a brown spot on her chin, a little upturned nose, a thin little voice, and talking like some spinster full of hackneyed sentimentality when she works in an office; her hair pulled back, perfume smelling like face powder, and a low-rent district voice when she becomes the owner of the brothel) (58).

Dora fantasizes about attaining such complete dominance over her persona that she can transform herself into a simulacrum of Eva Perón and assume her place (58). Although Bevilacqua is a credible chronicler and Dora an obvious falsifier, their procedures are similar. Both harbor a cache of documentary matter potentially useful in backing up allegations. Both try to mask the element of artful construction in their narratives, though Bevilacqua enjoys showing his hand privately. Both attain certain goals. Though Dora's assertions are dismissed, she succeeds in shaming and insulting her relatives. Bevilacqua suits the government, his employers, and the public; he derives an artisan's pride from his management of history. They both represent the benefits to be gained from an opportunistic use of the chronicle, whereas Berele, the naive believer in accurate reporting, wins only derision.

* * *

Having established the manipulability of history, the novel offers a spectacular example of this principle in its tangled, unstable account of the relations between the principal characters. To examine the complexities of the family bonds, one may construct a simplified scheme based on the preponderance of evidence in the novel and omitting contradictory clues. The novel then features the five Pechof siblings—Dora, Salmen, Natalio,

Jaime, and Itzik—as well as Natalio's son Berele and Salmen's daughter Rifque. The first indication that this scheme is too orderly is the irregular status of Itzik. Itzik might be called a half-character. He is grossly underdeveloped in body, half-witted at times, and apparently only a half-brother. He is not always a character in his own right and does not always count as a member of the family. In Berele's film, he is initially absent. Only some time into the documentary film does Itzik's mother berate her husband for leaving Itzik back in their Polish village (15). Itzik later makes an unexplained appearance in the story of the family's migration (58) and then disappears again (78–79) from the events.

Itzik's intimacy with Natalio grows into an irresolvable confusion. The two at times are close, rancorous brothers, but at other times, their identities are fused. The narrator, in riddling terms, speaks of their tendency to share a single identity: "Natalio tendrá dolor de muelas e Itzik sentirá olor del consultorio y el miedo al torno; Itzik pensará en Iom Quiper y Natalio se quedará en ayunas" (Natalio will have a toothache and Itzik will smell the dentist's office and feel the fear of the drill; Itzik will think of Yom Kippur and Natalio will be fasting), a circumstance capriciously attributed to "accidentes mutiladores" (mutilating accidents) (61).

Rifque's parentage is a similar imponderable. Salmen presents himself as her widowed father but is unable to establish one definitive version of his marriage and widowhood. As accounts vary and multiply, the narrator appears to delight in exposing the artificiality of Salmen's account. Mocking Salmen's accent, he says: "Se inventagá una punta de paguientes de su mujer muertos en un accidente colectivo el dos de enero de mil novecientos treinta y cuatro, para encubrir su soltería y el nacimiento de Rifque" (He will invent a bunch of relatives of his wife who all died in one accident the second of January of nineteen thirty-four, to cover up for his being single and for the birth of Rifque) (62).

A further complication is the occasional appearance of Itzik as Rifque's father and Dora as her mother (for example, see page 193). Dora's two principal scenes with Rifque emphasize this instability. In the earlier, she is Rifque's aunt, resented for her interference in the girl's affairs (113–15). In the later scene, she is Rifque's mother but neglects to show any concern for her (228–31). The most adequate explanation of Rifque's parentage is a fantastic one. Though impossible in real-world terms, this version accounts for the fact that each sibling has a different story of Rifque. As the narrator explains (78–79), Rifque was invented by the siblings on the boat to Argentina, each one developing the variant of her that best suited his purposes.

The pattern of variable history, remade to the needs of the moment, also

affects the story of the Pechofs' move to Buenos Aires from their original
rural settlement. The narrator states that the family moved to the city in
1932 (121). But this information soon loses any orienting usefulness. The
Pechofs keep this item of information flexible so as not to forego the use of
any historical material. Events that could have occurred, had they stayed in
the country, are hoarded along with those that transpired in the city. As a
result, the characters develop rural doubles whose phantom actions sometimes appear in the narrative.

The reader looks for a standard against which to assess competing
stories. The third-person narrator, by convention a probable source of
trustworthy propositions, declines to set the record straight. Refraining
from clarification, he confronts the reader with the massive disorder of
history after decades of self-serving versions. This is not to say, though, that
the reader cannot become oriented. The story of Rifque's origins, for
example, is useful in understanding the novel's tangled chronicles. The
principle that characters invent their relations with one another to gain
advantages explains many bizarre features of the plot. Dora appears as
Itzik's wife to exercise a uxorious domination, but she also wishes to retain
the power she derives from divulging her sisterly knowledge of Itzik's
childhood shames. Itzik's status as a half-person appears to suit his brothers
and sister, who thus have an inferior readily on hand.

It is also possible to identify the general outlines of the Pechofs' family.
Salmen and Dora were, for a time, involved in the management of brothels,
though Salmen denies the story and Dora melodramatically highlights it.
Jaime and Natalio worked as confidence men. All the brothers and their
sister have been miserly and opportunistic in their pursuit of upward social
mobility. These general features of their history, which stand in sharp
contrast to the incessantly upright conduct of *Los gauchos judíos,* help to
account for the characters' need to revise their personal chronicles.

* * *

What has *Mar Dulce* accomplished by representing Jewish Argentine
history with so little decorum, coherence, and narrative reliability? First,
Szichman modernizes the treatment of the subject matter, reflecting the six
decades that separate his novel from Gerchunoff's. *Los gauchos judíos* rests
on the assumption that literary writing should display perfect smoothness.
Mar Dulce results from a more current belief: that a fragmented form is
necessary to reflect the character of modern life. Nicolas Calas notes a
distrust of forms "too compact and too studied to reflect the immediacy

inherent in the actuality of the newspaper. . . . Immediacy is perhaps most strongly imparted through discontinuity. It is discontinuity that gives style."[17]

But more significant, Szichman's novel raises the issue of self-servingness in historical representation. Gerchunoff is mocked above all for his suppression of matters embarrassing to the government or revealing of the class and ethnic tensions that moved history. Szichman not only parodies the earlier writer but also includes in *Mar Dulce* what is absent from *Los gauchos judíos:* conflict between social groups, exploitation of immigrants, suppression of indigenous peoples, historically specific Argentine popular speech, opportunism, and deception. But even this willingness to air painful issues does not make history trustworthy.[18] *Mar Dulce,* for all its frankness, does not offer itself as a sure guide to history. Its narrator and characters all inspire distrust.

Instead of an established account of history, *Mar Dulce* provides a questioning look at the various accounts. Readers are urged toward a critical outlook on all versions of history. But why should this skepticism be necessary? Modern works with a high degree of instability are often seen as promoting the idea of the relativism of truths.[19] However, Szichman's novel does not make the relative value of truths a major concern.[20] Narrative data are unstable not because truth itself is unsteady but because human chroniclers, representing class and individual interests, skew them. Indeed, only one character in the novel, the hapless Berele, attempts to establish truths. The many quarrels between characters over what really happened are contests for the power to write history.

The novel does not leave the reader without hope of understanding the story of Jewish immigration to Argentina. As accounts clash, insights emerge. The novel makes the point that the story of immigrants involves the entire struggle between diverse class and ethnic sectors of the national society. The novel also establishes that to rise in competitive, stratified society, immigrants learn to remake their identities. The particulars of the story of the Pechofs, or of Eva Perón, or of Jewish immigration, may never be set straight. Yet a critical examination of the obfuscation surrounding events, taking into account the interests of various sectors of society, enables one to move beyond simple confusion and to perceive the larger story of social conflict behind the welter of competing versions.

POSTFACE

The 1976–1983 military government was disruptive to public discussion, the arts, and Jewish life. The regime's campaign to suppress left-wing guerrilla activity resulted in the apprehension of a broad variety of suspects and in many deaths among those detained. Because of the long-standing association in the public mind of Jews and socialism, Jewishness was one of the factors that could draw suspicion toward an individual and increase the severity of treatment in detention. Involvement in cultural and intellectual activity also carried a risk, as did being young. Many Jewish Argentine writers, particularly younger ones and those considered social critics, either curtailed their public expression or took up residence abroad during this period. Some who had already left the country for relief from the chaotic situation found it too difficult to return. In the best of cases, these writers produced an exile literature distinguished by frankness, possible to those publishing away from home, and by fresh reflections on the past century, expressed in hopes of understanding current repression. This exile writing, perhaps too new a phenomenon to permit full evaluation, is briefly surveyed here by discussing some of its contributions to the growth of Jewish Argentine literature.

One of the earliest examples of this literature, and one vividly illustrative of its critical powers, is *Caballos por el fondo de los ojos* (*Horses in the Depths of the Eyes*). This 1976 novel by Gerardo Mario Goloboff (1939–), who left Argentina in 1973 and established residence in France, was published in Barcelona. The text signaled Goloboff's shift from poetry, in which he had earlier elaborated his concerns, to the novel, thereafter his preferred genre. It is a work of often lyrical prose, elliptical and discontinuous in its narrative arrangement. The novel refrains from presenting its commentary in any too explicit a form; nonetheless, it is unambiguous in calling for a reexamination of Jewish Argentine participation in the last several decades of national life. It reviews, over a span of three generations in one family, the various programs that have especially attracted Jewish Argentines, from the settlers' trust in their new nation's plans for them, through socialism, Peronist populism, Zionism, entrepreneurialism, and psychoanalysis. Though these "isms" receive a tribute as historically necessary stages, none is in itself a solution. Even the correct assertions of the protagonist's psychoanalyst do the patient no good until he can arrive at these truths through his own efforts. The novel implies that programmatic solutions can never replace the continual process of individual thought required to deal with the historical problems exemplified in its central character's crisis. The stimulus that finally forces this character to struggle toward a critical reassessment is the contemplation of the blood-stained white sheet thrown over the body of his son, one of the many young people killed in the violence of the times. The implication is that the political situation of mid-1970s Argentina, so massively disordered as to affect even the stagnant mind of this character, can bring about a reconsideration of the Jewish Argentine experience, as well as, necessarily, that of the entire nation.[1]

Jewish tradition provided elements especially well suited to expressing the crisis of those years. The subjects of persecution, social disruption, outcast status, and exile, long elaborated in Jewish expression, quickly became Argentine themes, and indeed Latin American ones. Pedro Orgambide (1928–) pursued the expressive possibilities of these parallelisms in his 1977 *Aventuras de Edmund Ziller en tierras del Nuevo Mundo* (*Adventures of Edmund Ziller in the New World*), published in Mexico, where the author spent his exile. The novel's most obvious Jewish reference is its use of the Wandering Jew as its roguish hero. This choice entails the highlighting of such features as outcast status, ability to adapt to changing circumstances, powers of improvisation, and generally living by one's wits. Wherever Edmund materializes in the New World, he studies the local social hierarchy, with special attention to those who lack land, inherited entitlements, or such acquired privileges as military or ecclesiastical rank. He then masters many of the strategies developed to survive outside the protected realm of the elite. When possible, he works to move the deprived beyond measures of simple survival and toward a struggle to abolish privilege. Thus, while Edmund practices the tawdry tricks of a nomadic razzle-dazzle artist he urges those around him to question why they are perpetually disadvantaged. The picaresque adventures of the Wandering Jew, which allow the novel's Jewish allusions to represent its pan–Latin American subject matter, run parallel to another set of Jewish references, one concerned with texts and their study. Edmund maintains the tradition of the scholarly scribe—preserving, emending, glossing, and generating texts. Of his many projects, the most significant is the compilation of documents concerning and attributed to the historical Ziller. The modern scholar working on these papers, who supposedly supplies Pedro Orgambide with the material for *Edmund Ziller,* is yet another of Ziller's incarnations. Much of this material is documentation amassed by the Inquisition. In

Ziller, Orgambide for the first time makes Jewish allusions overt and prominent, though he has long shown an interest in such related issues as immigrant Argentines and the Inquisitorial mind. His sometimes roisterous novel is clearly driven by an urge to bring out the social ethics running through Ziller's disjointed past and to draw a lesson for contemporary Latin America.

Ziller illustrates, as does its author's career during the late 1970s, significant contemporary tendencies. It was written and published in Mexico City, which in the latter part of the 1970s was fast becoming a center of Argentine exile intellectual life. As well as representing the exiled intellectuals, Orgambide exemplifies in his person, as does David Viñas, the "mixed" population, the offspring of intermarriage that is a notable Jewish Argentine reality. Until the crisis of the 1970s and *Edmund Ziller,* though, Orgambide had made little literary use of Jewish awareness or knowledge. He was one of those creative figures who took the 1970s crisis as the moment to abandon any downplaying of their Jewish outlook. The publication of the novel marked the integration into Orgambide's creative work of a repertory of Jewish cultural information and a new Latin American interpretation of the meanings of Jewishness.[2]

Viñas was one of the most prominent intellectuals to go into exile and to contribute to the associated literature. He established residence in Mexico, teaching, researching, and writing. Surely the boldness of Viñas's 1979 novel *Jauría (Pack of Dogs)* can be attributed in part to its author's distance from Argentina and to the use of the Mexican branch of the Siglo Veintiuno publishing house. Reflecting Viñas's extensive knowledge of military elites and officer training, the novel gives an intimate portrait of a life among officers that includes homosexual activities accepted as a festive release among men whose everyday practice is to support a repressively strict morality. It prefigures the intense interest in military culture that would be characteristic of intellectual discussion following redemocratization.[3]

Mario Satz (1944–), a novelist of international reputation, might be considered something of an exile and something of an expatriate. The Argentine-born Satz had already spent extended periods abroad when, in 1976, he took up residence in Barcelona. He is principally distinguished for his vast, perhaps inherently inexhaustible, novelistic undertaking. Under the project title of *Planetarium,* Satz published lyrical, metaphorical novels of cosmic scope: *Sol,* 1975 (published in English as *Sol,* 1979); *Luna (Moon),* 1976; *Tierra (Earth),* 1978; *Marte (Mars),* 1980. The relation of these novels to the rest of Argentine literature presents a puzzle. Latin American allusions surface in Satz's work, in the elements of Aztec and Inca cosmology and the story of guerrilla activity in *Marte*. But they coexist with a multitude of allusions to other diverse traditions. The sweep of Satz's enterprise, which goes from the elements of earthly matter out through the solar system, makes it inherently difficult to emphasize particular cultural strains running through the novels. A critical examination of Satz's work giving special attention to these issues would be necessary to assess the ways in which and the degree to which this fiction may be considered part of Argentine, Jewish, and Jewish Argentine letters.

Although the issue of placing Satz's work remains unresolved, his cosmic novels and the ambitious project behind them deserve mention in the discussion of Jewish Argentine literature. Not only do the author's biographical circumstances support such a connection, but also his novels, with their intricate construction and effort to treat a subject of cosmic breadth, merit further consideration from readers and critics.[4]

Humberto Costantini (1924–1987), who had been contributing to Argentine literature since the 1950s, became a newly significant figure during the period of military rule. Costantini, who resided in Mexico during this period, was one of the fiction writers most able to convey the mixture of fear and absurdity resulting from the arbitrary identification of suspected subversives. His *De dioses, hombrecitos y policías* (1977; English translation, *The Gods, the Little Guys, and the Police,* 1984) was well received internationally for its inventive novelistic presentation of the massive but often haphazard campaign against subversion.[5] As Orgambide noted, after rereading Costantini's work from the perspective of the exile years, this author's Jewish identity acquired new meaning when the national crisis made fresh issues of persecution, exile, and the uses of immigration.[6]

The 1980 novel *Identidad (Identity)*, by Antonio Elio Brailovsky, deserves special mention for the circumstances of its publication. Though the author himself was in exile, the novel appeared in Buenos Aires among the offerings of the well-established Sudamericana publishing house. It is a classical example of the figurative expression that can at times elude the effects of repression. The novel's complicated plot involves the discovery of a Sephardic expedition from Inquisition-era Spain seeking the lost tribe of Israel rumored to have settled in the New World. Competing efforts to suppress and to maintain the Jewish people, along with the ideological and cultural principles motivating the struggle, give the novel a subject matter easily applicable to other situations. No parallel to contemporary Argentina appears overtly, but readers are given the opportunity to draw such an inference.[7]

The most internationally known contemporary text by any Jewish Argentine writer was not a literary work but a memoir, *Prisoner Without a Name, Cell Without a Number* (1981; first published in the United States and Britain), by the Buenos Aires newspaperman Jacobo Timerman (1923–). Timerman's detention while serving as editor of *La Opinión* made him an emblematic figure of the offenses against human rights. His difficulties began with his apprehension by an antisubversive squad. After six months of detention and torture, during which his whereabouts were unknown to his family and friends, Timerman reappeared, still in the custody of the military. He then spent two years under house arrest, until international pressure helped to secure his release in 1979. His account increased world awareness of the numerous Argentines detained without word on their status and of the persistence of anti-Semitism of both Left and Right.[8]

As military rule extended into the 1980s, literary work written and/or published abroad by Argentine exiles came to constitute a large category, including many works by Jewish Argentine authors. Mario Szichman, for example, composed portions of his 1981 novel *A las 20.25, la señora entró en la inmortalidad* (English translation, *At 8.25, Evita Became Immortal,* 1983) in the United States, where both the Spanish- and English-language versions appeared.[9] A complete register of such exile publications would be lengthy indeed.

By 1982, the military's authority was being undermined by lack of public confidence. Public criticism began to emerge again; there was no choice but to call elections, bringing a return to civilian government in December 1983. Released from limitations on expression, and in many cases recently returned from exile, Argentine intellectuals were eager for public discussion of the events of the previous seven years. To appreciate the originality of the renewed discussion of Jewish Argentine issues, one should contrast it with the Jewish response to the crises of the early 1970s. Then, as the situation had become more precarious the official word from Jewish organizations became notably cautious, inhibited by the notion that such associations had no proper role in the criticism of national affairs. There was hope that by separating Jewish issues from Argentine ones and concentrating on the former, the community could avoid aggravating hostility and suspicion toward its members. Outside the community as such, those involved in dissent, whether in their writing or in their activist involvement, tended to deny any debt to Jewish thought.

The intervening years showed these strategies for self-protection to have been inefficacious. If anything, they had been counterproductive in that they prevented Jewish associations from establishing bonds with those groups pressing for improvements in the human rights situation and for restoration of representative government. In the climate of redemocratization, Jewish community organizations and spokesmen relaxed the constraints on frank discussion of national matters. Not only was insularity being abandoned as a defense against anti-Semitism, but also a new hope rose that through a Jewish Argentine perspective on the nation's troubled history, fresh insights could emerge. This gave rise to such mid-1980s innovations as the discussion of Argentine literature, culture, and society under the aegis of the large Jewish community organization Asociación Mutual Israelita Argentina, previously known for its caution in commenting on national matters.[10] The long struggle not to acknowledge Argentine anti-Semitism began to cede to an effort to understand its historical causation. This shift included a renewed effort to impress on non-Jewish Argentines the seriousness of the nation's long history of anti-Semitism and to seek to end it through such measures as the legislation, passed in August 1988, banning discrimination on the basis of race, religion, or national origin.

Strongly related to this shift in organizational policy was a new readiness among individual discussants to acknowledge the Jewish sources of their intellectual style or sense of social ethics. The post-1955 generation of intellectuals had pointed out how Jewish questions became national ones when seen in historical perspective. Although respecting this principle, the mid-1980s commentators showed a greater liberty to focus on Jewish aspects of issues, even if they did not immediately lead to an insight applicable to the entire society. An analyst of the Argentine cultural situation could express, as did Goloboff, a resolve to cultivate the distinct outlook on language and society allowed by a background in Jewish thought and expression.[11]

At the same time, extensive efforts were made to recover elements of Jewish Argentine history in danger of being lost. Sara and José Itzigsohn, Leonardo and Beatriz Senkman, Jaime Barylko, Isidoro Niborski, and others have worked vigorously to assemble participant accounts and documentary sources on Jewish Argentine culture.[12] With ever fewer living witnesses to the period of massive immigration and the founding of rural colonies, it became important to set down reliable accounts of these experiences. There was a flourishing of such activities as the establishment of documentation centers and groups, round tables, workshops, and other fora designed to bring about a reconsideration of Argentine history and the Jewish presence in it. In the United States, the Latin American Jewish Studies Association (LAJSA; Judith Laikin Elkin, founder), based in Ann Arbor, Michigan, has coordinated meetings with other scholarly associations and has held its own conferences.

The post-Peronist intellectuals, with their practice of contextualizing

Jewish issues in national history, have come in for a revival during this resurgence of social criticism. Viñas has reappeared as an active figure on the Buenos Aires intellectual scene. He assumed the chair in Argentine Literature of the Nineteenth Century at the Universidad de Buenos Aires. In talks and interviews, Viñas warned against premature celebration of redemocratization and insisted that retrospective commentary go beyond a simple airing of traumas. He has often been a dissident critic of the current discussion of national affairs. His concern is that Argentines may be too easily satisfied with the improved state of political life and, in relief at the relaxation of tensions, may neglect unresolved issues. The problems that Viñas fears may go unexamined include, from the recent past, the causes and aftereffects of the repression, which he considers the nation too quick to dismiss. In the longer historical view, he encourages an awareness of the lingering effects of nineteenth-century notions of progress through enlightened elite governance.

León Rozitchner (1924–), mentioned earlier for his participation in the parricide movement and his 1967 essay *Ser judío* (*To Be a Jew*), has also been newly visible. He continues to pursue the lines suggested by his early work. For example, he is still seeking a form of psychoanalytic thought compatible with Marxist theory and applicable to collective political behavior, and he still maintains a critical vigilance over the Left.

Marcos Aguinis (1935–) entered public affairs as an appointee in the Ministry of Culture, heading that agency during 1986–1987. He subsequently became head of the governmental organization instituted to promote the redemocratization of national culture. The anti-Jewish sentiment obvious in some of the criticism he received drew attention to the persistence of the problem. Aguinis's speeches and occasional writings showed his thoughtful concern for the development of an open and pluralistic national culture. He brought his knowledge of geopolitics and contemporary political and psychoanalytic thought to his persuasive, tactful essays and journalism. Aguinis's 1983 essay *Carta esperanzada a un general* (*Hopeful Letter to a General*) was one of the first important works to emerge from the discussion opened by redemocratization.[13] Here, Aguinis locates a source of the nation's troubles in the system of officer training. His complaint is not about any one feature of the typical officer, such as a tendency to anti-Semitism or a distrust of intellectuals and artists. Rather, Aguinis takes a larger view and subsumes all these frequently denounced features of the military population to one overriding deficiency of military training: its inhibition of the capacity for critical questioning of social structures. Because this essay sets in larger perspective the problem of the military, it is likely to be one of the landmarks of this period.

The new prominence of Aguinis, Rozitchner, and others marks a revival of interest in adapting psychoanalysis to the diagnosis of social ills. It is an area in which Jewish intellectuals have been especially able to make contributions, owing in part to the high incidence of professional psychoanalytic training among this group and in part to the contact with the European tradition of socially aware forms of this analysis. Rozitchner in his coordination of Marxism and psychoanalytic ideas, Aguinis in his novels and social criticism, and Eduardo Pavlovsky in his theater and writings on psychodrama are three visible examples of this tendency.

One segment of writing published since redemocratization (or, in some cases, even before elections became a reality) treats the events of the previous decade so as to see them plainly and to avoid their recurrence. Aguinis's work on the military mind was one of several significant contributions to this discussion by Jewish Argentine authors. One of the earliest works to reassert freedom of expression, even before the return to civilian rule, was Daniel Kon's best-selling *Los chicos de la guerra* (1982; English translation retained the original Spanish title, 1983), an exposé of the ill-conceived 1982 invasion of the Falkland/Malvinas islands.[14] Kon obtained frank testimony from enlisted men unconcerned with defending the military command. Also notable for its early expression of critical views was Santiago Kovadloff's 1982 *Argentina, oscuro país* (*Argentina, Dark Country*), heralding the many introspective essays on national history, attitudes, and institutions that would appear after 1983.[15] A more literary treatment of the shameful aspects of the immediate past is Aída Bortnik's screenwriting for the internationally successful *La historia oficial* (*The Official Story*), published in 1985, which gave a dramatic account of the struggle to come to terms with the damaging effects of the antisubversive campaign.[16] In addition to these new writings, works originally published abroad because of their critical observations on sensitive national questions now appeared in Argentine editions, generating fresh commentary.

Many other newly returned or emboldened Jewish Argentine intellectuals took part in the renewed public discussion, by both written and oral means, of Argentine political culture, including Goloboff, Costantini, Alicia Steimberg, Ricardo Feierstein, and Saúl Sosnowski. Characteristic of this exchange was a fresh willingness to raise Jewish-related aspects of questions. For example, the experimental prose writer and critic Tamara Kamenszain, who had not been strongly associated with Jewish forms of expression since early in her career, now meshed this concern with the feminist and deconstructionist ideas she had been working with during the 1970s and 1980s.[17]

Whereas for some purposes 1983 was a fresh start for Argentine intellectual life, much writing published in this and subsequent years simply continued projects already under way but out of public view during the years when authors were unwilling or unable to publish their bolder material. Cecilia Absatz (1943–), for example, in her 1984 *Los años pares* (*The Even-Numbered Years*), extended her literary commentary on the perplexity of middle-class women conducting their careers and amorous lives in a rapidly changing social environment. In this novel, though, the heroine leaves the usual setting of Buenos Aires. She first encounters the interior, where she experiences firsthand how unlike Europe Argentina is and how grave the divisions within the nation continue to be. Later travels into the Andean region force her to consider the paradox her European appearance and manner create when she seeks to feel part of Latin America. Though as witty and urbane as Absatz's earlier writing, the 1984 novel has less of the flippancy that has probably prevented the entry of the author's work into the category of more seriously regarded literature.[18]

Ricardo Feierstein (1942–), long a writer, achieved prominence in the mid-1980s for the trilogy of novels collectively titled *La sinfonía inocente* (*The Innocent Symphony*): *Entre la izquierda y la pared* (*Between the Left and the Wall,* the first volume, or "movement," though not published until 1983); *El caramelo descompuesto* (*The Spoiled Caramel,* 1979); and *Escala uno en cincuenta* (*One to Fifty Scale,* 1984). Rather than the journey into exile frequently described by writers of this generation, Feierstein's novels center on a move intended to bring redemption from exile. Together they tell a story of 1960s activism, immigration to Israel, an eventually unsatisfactory attempt at kibbutz life, and the return to a professional career in Buenos Aires. The protagonist retains an undiminished confidence in the political discussion that typified left-wing student culture of the 1960s, characterized by a search for political meaning in personal experiences. Despite efforts to analyze his recent past and engage others in its interpretation, he proves unable to grasp his disappointments in Israel and Argentina. Lengthy sections of the novels transcribe the conversations and inner musings the main character carries on in the hope of clarifying his situation. The dialogue provides a sample of the styles adopted through the years for the discussion of issues the hero would most like to understand: Jewish identity, the nature of community, the current worth of the kibbutz ideal, and the geopolitical role of modern Israel. In the last of the novels, this character, with his intact faith in the power of shared introspection, finds himself isolated amid contemporaries disinclined to help him to scrutinize the events of his life. The novels are of greatest interest for their unusual structural design and for the examples they offer of shifting modes in the discussion of social and political matters, especially Jewish-related ones, over the past two decades. The hero's quickness to succumb to shifting fashions in rhetoric and political style gives a human poignancy to novels that might otherwise be somewhat congested with dialectical exchanges and soliloquies.[19]

Edgardo Cozarinsky, a Jewish Argentine writer who took up residence in Paris during the early 1970s, presented in the 1985 *Vudú urbano* (*Urban Voodoo*) the fragmentary prose pieces he calls "postcards." This designation draws attention to one of his central preoccupations, the isolation caused by the displacement of individuals and populations and by the commercialization of national and regional cultures. A typical Cozarinsky vignette presents a foreigner's growing awareness that he is viewing the scene around him through the eyes of an outsider and portrays his efforts to explore both the distortions and the insights that his alien sensibility imparts. However, the scenarios this distanced observer surveys are in themselves far from pure in their cultural makeup. They may be enclaves of immigrants, as are the Arabs that Cozarinsky has studied as part of the uneasily diverse Paris population. They may be people living in what is presumably their homeland but set at a remove from their own culture by such intervening factors as the display of exoticism for commercial purposes. The result is an unstable mix of the provincial, the cosmopolitan, and the salesmanly, creating a shifting cultural landscape wherever one may go—Buenos Aires, Europe, or the Eastern Mediterranean. *Vudú* presents a different, more ambiguous figure of the Argentine exile, one whose departure was a response to various motives and thus one who remains displaced.

The collection contains few, but telling, allusions to Jewish matters. Characters' casual discussion of Argentina's period of political repression brings out the much-noted circumstance that, during the antiterrorist sweeps, Jewish detainees ran an increased risk of severe treatment. The Jewish currents running submerged throughout Argentine history make themselves manifest in odd glimpses. In a text summarizing the nation's aristocracy, offspring of the elite inadvertently bring the denied past to light by opening an ancestral trunk containing Jewish religious articles. Such allusions, appearing briefly in Cozarinsky's sketches, spread the deep-reaching notion that Jewish issues form part of the social and cultural history, whether recent or remote, Argentine or European.[20] A confirmation of Cozarinsky's more than passing concern with Jewish matters is his participation in events designed to further discussion of present-day Jewish culture, such as the encounters of Israeli and Latin American Jewish writers.

It is still too soon to begin assessing the achievement of the Jewish

Argentine writers who are writing in the immediate wake of the 1976–1983 military government and the subsequent return of civilian rule. However, some of the common outstanding features of this new writing can be identified. There is evidently less concern that the consideration of Jewish issues could, if pursued too vigorously, detract from the larger view of the historical problems of the entire society. The converse of this tendency is a rejection of the possibility of discussing Jewish Argentine matters in isolation from the overall process of history. A powerful ideal is to make Jewish Argentine questions one point of entry into the larger dynamic that is the development of national, and in many cases international, cultural and social history. Indeed, this way of viewing the larger scene is considered exceptionally promising because it has not yet been fully explored. It reverses a long-standing and understandable reluctance, especially in troubled periods, to raise, as part of the discussion of Jewish topics, issues politically sensitive and painful to the mainstream society.

NOTES

NOTES FOR INTRODUCTION

1. For a summary of Sephardic immigration to pre-Independence Argentina, see Robert Weisbrot, *The Jews of Argentina: From the Inquisition to Perón*, 15-25; a review of subsequent Western European Jewish immigration follows on 26-38. For the statistical results of the successive waves of Jewish immigration to Argentina, see Judith Laikin Elkin, "A Demographic Profile of Latin American Jewry," *American Jewish Archives* 3, no. 2 (1982): 231-48, particularly interesting for her estimates of the current population. For general information and sources, see also idem, *Jews of the Latin American Republics;* idem, "Latin America's Jews: A Review of Sources," *Latin American Research Review* 20, no. 2 (1985): 124-41; Daniel J. Elazar with Peter Medding, *Jewish Communities in Frontier Societies: Argentina, Australia and South Africa;* Eugene Sofer, *From Pale to Pampa: The Jewish Immigrant Experience in Buenos Aires;* Irving Louis Horowitz, "The Jewish Community of Buenos Aires"; and Haim Avni, "Argentine Jewry: Its Socio-Political Status and Organizational Patterns." For further studies, see the bibliography.

2. On the Baron Maurice de Hirsch and his Jewish Colonization Association, see Elkin, *Jews of the Latin American Republics,* 127-42, an account especially valuable for its careful examination of statistical evidence, and Weisbrot, *Jews of Argentina,* 44-45.

3. Victor A. Mirelman, "Early Socialists and the Jews in Argentina," photocopied typescript of article, courtesy of author. See also Mirelman, *En búsqueda de una identidad, los inmigrantes judíos en Buenos Aires, 1890-1930.* The recommendations of the Socialist party congressman Adolfo Dickmann, who sought the incorporation of Jewish and other new immigrants into the Argentine Left, appear in his *Nacionalismo y socialismo, los argentinos naturalizados en la política* (Buenos Aires: Porter, 1933). His brother Enrique's *Recuerdos de un militante socialista* (Buenos Aires: La Vanguardia, 1947) includes discussion of the alliances between radicalized immigrants and the Socialist party.

4. For an overview of Gerchunoff's place in Argentine literary history, see Francisco Herrera, "Alberto Gerchunoff," in Pedro Orgambide and Roberto Yahni, eds., *Enciclopedia de la literatura argentina,* 269-70.

5. On the problem posed by *La Bolsa,* see Beatriz de Nobile, *Análisis de La Bolsa* (Buenos Aires: Centro Editor de América Latina, 1968), 29-30, and Carmelo M. Bonet, introduction to Julián Martel, *La Bolsa* (Buenos Aires: W. M. Jackson, 1944), xv-xvi. See also Gladys S. Onega, *La inmigración en la literatura argentina 1880-1910,* 63-72, and Germán García, "El chauvinismo racista," *El inmigrante en la literatura argentina,* 93-99.

6. Saúl Sosnowski, "Contemporary Jewish-Argentine Writers: Tradition and Politics," 3.

7. Leonardo Senkman, *La identidad judía en la literatura argentina,* 17-57, 199-256.

8. On Jewish Argentine community organizations, see Weisbrot, *Jews of Argentina,* 57-83.

9. For further information on both Yiddish- and Spanish-language periodical publications, see ibid., 109-13, and Senkman, *La identidad,* 476-77.

10. Gerchunoff's occasional writings on Jewish Argentine topics are collected in a posthumous volume edited by Manuel Kantor, *El pino y la palmera.*

11. Juan B. Justo, "Por qué no me gusta escribir en una hoja que se dice israelita," reprinted in *El marxismo y la cuestión judía* (Buenos Aires: Plus Ultra, 1965), 170-75, originally printed in *Vida Nuestra* (Buenos Aires) in 1923.

12. Senkman, *La identidad,* 218, gives examples of Gerchunoff's overstatement of Jewish-Christian commonalties and notes the adverse response of the Jewish community.

13. Manuel Gálvez's treatment of Jewish themes is exemplified by, in the genre of the essay, "Antisemitismo," *Criterio* (Buenos Aires) 239 (1923): 32–36, and, in the genre of the novel, *El mal metafísico,* originally published in 1922 and reprinted in his *Obras escogidas* (Madrid: Aguilar, 1949), 395–691. For critical discussion of Gálvez's attitudes and their expression, see Kessel Schwartz, "The Jew in Twentieth-Century Argentine Literature," 9–10; Rose S. Minc, "*El mal metafísico:* Hacia una revalorización"; and Senkman, "El judío en la obra de Manuel Gálvez," *La identidad,* 13–30.

14. Gerchunoff's statement declining to assume the seat accorded him in the Academia Argentina de Letras was published under the title "Presentó su renuncia uno de los miembros," *La Nación* (Buenos Aires) 21 August 1931, 4.

15. In 1980, Ediciones Nueva Presencia reissued León Dujovne, *El judaísmo como cultura: De la filosofía milenaria a la resurrección nacional.* The republication signals a desire on the part of a young Jewish intellectual public to know the leading historical figures of Jewish Argentine culture, including those perhaps too easily dismissed as posing no challenge to established ways.

16. In César Tiempo's 1974 *Clara Béter y otras fatamorganas,* he officially confessed to perpetrating the Clara Beter deception. The 1926 *Versos de una . . . ,* long thought of as principally a complex hoax, has in recent years begun to be read as a poetic text constituting a social statement. In 1977, Editorial Rescate of Buenos Aires reissued the work, along with extensive critical background material by Estelle Irizarry. Senkman, in *La identidad,* observes that *Versos* contains the elements suppressed in Tiempo's "own" poetry to produce a cheerful vision of the ghetto. Clara Beter's account of her life as a Jewish prostitute in Buenos Aires, Senkman notes, gives an accurate composite of contemporary social realities (169–72). Beginning in 1985, David Viñas raised fresh controversy over *Versos* by speaking of the collection as equal in significance to Ricardo Güiraldes's novel *Don Segundo Sombra,* long considered the great national work to appear in 1926. The ensuing polemical exchange between Viñas and the nationalist Raúl Puigbó, which quickly spread to include many other discussants, is summarized and analyzed by Senkman in "Dos dilemas básicos," in the Asociación Mutual Israelita Argentina's multiauthored volume *Pluralismo e identidad: Lo judío en la literatura argentina* (Buenos Aires: Milá, 1986), 50–52.

17. César Tiempo and Pedro-Juan Vignale, eds., *Exposición de la actual poesía argentina (1922–1927),* is most indicative of Tiempo's connections with the youthful avant-garde and social literature movements, for he was able to obtain contributions from leading members of both factions. A good sampling of his literary journalism appears in Roberto F. Giusti, ed., *Nosotros* (Buenos Aires), available in Kraus Reprints. Here Tiempo shows that, as well as the writing of his contemporaries, he knows a good deal about modern literature from Central and Eastern Europe, particularly that touching on progressive social tendency or Jewish themes. Tiempo's contemporary Alberto Pineta notes his ability to move between literary groups; see the latter's overview of the 1920s scene, "La promesa de la nueva generación," *Síntesis* (Buenos Aires), 29 (1929), unpaginated. The same comment is made retrospectively by Adolfo Prieto in "Boedo y Florida," in his *Antología de Boedo y Florida* (Córdoba: Universidad Nacional de Córdoba, 1964), 6, 28–29. For a general overview in English of Tiempo and his importance in Argentine literary culture, see Donald D. Walsh, "César Tiempo."

18. Senkman, *La identidad,* 153–68, finds the rosy view of the ghetto in Tiempo's Sabbath poems a form of capitulation to the non-Jewish reader's desire for reassurance that the Jewish population was satisfied with its place in national society. Beyond any doubt, Tiempo's apparent satisfaction with the status of the Jewish Argentine population greatly impressed many non-Jewish readers. See, for example, Julio Noé, "La poesía," in Rafael Alberto Arrieta, ed., *Historia de la literatura argentina.*

19. Jacobo Fijman, *Molino rojo* (Buenos Aires: Editorial "El Inca," 1926); *Hecho de estampas* (Buenos Aires: n.p., 1930; Buenos Aires: Ediciones Mano de Obra, 1981); *Estrella de la mañana* (Buenos Aires: Editorial Número, 1931). The most accessible edition of all three is *Obra poética*, ed. E. Vásquez (Buenos Aires: Ediciones La Torre Abolida, 1983).

In *El pensamiento de Jacobo Fijman: O, el viaje hacia la otra realidad* (Buenos Aires: Rodolfo Alonso, 1970), edited interviews by Vicente Zito Lema, Fijman objects to an allusion to his conversion as being from a Jew to a Catholic, insisting, "lo de judío no se pierde" (being a Jew isn't lost) (78). Fijman speaks of his debt to Jewish thought on page 67.

20. Samuel Eichelbaum, *Nadie la conoció nunca* (Buenos Aires: Carro de Tespis, 1957). On the involvement of Eastern European Jewish women in Buenos Aires prostitution and the literary reflections of this phenomenon, see Nora Glickman, "The Jewish White Slave Trade in Latin American Writings," *Jewish American Archives* 34, no. 2 (1982): 178–89.

21. Lázaro Liacho, *Siónidas desde la pampa y Sonata judía de Nueva York* (Buenos Aires: Candelabra, 1969).

22. Jorge Luis Borges, "Patria," preface to Carlos M. Grünberg, *Mester de judería* (Buenos Aires: Editorial Argirópolis, 1940).

23. Carlos M. Grünberg, *Junto a un río de Babel* (Buenos Aires: Acervo Cultural, 1965).

24. Senkman, *La identidad,* 174–75. 25. Ibid., 176–87.

26. Bernardo Kordon, "Kid Ñandubay," *A punto de reventar, seguido de Kid Ñandubay* (Buenos Aires: Losada, 1971), 111–68. For further commentary on the treatment of Jewish themes in Kordon's work, see Senkman, *La identidad,* 135–37, 382–84.

27. During the 1946–1955 Peronist regime, Gerchunoff and Tiempo were by far the two most prominent Jewish literary intellectuals. Gerchunoff's relations with the Peronist party and government are easy to characterize; he shared the anti-Peronism common among members of the cultural elite. Tiempo had more contact with the Peronists, especially through his editorship of the cultural supplement to the Peronist-owned *La Prensa.* Interpretations of this bond and Tiempo's attitude toward Peronism vary widely. For example, Senkman, *La identidad,* 187, says: "César Tiempo backs Peronism . . . and Peronism consecrates him as a figure of national culture . . . when it designates him as editor of the prestigious cultural supplement of the newspaper *La Prensa.*" The competing belief that Tiempo merely placated the Peronists is summed up by Marcos Glauberman when he refers to "César Tiempo, a Jewish writer who, despite the adversity of having to please a fascist Peronism, managed to become cultural editor of the newspaper *La Prensa*" (AMIA, *Pluralismo e identidad,* 168).

28. Emir Rodríguez Monegal, *El juicio de los parricidas: La nueva generación argentina y sus maestros* (Buenos Aires: Editorial Deucalión, 1956).

29. Natalio Budasoff, *Lluvias salvajes* (Buenos Aires: Mosaicos, 1962); Pablo Schvartzman, *Cuentos criollos con judíos* (Buenos Aires: Instituto de los Amigos del Libro Rioplatense, 1967).

30. José Chudnovsky, *Dios era verde* (Buenos Aires: Américalee, 1963) and idem, *Pueblo pan* (Buenos Aires: Losada, 1967).

31. Germán Rozenmacher, *Réquiem para un viernes a la noche* (Buenos Aires: Talía, 1971).

32. Saúl Sosnowski, "Contemporary Jewish-Argentine Writers: Tradition and Politics," 4–7, and idem, "Germán Rozenmacher: Tradiciones, rupturas y desencuentros."

33. León Rozitchner, *Ser judío,* 2d ed. (Buenos Aires: Ediciones de la Flor, 1967; reissued 1988).

34. Albert Memmi, *Portrait of a Jew,* trans. Elisabeth Abbott (New York: Viking, 1971) and idem, *The Liberation of the Jew,* trans. Judy Hyun (New York: Grossman Publishers, 1966). The original *Portrait d'un juif* and *La libération du juif* appeared in 1962 and 1966 respectively.

35. Juan José Sebreli, ed., *La cuestión judía en la Argentina* (Buenos Aires: Tiempo Contemporáneo, 1968).

36. Marcos Aguinis, *Refugiados* (Buenos Aires: Losada, 1969); revised edition, *Refugi-*

ados: Crónica de un palestino (Buenos Aires: Planeta, 1976); and idem, *La cuestión judía vista desde el Tercer Mundo* (Río Cuarto, Argentina: Librería Superior Editora, 1974; rev. ed., 1974).

37. On Yiddish-language cultural activity in Buenos Aires, see Weisbrot, *Jews of Argentina,* 76–77, 122–23, 141–42, 283–89.

38. Senkman, *La identidad,* 106.

39. Luis Emilio Soto, in Arrieta, ed., *Historia de la literatura argentina,* 4:359.

40. Dorothy Seidman Bilik, *Immigrant-Survivors: Post-Holocaust Consciousness in Recent Jewish American Fiction* (Middletown, Conn.: Wesleyan University Press, 1981), 5.

41. Personal communication from Marcos Ricardo Barnatán to author, April 1985.

42. Gerardo Mario Goloboff, a lawyer by profession, attained his current fame as a novelist but first came to the attention of the literary public with his collection of poetry *Entre la diáspora y octubre* (Buenos Aires: Stilcograf, 1966). For discussion of issues central to Goloboff's early poetry as they are later developed in his novel *Caballos por el fondo de los ojos* (Barcelona: Seix Barral, 1976), see Saúl Sosnowski, "Gerardo Mario Goloboff: Hacia el décimo mes en la diáspora." Senkman, *La identidad,* 329–31, discusses the 1966 collection.

43. Alicia Steimberg, *De músicos y relojeros* (Buenos Aires: Centro Editor de América Latina, 1971) and idem, *Su espíritu inocente* (Buenos Aires: Pomaire, 1981). For commentary on Steimberg's daringly critical treatment of everyday Jewish Argentine life, see Senkman, *La identidad,* 283–95, and Sosnowski, "Contemporary Jewish-Argentine Writers," 8–9.

44. Cecilia Absatz, *Feiguele y otras mujeres* (Buenos Aires: Ediciones de la Flor, 1976) and idem, *Té con canela* (Buenos Aires: Sudamericana, 1982).

45. Tamara Kamenszain fuses traditional Jewish religious culture with avant-garde concepts of the literary text to produce *De este lado del Mediterráneo* (Buenos Aires: Ediciones Noé, 1973).

46. Eugenia Calny, *Clara al amanecer* (Buenos Aires: Ediciones Crisol, 1972).

47. Nora Glickman, *Uno de sus Juanes* (Buenos Aires: Ediciones de la Flor, 1983).

NOTES FOR CHAPTER 1: ALBERTO GERCHUNOFF

1. Alberto Gerchunoff, *Los gauchos judíos* (Santiago de Chile: Ercilla, 1940). Subsequent citations in the text will give page numbers from this edition.

2. The progovernment slant of *Los gauchos judíos* and its suppression of social conflict have been noted by critics. Gladys S. Onega, "Lugones: La tetralogía del Centenario," *La inmigración en la literatura argentina, 1880–1910,* 123–25, criticizes both Gerchunoff's work and Leopoldo Lugones's *Odas seculares* for presenting the beleaguered immigrant as painlessly adapting. In both texts, the new arrivals "are perfectly integrated into the life of the country from which they have absorbed certain purifying essences and to which they have brought productive habits desirable in the new era of prosperity." David Viñas, "Gerchunoff: gauchos judíos y xenofobia," *Literatura argentina y realidad política: Apogeo de la oligarquía,* finds Gerchunoff's portrayal of immigrant life tranquil to the point of torpor, even when treating inherently conflict-filled subject matter.

3. An ideological analysis focused on Jewish issues is Saúl Sosnowski, "Contemporary Jewish-Argentine Writers: Tradition and Politics," 1–4. Sosnowski observes that by suppressing the fact that Jewish immigration furthered the government's plan to Europeanize the interior, Gerchunoff's novel disguises official racism and makes the Jews appear beholden to a disinterestedly benevolent host nation. Sosnowski objects to Gerchunoff's promotion of officially encouraged assimilationism. Viñas and Onega both underline the novel's strong connection with the patriotic celebration of the Argentine centennial, whose cultural observances were organized by Gerchunoff's friend Lugones.

4. Kessel Schwartz, "The Jew in Argentine Literature," 9.

5. Both Viñas's and Onega's analyses contain strong statements not only linking the work

to the centennial spirit but also calling it ideologically equivalent to Lugones's *Odas seculares,* a work conceived and elaborated as a stimulus to Argentine patriotism. An exception to the tendency to equate Gerchunoff's novel with Argentine centennial fervor is Héctor P. Agosti's undeveloped reference situating the novel in the context of Jewish thought. See pages 54–55 of his essay *"Los gauchos judíos,"* in his *Cantar opinando.*

6. Saul Tchernihowsky, "They Say There Is a Country . . . ," translated and included by Esor Winer Ben-Sorek in his *Poems and Poets of Israel: Selected Masterpieces,* rev. ed. (Boston: University of Boston Bookstores, 1967), 86–87. Of interest in this respect is the comment by Eisig Silberschlag that Ben-Sorek cites on page 84 of this volume, bringing to the fore the notion of a remade Jewish world: "It was Tchernihowsky who discovered a 'new realm of being' in the beginnings of the Jewish nation and reinforced modern Judaism with the hoary, half-mythical past." Tchernihowsky's belief that Jewish tradition once had a vitality that, though lost, might be recovered has strong parallels with the speech of Gerchunoff's fictional rabbi, in which current Jewish life is seen as diminishing ancient strengths.

7. Nathaniel Kravitz, *1,000 Years of Hebrew Literature* (Chicago: Swallow, 1972), 482.

8. Irving Louis Horowitz, "Organization and Ideology of the Jewish Community of Argentina," in his *Israeli Ecstasies/Jewish Agonies,* 138. Horowitz states that this attempt at remaking the Jewish image and the plan to settle the Jewish immigrants in agricultural areas "essentially have failed."

9. Viñas, "Gerchunoff," 172.

10. Ibid. The discussion of this ritualistic and magical vision of nature continues on 171–76.

11. Jorge Luis Borges, as quoted in Fernando Sorrentino, *Siete conversaciones con Jorge Luis Borges* (Buenos Aires: Casa Pardo, 1973), 36.

12. Schwartz, "Argentine Literature," 9. Though, as this study argues, *Los gauchos judíos* resolves the conflict between assimilation and talmudic and other traditions, Gerchunoff later rejected this early solution as too destructive of Jewish ways. He advocated a greater reluctance to abandon tradition for the modes of the dominant Christian culture.

NOTES FOR CHAPTER 2: CÉSAR TIEMPO

1. César Tiempo, *Sabatión argentino: Antiguas y nuevas dones para la pausa del sábado* (Buenos Aires/Montevideo: Sociedad Amigos del Libro Rioplatense, 1939). Subsequent citations in the text will give page numbers from this edition.

2. Oliverio Girondo, "Manifiesto de Martín Fierro," *Martín Fierro* (Buenos Aires) 4 (1924), unpaginated. The manifesto is currently available in Adolfo Prieto, ed., *El periódico Martín Fierro 1924–1927* (Buenos Aires: Galerna, 1968), 13–15.

3. Consider, for instance, that the imaginative writing on which Luis Borges's fame most solidly rests, the 1944 collection *Ficciones,* contains a number of celebrated short stories whose nucleus is either a theological problem or an issue of human religious behavior: "El acercamiento a Almotásim," "Las ruinas circulares," "El milagro secreto," "Tres versiones de Judas," and "La secta del Fénix."

4. Mordecai M. Kaplan summarizes the meaning he gives to his famous phrase and his reasons for preferring this definition of Judaism in Mordecai M. Kaplan and Arthur A. Cohen, *If Not Now, When? Toward a Reconstitution of the Jewish People* (New York: Schocken, 1973), 23–24, 29–32, 100–101. Kaplan's classic presentation of his idea is his *Judaism as a Civilization: Toward a Reconstitution of American Jewish Life,* rev. ed. (New York: T. Yoseloff, 1957).

5. Tiempo himself became involved in the early film industry and played several screen parts. See Pedro Orgambide, "César Tiempo," in Pedro Orgambide and Roberto Yahni, eds., *Enciclopedia de la literatura argentina.*

6. César Tiempo, "Chaplín," in his *Clara Beter y otras fatamorganas,* 51–56.

7. Juan Pinto, *Pasión y suma de la expresión argentina,* 121, observes that the Lacroze

streetcars were, during the 1920s, "objetos de caricaturas y chistes en el teatro y en las revistas por su deplorable estado de conservación" (the butt of cartoons and jokes in the theater and magazines because of their deplorable state of disrepair). Pinto notes that Tiempo is faithful to period details in his description of the ghetto of the 1920s.

8. Bernardo Verbitsky, *Es difícil empezar a vivir.* The treatment of the term *ghetto* in the novel is discussed in the next chapter of this study.

9. Tiempo favors the proposition that open discussion of "shameless" behavior can benefit a society afflicted with primness. His drama *Quiero vivir* features a schoolteacher mistaken for the prostitute-poet Clara Beter. The resulting scandal awakens the heroine to the stimulating variety of life and makes her "want to live." Tiempo and Arturo Cerretani, in their stage version of Sarah Bernhardt's life, *La dama de las comedias,* set the heroine's "scandalous" life in favorable contrast to the straight-laced bourgeois morality of her time.

10. Robert Alter, "Varieties of Jewish Verse," *Commentary* 72, no. 1 (July 1981): 55.

11. Abraham Joshua Heschel's thought is summarized by S. Daniel Breslauer in *The Ecumenical Perspective and the Modernization of Jewish Religion* (Missoula, Mont.: Brown Judaic Studies Series, No. 5, 1978). The classic Heschel work Breslauer draws on is *The Sabbath: Its Meaning for Modern Man,* rev. ed. (New York: Farrar, Straus, 1963).

NOTES FOR CHAPTER 3: BERNARDO VERBITSKY

1. Bernardo Verbitsky, *Es difícil empezar a vivir* (Buenos Aires: Losada, 1941), 209–12. Subsequent citations in the text will give page numbers from this edition.

2. Juan Pinto, *Pasión y suma de la expresión argentina,* 36. Commentary on the novel emphasizes its documentary or testimonial quality. For Carmelo M. Bonet, "La novela," in Rafael Alberto Arrieta, ed., *Historia de la literatura argentina,* 4:211–13, the work is a "chronicle" and a "realistic text." Germán García, in *La novela argentina: Un itinerario,* 231, says that the novel "documents," and he likens it to reportage and journalism. Fernando Alonso and Arturo Rezzano, "Bernardo Verbitsky," *Novela y sociedad argentina,* praise Verbitsky for his realistic presentation of social problems. David William Foster, in *A Dictionary of Contemporary Latin American Authors* (Tempe, Ariz.: Center for Latin American Studies, 1975), 106, calls Verbitsky "along with David Viñas, perhaps the best example of an exponent of social realism in the Argentine novel. . . . True to the tradition of Lukács, Verbitsky presents . . . typical individuals, 'heroes,' who . . . give specific human representation to the social problems involved." Verbitsky's ability to bear witness to society's situation at a given moment is the focus of Pinto's commentary in *Breviario de la literatura argentina* (Buenos Aires: La Mandrágora, 1958), 121, and José Barcia, "Bernardo Verbitsky," in Pedro Orgambide and Roberto Yahni, eds., *Enciclopedia de la literatura argentina,* 616–18. Verbitsky's own book of commentary on Argentine literature, *Literatura y conciencia nacional,* displays the outlook of a committed social realist and stresses the writer's obligation to increase awareness of ethical problems confronting society.

3. Saúl Sosnowski, "Germán Rozenmacher: Tradiciones, rupturas y desencuentros."

4. Kessel Schwartz, "The Jew in Twentieth-Century Argentine Literature"; Nora Glickman, "The Image of the Jew in Brazilian and Argentine Literature," 68–72.

5. A central concern of Robert Weisbrot in *The Jews of Argentina: From the Inquisition to Perón,* is that younger Jewish Argentines may lose their identity largely from lack of sufficient information about the religious and cultural tradition involved. See especially his chapter "Education," 137–54.

6. The fragmented character of the narrative has elicited commentary from Pinto, *Pasión y suma,* and Bonet, "La novela."

7. Bonet, "La novela," 211, 213.

NOTES FOR CHAPTER 4: DAVID VIÑAS

1. *Literatura argentina y realidad política* is the overall title for Viñas's projected series of ten volumes offering a historical analysis of Argentine literary culture in relation to social change. He has published the following volumes of criticism: *Literatura argentina y realidad política* (1964), revised as *Literatura argentina y realidad política: De Sarmiento a Cortázar* (1971); *Laferrère: Del apogeo de la oligarquía a la crisis de la ciudad liberal* (1965); *Literatura argentina y realidad política: La crisis de la ciudad liberal* (1973); *Literatura argentina y realidad política: Apogeo de la oligarquía* (1975); and *Grotesco, inmigración y fracaso: Armando Discépolo* (1973). He edited the three-volume *Obras escogidas de Armando Discépolo* (1969), rediscovering a technically innovative and socially aware dramatist whose work had been undervalued. David William Foster has examined Viñas's critical work in "*Literatura argentina y realidad política:* David Viñas and Sociological Literary Criticism in Argentina." Shorter summaries of Viñas's critical undertaking appear in David William Foster, "David Viñas," *A Dictionary of Contemporary Latin American Writers,* 107; Francisco Herrera, "David Viñas," in Pedro Orgambide and Roberto Yahni, eds., *Enciclopedia de la literatura argentina,* 625–26; and Humberto Mario Rasi, "David Viñas, novelista y crítico comprometido." For a characterization of the movement of socially committed critics from which Viñas emerged, see Emir Rodríguez Monegal, *El juicio de los parricidas: La nueva generación argentina y sus maestros* (Buenos Aires: Deucalión, 1956); María Luisa Bastos, "*Contorno, Ciudad, Gaceta Literaria:* Tres enfoques de una realidad," *Hispamérica* 4–5 (1973): 49–64; and the bibliographic compilation by Gustavo Valadez, "David Viñas y la generación del 55." Of interest also to a reader seeking a picture of Viñas's critical mission is the interview of him by Mario Szichman, "David Viñas (entrevista)," in *Hispamérica,* which provoked a statement in self-defense from Julio Cortázar, *Hispamérica* 2 (1972): 55–58.

It is interesting to see Viñas's vision of history developed without emphasis on literature in his *Rebeliones populares argentinas: De los montoneros a los anarquistas* (Buenos Aires: Carlos Pérez, 1971).

2. General characterizations of Viñas's narrative work are available in Rasi, "David Viñas"; Herrera, "David Viñas"; and Emir Rodríguez Monegal, "David Viñas en su contorno," 75–84. Saúl Sosnowski has taken a closer look at particular features of Viñas's writings in "*Jauría,* de David Viñas: Continuación de un proyecto desmitificador."

3. Rasi, "David Viñas," 261, states: "The assumptions that form the ideological basis for Viñas's narrative stand out with greater clarity in his essays in literary criticism." Whatever judgment may underlie this comment, one should note that as a creative writer Viñas enjoys the right to employ less rational and linear arguments.

4. David Viñas, *Dar la cara* (Buenos Aires: Centro Editor de América Latina, 1967), 140. Subsequent citations in the text will give page numbers from this edition.

5. Rasi, "David Viñas," 262.

6. It is beyond the scope of this book to examine the relation among the traditional Jewish responsibility for the community's well-being, the responsiblity to maintain a special awareness of social injustice, and the extension of these responsibilities to include radical action. Suffice it to note that the idea that the exceptional mission of the Jewish people includes a social conscience is one with long-standing support both in mainstream surveys of Jewish thought and in writings with a radical tendency. See, for nonradical examples, Bernard J. Bamberger, "The Chosen People," *The Search for Jewish Theology* (New York: Behrman House, 1978), 51–65, and André Chouraqui and Jean Daniélou, *The Jews: Views and Counterviews, A Dialogue* (New York: Newman Press, 1967), 56. Extension of Jewish responsibility to include radical action is the topic of Percy Cohen, *Jewish Radicals and Radical Jews* (New York: Academic Press/Institute of Jewish Affairs, 1980).

In his last writings Verbitsky, stung by the equation of Zionism with imperialism, boldly asserted a link between Jewish social thought and a Marxist vision of society. Verbitsky promotes the critique of society. His 1972 novel *Etiquetas a los hombres,* 21, brings the idea a step further as a character articulately unites Jewish ethics and the origin of socialism: "Su idea era que . . . debe reconocerse en la Biblia un antecedente aún más preciso [que la antigüedad clásica] del socialismo. Los judíos dieron al mundo el sentimiento y la noción de justicia, y ése es precisamente el antecedente inequívoco de toda concepción del mundo basada en la razón y la justicia" (His idea was that . . . the Bible should be recognized as an even more direct antecedent [than classical antiquity] of socialism. Jews gave the world the feeling and the idea of justice, and this is precisely the exact antecedent of every conception of the world based on reason and justice).

7. Viñas, *De Sarmiento a Cortázar,* 53.

8. The exclusivity of elite publications, and their cultural influence, are long-standing critical preoccupations of Viñas's. See his analysis of Argentina's foremost elite literary magazine ("*Sur:* Sobrevivencia y reemplazo del escritor. Mallea," *De Sarmiento a Cortázar,* 83–89), as well as his remarks on the literary supplements to the newspapers *La Nación* and *La Prensa* (ibid., 57).

9. Viñas observes that criteria of elegant expression shift continually but always benefit the elite that has mastered the preferred manner. See his comments on "lenguaje afrancesado" (Frenchified language) of the 1880s in ibid., 39. Whereas Sabul sees Frenchified Spanish as inherently and timelessly tainted, Viñas shows that ideals of linguistic purity or eclecticism fit a historical moment.

10. See David Viñas, "Gerchunoff: Gauchos judíos y xenofobia," *Literatura argentina y realidad política: Apogeo de la oligarquía.*

11. In Viñas's analysis of literary culture, he points to the concept of "generational conflict" as a pseudoproblem masking the deeper contradictions in the relations between literature and society. See his discussion in *De Sarmiento a Cortázar,* 19–20, 62.

NOTES FOR CHAPTER 5: JOSÉ RABINOVICH

1. Enrique de Gandia, "Prólogo" to José Rabinovich, *Sobras de una juventud,* 5, asserts that the poet is unlike contemporaries in that "he has no influences from other writers. He doesn't imitate and indeed he can't imitate because he doesn't read his colleagues." However vigorously Gandia initially asserts Rabinovich's lack of "outside pressure, be it from books, from schools, from doctrines, or from principles," his remarks reveal a recognition of the traces of theological study in the poet's work (10). Luis Emilio Soto, "José Rabinovich," in Rafael Alberto Arrieta, ed., *Historia de la literatura argentina,* 4:359, finds Rabinovich "showing the misfortune of the Jewish proletarian who feels the impact of the difficulty of assimilating to the country and the burden of racial inhibitions, and whose conflicts generate the piercing realism of his books." Ulises Petit de Murat's prologue to the first edition of *Sobras de una juventud, memorias,* 7–9, emphasizes the vivid directness with which Rabinovich's writing appears to reflect real-world matters. Gandia, "Prólogo," 5, remarks that Rabinovich was discovered by Elías Castelnuovo, a leading figure in the proletarian realist movement. Castelnuovo wrote promotional introductions for Rabinovich's 1943 *Cabizbajos* (*Heads Bowed*) and 1944 *Tercera clase* and helped to launch Rabinovich among realists. Another endorsement is Ricardo Baeza's enthusiastic prologue to the 1947 *Los acusados,* reprinted in the 1969 reissue of *Tercera clase.* Also see César Tiempo's introductory interview with Rabinovich for Rabinovich's 1968 *El perro de Maidenek* (*The Dog From Maidenek*). All bring to the fore representational and documentary qualities. Rabinovich continues the experiment begun in the 1920s in Argentina by proletarian writers. Consider, for example, the relation between what Rabinovich does in *El violinista bajo el tejado* and Leónidas Barletta's effort toward a realistic form of verse in *Canciones agrias* (Buenos Aires: Editorial El Libro Moderno, 1924) or Tiempo's work in *Versos de una . . . .* For two modern samp-

lers, see Raúl González Tuñón's early work as anthologized in *La luna con gatillo: Selección de poemas líricos, sociales y políticos* (Buenos Aires: Editorial Cartago, 1957) and Susana Pereira's *Literatura testimonial de los años 30* (Buenos Aires: A. Peña Lillo, 1979). On the attempt to develop a proletarian poetry, see Adolfo Prieto's introductory essay and selection of examples in his *Antología de Boedo y Florida* (Córdoba: Universidad Nacional de Córdoba, 1964).

2. C. K. Weatherhead denounces the neglect of literal types of expression in poetry and urges a greater respect for poems that allude more directly to real-world matters; see *The Edge of the Image* (Seattle: University of Washington Press, 1968). Uriel Weisstein, "Realism," in Alex Preminger, ed., *Princeton Encyclopedia of Poetry and Poetics*, rev. ed. (Princeton: Princeton University Press, 1974), 685, notes the relative scarcity of realism in poetry. Telling is the *Encyclopedia*'s less than one-page treatment of realism. Weisstein must characterize many of the instances he cites as realistic only in certain respects. Damian Grant describes the term *realism* itself as having an unmanageable "elasticity" and "chronic instability"; see *Realism* (London: Methuen, 1970), 1–3. The bewildering variety of concepts of realism is well represented by George T. Becker, ed., *Documents of Modern Literary Realism* (Princeton: Princeton University Press, 1963). One should note that early poetic realism in Argentina was most frequently tendentious, aimed at awakening the humanitarian conscience of readers, and little resembled realism that seeks only to reflect existing conditions. In addition, Rabinovich makes an undisguised use of certain techniques clearly typical of avant-garde or experimentalist poetry. The creation of lengthy series of innovative metaphors, as in the figurative equivalents of the Hebrew alphabet given in "Abecedario judío" ("Jewish Alphabet") in Rabinovich's *El violinista bajo el tejado*, 66–69, are inescapably reminiscent of the major Argentine avant-garde movement of the 1920s and its less-noted sequel, the Generation of 1940. Such linguistic playfulness places Rabinovich outside any concept of realism that rejects the cultivation of aesthetically daring novelties. For a summation of the argument against allowing avant-garde innovation in social realism, see Georg Lukács, "The Ideology of Modernism," *The Meaning of Contemporary Realism*, trans. John and Necke Mander (London: Merlin Press, 1962), 17–46.

3. José Rabinovich, *El violinista bajo el tejado* (La Plata: Platense, 1970). Subsequent citations in the text will give page numbers from this edition.

4. On the stylistic forms typical of biblical argumentation, see James Muilenberg, *The Way of Israel: Biblical Faith and Ethics* (New York: Harper and Row, 1961), 24–29. Consider, for example, Rabinovich's denunciation of Catholic officials' insistence that the faithful confess by means of a priest. Such statements resemble, with due changes, the biblical wishing of ill upon misleading authorities and those claiming illegitimate authority. The encouragement to readers to communicate directly with God places the poem in the line of exhortation; see ibid., 26–27. In the analysis of biblical texts, it is possible to separate these conventional forms of aggressive argumentation.

5. A study could well be made of Rabinovich's free adaptation and transformation of biblical forms. Muilenberg, ibid., 26, notes that "while these are stylistic forms, they undergo transformation in the course of Irael's history." In "Responso" there is a remarkable correspondence between Rabinovich's use of blessing and the biblical form. Muilenberg, ibid., 26, states: "In the Psalter, we receive a clear picture of who are blessed and what the nature of the blessing is. He is blessed (or happy) who obeys Yahway's law (Ps. 1:1–13), for he has living resources, like a tree planted by channels of water, and whatever he does prospers (cf. Jer. 17:7–8)."

6. One may observe that the issues Rabinovich's poetry raises are especially close to those handled by the figures associated with socialist realism. See Friedrich Engels, "On Socialist Realism," 483–85, and Maxim Gorky et al., "Comments on Social Realism," 486–88, both in Becker, ed., *Documents of Modern Literary Realism*. The official "Comments on Socialist Realism," by Gorky and his colleagues, speaks of a directed, organized movement in art,

unlike Rabinovich's individualistic and sometimes idiosyncratic realism; yet some of their statements describe the functioning of the Argentine poet's work. Rabinovich's creation of highly exemplary figures, such as the altruistic blacksmith of "Responso," can be justified using the words of Gorky et al.: "Indeed a time has come when we need the heroic: everyone wants the stimulating, the colorful—something, you know, that would not resemble life, but would be higher than life, better, more beautiful. It is absolutely necessary that today's literature begin to embellish life somewhat, and as soon as it does so, life will be embellished, i.e., people will begin to live more swiftly, more brightly." Rabinovich favors a startling mixture of this larger-than-life depiction with what W. K. Wimsatt and Cleanth Brooks have called "drab realism"; see *Literary Criticism* (New York: Knopf, 1957), 102.

7. It would be possible to argue that poems like "Responso" present a poetic adaptation of the idea, prevalent in Marxist thought, of nonalienated labor. See, for example, István Mészáros, *Marx's Theory of Alienation* (London: Merlin, 1970), and Ollman Bertell, *Alienation: Marx's Conception of Man in Capitalist Society* (Cambridge: Cambridge University Press, 1971).

8. Szymon Bojko, *New Graphic Design in Revolutionary Russia,* trans. Robert Strybel and Lech Zembrzuski (New York: Praeger, 1972), 13, 17.

9. See Saul Tchernihowsky, "They Say There is a Country . . . ," translated and included by Esor Winer Ben-Sorek in his *Poems and Poets of Israel: Selected Masterpieces,* rev. ed. (Boston: University of Boston Bookstore, 1967), 86–87; the text is transcribed in chapter 1 of this study.

NOTES FOR CHAPTER 6: JOSÉ ISAACSON

1. José Isaacson, *Cuaderno Spinoza* (Buenos Aires: Marymar, 1977). Subsequent citations in the text will give page numbers from this edition.

2. For discussions of the audience addressed by literary work, see Walter J. Ong, "The Writer's Audience is Always a Fiction," *PMLA,* 90, no. 1 (1975): 9–21. See also idem, *The Presence of the Word* (New Haven: Yale, 1967), especially 115–20, on the indications, manifest in the text, of the type of audience to be addressed and how that audience is to be addressed. The most famous discussion of the "mock reader," or the reader implicit in the text, may well be Wayne Booth, *The Rhetoric of Fiction* (Chicago: University of Chicago Press, 1961), 49–52, 363–64.

3. Leonard Senkman, *La identidad judía en la literatura argentina* (Buenos Aires: Pardes, 1983), 353. Senkman's remarks on *Cuaderno Spinoza,* 353–63, indicate a lack of confidence in the work's ability to provide readers with insights into the questions it addresses. Instead, he sees the work as a symptom of the real-life Isaacson's anxieties and efforts to regain a feeling of worth. Senkman criticizes the work on ideological grounds as a vestige of outmoded liberalism, a complaint not germane to the present study.

4. Mortimer J. Adler and Charles Van Doren, *How to Read a Book,* rev. ed. (New York: Simon and Schuster, 1972), 84. This very basic and general exposition of the forms of philosophical discourse is especially useful because it is designed to summarize the judgments most widely agreed on.

5. Senkman, *La identidad,* 353–54. Note that Senkman makes a similar complaint against another writer concerned with his Sephardic roots, Marcos Ricardo Barnatán; see 341–44. Senkman's objection is to the vaunting of Sephardic ancestry over a comprehensive view of Jewish identity.

6. Samuel and Tamar Grand, *Exploring the Jewish Heritage in Spain* (Bilbao: Secretaría de Estado de Turismo, 1980), start their beginner's guide to Sephardic matter with a warning that Sepharad was *not* Spain: "Technically, the word *Sephardim* means Spaniards. It comes from *Sepharad,* the Hebrew word for Spain. In practice, however, the term *Sephardim* refers to Jews of Spanish and Portuguese origin, whose ancestors were expelled from Spain

in 1492. Such an explanation of the distinction between literal and usage-determined meanings would be found only in the most introductory of discussions.

7. Yosef Hayim Yerushalmi, *From Spanish Court to Italian Ghetto. Isaac Cardoso: A Study in Seventeenth-Century Marranism and Jewish Apologetics,* rev. ed. (Seattle: University of Washington Press, 1981), 193. It should be noted that the traditional denial of the importance of Jewish culture as part of Spanish civilization has, in recent decades, been countered by a massive effort to reclaim this heritage. The name of Américo Castro should surely be mentioned in this respect.

8. Frederick Pollock, *Spinoza: His Life and Philosophy,* 2d ed. (New York: Macmillan, 1899), 11, notes that it is impossible to ascertain Spinoza's exact mother tongue; of Spanish and Portuguese, "one or both . . . were native to him." Pollock's treatment is of interest because of its traditionally humanistic and interpretive coverage of Spinoza, unlike the more specific and technical discussions typical of the modern era.

9. Ibid., 9–10.

10. See especially Ezequiel Martínez Estrada, *Radiografía de la pampa* (Buenos Aires: Babel, 1933), and Héctor A. Murena, *El pecado original de América* (Buenos Aires: Sur, 1954).

11. Spinoza's correspondence is generally available and commented on through the selection and edition orginally made by E. Van Vloten and H. Land, the one clearly used by Isaacson in his re-creation of the letters. For an example of this selection of letters and typical commentary on them, see, respectively, "Spinoza's Correspondence," in *The Chief Works of Benedict de Spinoza,* trans. R. H. M. Elwes (New York: Dover, 1951), 2:273–420, and Frederick Pollock, "Spinoza's Correspondence," 44–75.

12. Benedict de [Baruch] Spinoza, *Ethics,* in *Chief Works,* 2:43–81, displays the famous format.

13. Benedict de [Baruch] Spinoza, "Letter II: Spinoza to Oldenburg," in *Chief Works,* 2:276–79, begins with conventional flattery: "How pleasant your friendship is to me, you may yourself judge, if your modesty will allow you to reflect on the abundance of your own excellences" (276). Spinoza makes polite protestations of modesty and expresses reluctance to criticize the work of his illustrious predecessors. Isaacson eliminates these manifestations of civility, producing a more abrupt, no-nonsense Spinoza intent on making his views known.

14. Adler and Van Doren, *How to Read,* 271.

15. The opinions of the intellectual historian Enrique Krauze and the famous amateur of philosophy Jorge Luis Borges are found in their dialogue on Spinoza, "Desayuno *more geometrico,*" *Vuelta* 3, no. 29 (1979): 28–31. Borges argues that despite Spinoza's condemnations of Kabbalah and mysticism in general, his work is pervaded by them. Krauze is less willing to draw conclusions but mentions the interesting hypothesis that Spinoza's pseudo-geometrical writing was Kabbalistically inspired.

16. Nicolas Calas emphasizes the importance of antirational language and treatment of media in his summary and assessment of the avant-garde, *Art in the Age of Risk* (New York: Dutton, 1968).

17. Senkman, *La identidad,* 353, 359.

NOTES FOR CHAPTER 7: MARCOS RICARDO BARNATÁN

1. Marcos Ricardo Barnatán, *El laberinto de Sión* (Barcelona: Barral Editores, 1971). Subsequent citations in the text will give page numbers from this edition.

2. Frank Kermode, *The Genesis of Secrecy: On the Interpretation of Narrative* (Cambridge: Harvard University Press, 1979), emphasizes that wisdom literatures seek both to exclude idle readers and to reveal secrets to more arduous ones. See especially his chapter "Loti's Business: Why Are Narratives Obscure?," 23–47.

3. Harold Bloom, *Kabbalah and Criticism* (New York: Seabury, 1975), 17–18. Subsequent citations in the text will give page numbers from this edition.

4. This is not to say that literary treatments of Kabbalism and related mystical systems are inherently novel but that the innovative aspect of the hero's presentation resides in the literary area. Bloom, ibid., 28, notes the diverse contemporary fiction works that have been deemed Kabbalistic. An especially relevant example of the critical search for Kabbalistic elements in literary work is Saúl Sosnowski, *Borges y la cábala,* to cite only the most detailed treatment of Borges's borrowings from Kabbala; Sosnowski treats a utilization of Kabbalistic elements at least as idiosyncratic and deviant as that found in *Laberinto*. Bloom himself has extended his interpreter's interest in Kabbalah and Gnosticism into the writing of a novel, *The Flight to Lucifer: A Gnostic Fantasy* (New York: Farrar, Straus, Giroux, 1979). See also Marcos Ricardo Barnatán, *La Kábala: Una mística del lenguaje.*

5. Gershom G. Scholem, *Major Trends in Jewish Mysticism* (Jerusalem: Schocken, 1941). Subsequent citations in the text will give page numbers from this edition. This work was chosen for the wide scope of phenomena treated, as well as for its renown. On Kabbalah alone, see idem, *Kabbalah* (New York: New York Times/Quadrangle Books, 1972).

6. Leonardo Senkman, *La identidad judía en la literatura argentina,* 341–44, expresses his negative judgment of *El laberinto de Sión* and, even more severely evaluated, of Barnatán's *Gor* (Barcelona: Barral Editores, 1973). Senkman complains that Barnatán's work "is marred . . . by a certain showmanship, that of a Kabbalist playing at being a prestidigitador, frivolous to the point of camp" (344). He sees Barnatán's exaltation of distinguished Sephardic lineage as an obstacle to a serious comprehension of Jewish identity.

7. Since the hero's interest is not limited to Kabbalism proper but includes many forms of mysticism, some suspicion is raised by not finding among his abundant citations such sources as Evelyn Underhill, *Mysticism, A Study in the Nature and Development of Man's Spiritual Consciousness* (London: Methuen, 1911), a scholarly classic. One likewise wonders why none of Martin Buber's writings are cited. The answer to these and other similar questions seems to be that the hero does not care to know what is mainstream, central to tradition, or widely known to others.

8. A zealous promotion of the tenet that correspondences link all mystical systems is found in Arthur Edward Waite, *The Holy Kabbalah, A Study of the Secret Tradition in Israel* (London: Williams and Norgate, 1929).

9. See, for example, Scholem's dedication of *Major Trends in Jewish Mysticism* to Walter Benjamin.

10. Underhill, *Mysticism,* stresses that great mystics tend to be fully part of major religious traditions, however uneasy they may make the official representatives of those traditions. For an example of a Kabbalistic commentary that properly exalts Halakhic observance, see Adin Steinsaltz, *The Thirteen-Petalled Rose,* trans. Yehuda Hanegbi (New York: Basic Books, 1980).

11. On the goddess cultism that was strenuously weeded out of mainstream Judaism, see Raphael Patai, *The Hebrew Goddess* (New York: Ktav Publishing House, 1967). Patai is like the hero of *Laberinto* in his effort to reclaim as part of Jewish culture this element of worship, generally held to be idolatrous and unhealthy; but unlike the novel's narrator, he takes a scholarly interest in the exact identification of goddess figures. *Laberinto* obscures the issue of which goddesses are being rediscovered, except in occasional instances of clear labeling (for example, Juno). Luna remains a generalized moon goddess, whereas the mythic figures that Max creates from celebrity gossip are even more vaguely identified deities.

12. Harold Bloom, *The Anxiety of Influence* (New York: Oxford, 1973).

13. Charles C. Lehrmann, *Jewish Influences on European Thought,* trans. George Klin and Victor Carpenter (Rutherford/London: Fairleigh Dickinson University Press/Associated University Presses, 1976), 227

14. Kermode, *Genesis of Secrecy.*

NOTES FOR CHAPTER 8: MARIO SZICHMAN

1. Mario Szichman, *Los judíos del Mar Dulce* (Buenos Aires/Caracas: Galerna/Síntesis 2000, 1971), and Alberto Gerchunoff, *Los gauchos judíos* (Santiago de Chile: Ercilla, 1940). Subsequent citations in the text will give page numbers from these editions.

2. Edna Aizenberg's very interesting analysis "Parricide on the Pampa: Deconstructing Gerchunoff and His Jewish Gauchos" applies Harold Bloom's concept of the newly emergent writer's struggle not to be overwhelmed by his predecessors. Following her line of argument, Szichman must naturally oppose Gerchunoff in order to establish the need for his own work's existence. At the same time that Aizenberg views this "parricide" as inevitable, she also supports the widespread belief that Gerchunoff's distortions of history require correction.

3. On centennial-era writings reflecting the official version of European immigration to Argentina, see Gladys Onega, "El Centenario," *La inmigración en la literatura argentina 1880–1910,* 195–220. David Viñas, "Gerchunoff: Gauchos, judíos y xenofobia," *Literatura argentina y realidad política: Apogeo de la oligarquía,* 165–85, notes Gerchunoff's habit of endorsing the behavior of those in power, extending even to a royalist treatment of Spain. Saúl Sosnowski criticizes Gerchunoff's inability to question official policy; see "Contemporary Jewish-Argentine Writers: Tradition and Politics." Juan Carlos Ghiano, "Una lección de Gerchunoff," *Relecturas argentinas: De José Hernández a Alberto Girri* (Buenos Aires: Ediciones Mar de Solís, 1978), 98, compares *Los gauchos judíos* with other centennial works for their shared vision of Argentine social history purged of negative elements, "as if the celebrations had imposed a pious forgetting of the critical situations of the country, aggravated in the last two decades of the previous century and not resolved by the first decade of the new century."

4. Gerchunoff's strategies to present a "perfect," sumptuously lyrical mode of expression reflect a Modernist ideal of literary art, which Szichman rejects as vigorously as he does the official version of Jewish Argentine history.

5. Viñas, "Gerchunoff," 345–50.

6. Eric S. Rabkin, "The Descent of Fantasy," in George E. Slusser, Eric S. Rabkin, and Robert Scholes, eds., *Coordinates: Placing Science Fiction and Fantasy* (Carbondale: Southern Illinois University Press, 1983), 22.

7. Gerchunoff's biblical style is noted by Germán García, "Los judíos," *El inmigrante en la literatura argentina,* 62–64. Viñas, "Gerchunoff," 346–47, remarks on a similarity between Gerchunoff's language and liturgical readings. Ghiano, "Una lección," 95–96, finds Gerchunoff relying on his reading of the Bible not only for style but also for his sense of the meaning of history. Stephen A. Sadow, "*Judíos y gauchos:* The Search for Identity in Jewish-Argentine Literature," finds Gerchunoff casting the gauchos in the role of biblical-era Hebrews.

The traces of rabbinic writings have also drawn attention. Kessel Schwartz notes that Gerchunoff's admiration for Talmud kept him from falling into an assimilationist stance; see "The Jew in Twentieth-Century Argentine Literature." Sadow, "*Judíos,*" 166, remarks on the influence of Talmudic legal commentary and Haggadic lore.

Talmud would especially interest Gerchunoff because of his desire to understand how the Jews maintained their community during the Exile and the work of regathering. André Chouraqui, *A History of Judaism,* trans. Yvette Wiener (New York: Walker and Co., 1962), 70, explains that the "rabbis had succeeded in giving firm cohesion to Judaism in exile by relating its fate among the nations to that of the revealed Word," accounting for the usefulness of the Talmud to dispersed Jewry.

8. Gerchunoff makes tendentious use of Jewish history, but in a sense his procedure is compatible with the tradition of reinterpreting this history to confer meaning on current events. See Elmer Berger's discussion of this polemical tradition, *A Partisan History of Judaism* (New York: Devin-Adair, 1951), 7–53.

9. Sosnowski, "Jewish-Argentine Writers," and Viñas, "Gerchunoff." Note also that Gerchunoff accepts the principle, fundamental to Argentine immigration policy, that Europeans bring civilization to areas afflicted with gaucho nomadism. However, in his idyllic rendering, Jews do not displace gauchos but encourage them to establish settled patterns of life, as illustrated in the scenes between the Jews and the land-owning gaucho Don Estanislao. Gerchunoff appears to be utilizing the concept of the Jews as an exemplary people, whose mandate "obliged Israel to heavier duties," including "in regard to the other nations," as summarized by André Chouraqui and Jean Daniélou, *The Jews: Views and Counterviews: A Dialogue* (New York: Norman Press, 1967), 56.

10. It is worth noting that Judah Halevi's words are here used to dismiss the need for a return to Palestine, whereas the normal understanding is that Halevi, himself a pilgrim to Jerusalem, strongly advocated a return to the biblical homeland.

11. This episode was based on the murder of Gerchunoff's own father. José Chudnovsky's *Pueblo Pan* (Buenos Aires: Losada, 1967), a semidocumentary novel, gives a different account of the Jewish community's response. His version has nothing of the tranquil resignation that pervades Gerchunoff's but speaks of "el padre de Alberto Gerchunoff, también víctima de un bebido feroz que casi extermina a la familia (luego muerto a palos por el vecindario)" (the father of Alberto Gerchunoff, also the victim of a fierce drunk who almost exterminated the family [later beaten to death by those from the area]) (186).

12. The argument that Spanish Christians carried out a divine punishment of the Jews is problematical indeed. It fails to account for the simultaneous expulsion and harassment of peninsular Arabs, who can hardly be seen as having fallen short of specified Jewish standards. Moreover, it is strange to find Jewish urban culture called a mistake or a sin. In accounts of Jewish cultural history, the Berlin Haskalah, Jewish Vienna in its prime, and Jerusalem in its moments of splendor receive special attention. The rabbi's speech, then, testifies to Gerchunoff's fervent desire to find a divine mandate for Jewish rural settlements in Argentina.

13. Charles C. Lehrmann, *Jewish Influences on European Thought* (Rutherford/London: Fairleigh Dickinson University Press/Associated University Presses, 1976), 25–26.

14. Sosnowski, "Jewish-Argentine Writers," 4, accounts for the blatant inaccuracies of the novel by saying that Gerchunoff's "apparent longing to join that [ruling] class, a misdirected sense of gratitude and loyalty to his adopted country prevented him from an accurate reading."

15. Chudnovsky, *Pueblo Pan,* often covers the same subject matter as does *Los gauchos judíos* but without the extreme idealization that characterizes the earlier novel. Although sanguine about the idea of Jewish life in Argentina, *Pueblo Pan* stresses the confusion and frustration of the Jews who, arriving in Argentina, found the settlement program in disorder. The Baron Hirsch, exalted in *Los gauchos judíos,* appears as a well-meaning benefactor lacking contact with the actual operations he funds, whereas those charged with implementing the settlement program are often dishonest, ineffective, or both.

16. The variability of Eva Perón's public image has drawn considerable commentary. Not only was Eva Perón's personal history altered in its official version, but also the woman herself changed aspects of her appearance and behavior to suit various purposes. Further multiplicity arose as stories about Eva Perón were generated by her admirers and enemies. For a recent examination of these issues, see E. P. Taylor, *Eva Perón: The Myths of a Woman* (Chicago: University of Chicago Press, 1977).

17. Nicolas Calas, *Art in the Age of Risk* (New York: Dutton, 1968), 190. Calas makes the point that even Cubism was rejected, by subsequent innovators, for its excessive studiedness and coherence; the remarks apply even more to the ideal of polished prose implicit in *Los gauchos judíos*.

18. Over the six decades between Gerchunoff's and Szichman's novels, there was a period of widespread belief that Jewish Argentine experience could be clarified by realistic repre-

sentation. The move toward documentary realism as a corrective to earlier obfuscations is discussed by Julio Noé, "La poesía," in Rafael Alberto Arrieta, ed., *Historia de la literatura argentina* (Buenos Aires: Peuser, 1959), 4:117–24. It should be noted that Szichman breaks with the realist imperative, in which the novel illuminates the truth of matters for the reader. His own novel refuses to perform the work of untangling history, leaving the reader to attempt the task.

19. Calas, *Age of Risk,* tends to link modern innovation with a widespread conviction that truths are relative.

20. The novel does touch on a related issue: the importance of the element of discourse in historiography. In this respect, Szichman resembles those historiographers who examine chronicles for their "literary" shaping of events. See Hayden V. White, *Metahistory: The Historical Imagination in Nineteenth-Century Europe* (Baltimore: Johns Hopkins University Press, 1973).

NOTES FOR POSTFACE

1. Gerardo Mario Goloboff, *Caballos por el fondo de los ojos* (Barcelona: Seix Barral, 1976). For commentary tracing the concerns key to the novel that are evident in Goloboff's earlier poetry, see Saúl Sosnowski, "Gerardo Mario Goloboff: Hacia el décimo mes en la diáspora."

2. Pedro Orgambide, *Aventuras de Edmund Ziller en tierras del Nuevo Mundo* (Mexico City: Nueva Imagen, 1984; original publication, 1977). For an early response to this novel, see Saúl Sosnowski, "¿Quién es Edmund Ziller?" *Semana de Bellas Artes* (Mexico) 8 (1978): 8–11.

3. David Viñas, *Jauría* (Mexico City: Siglo Veintiuno, 1979).

4. Mario Satz, *Sol* (Barcelona: Noguer, 1975), English translation, *Sol,* trans. Helen R. Lane (Garden City, N.Y.: Doubleday, 1979); *Luna* (Barcelona: Noguer, 1976); *Tierra* (Barcelona: Noguer, 1978); *Marte* (Barcelona: Barral, 1980).

5. Humberto Costantini, *De dioses, hombrecitos y policías* (Mexico City: Nueva Imagen, 1977). This novel had a U.S. success as *The Gods, the Little Guys, and the Police,* trans. Toby Talbot (New York: Harper and Row, 1984).

6. Pedro Orgambide, "Notas sobre un poema de Humberto Costantini," *Hispamérica* 36 (1983): 45–49.

7. Antonio Elio Brailovsky, *Identidad* (Buenos Aires: Sudamericana, 1980).

8. Jacobo Timerman, *Prisoner Without a Name, Cell Without a Number,* trans. Toby Talbot (New York: Knopf, 1981). The original Spanish version appeared in 1982 in Buenos Aires, published by El Cid Campeador with the title *El caso Camps: Punto inicial* on the cover and *Preso sin nombre, celda sin número* on the title page.

9. Mario Szichman, *A las 20.25, la señora entró en la inmortalidad* (Hanover, N.H.: Ediciones del Norte, 1981); *At 8:25, Evita Became Immortal,* trans. Roberto Picciotto (Hanover, N.H.: Ediciones del Norte, 1983).

10. For example, the proceedings of a symposium sponsored by the Asociación Mutual Israelita Argentina and Centro Cultural San Martín were published as Santiago Kovadloff et al., *Pluralismo e identidad: Lo judío en la literatura argentina* (Buenos Aires: Milá, 1986).

11. Gerardo Mario Goloboff, "De una lengua impura," in ibid., 123–27.

12. Leonardo Senkman, Ricardo Feierstein, Isidoro Niborski, and Sara Itzigsohn, eds., *Integración y marginalidad: Historias de vidas de inmigrantes judíos a la Argentina* (Buenos Aires: Pardés, 1985) is a good example of the oral history gathered from the period when new immigrants were most numerous.

13. Marcos Aguinis, *Carta esperanzada a un general: Puente sobre el abismo* (Buenos Aires: Sudamericana/Planeta, 1983). For a good example of Aguinis's public statements made during this period, including his commentary on anti-Semitic reactions to his work as

Minister of Culture, see his interview with Gerardo Yomal, "Priorizamos la lucha contra el autoritarismo," *Nueva Presencia* (Buenos Aires) 29 August 1986, 6.

14. Daniel Kon, *Los chicos de la guerra: Hablan los soldados que estuvieron en la guerra* (Buenos Aires: Galerna, 1983; original edition, 1982).

15. Santiago Kovadloff, *Argentina, oscuro país* (Buenos Aires: Torres Agüero, 1982).

16. Aída Bortnik and Luis Puenzo, *La historia oficial* (Buenos Aires: Ediciones de la Urraca, 1985).

17. Tamara Kamenszain, "Toda escritura es femenina y judía, in Kovadloff et al., *Pluralismo e identidad*, 129–32.

18. Cecilia Absatz, *Los años pares* (Buenos Aires: Sudamericana, 1984).

19. Ricardo Feierstein, *Entre la izquierda y la pared* (Buenos Aires: Pardés, 1983); *El caramelo descompuesto* (Buenos Aires: Nueva Presencia, 1979); and *Escala uno en cincuenta* (Buenos Aires: Pardés, 1984). The 1985 joint publication of this trilogy as *La sinfonía inocente* (Buenos Aires: Pardés) carries a prefatory study by Andrés Avellaneda, "Para leer una trilogía," v-xv, explicating the segmented construction.

20. Edgardo Cozarinsky, *Vudú urbano* (Barcelona: Anagrama, 1985).

SELECTED BIBLIOGRAPHY

These items were selected to provide, most importantly, a guide to works by and commentary on the authors featured in this study; secondarily, an orientation to works on Jewish Argentine literature in general; and lastly, an indication of where to find background on Argentine Jewry.

Preference has been given to items a reader might find using the U.S. library system. Only English- and Spanish-language works appear. An exception was made for the Yiddish translations of Alberto Gerchunoff's work, which are important in tracing his changing relations with specifically Jewish publics.

Coverage of a related area, Jewish subject matter in the works of non-Jewish Argentine authors, has been restricted to a few items particularly able to illustrate this critical problem.

GENERAL BACKGROUND ON ARGENTINE JEWRY

Periodical Sources

(For a full listing of magazines, annuals, and other original documents, see Leonardo Senkman, *La identidad judía en la literatura argentina*, 475–78. Buenos Aires: Pardés, 1983.)

American Jewish Archives Vol. 34, no. 2 (1982). Judith Laikin Elkin, guest ed., *New Perspectives on Latin American Jewry.*
Comentario. Published by Instituto Judío Argentino de Información, 1953–1971.
Davar. Published by Sociedad Hebraica Argentina, Buenos Aires, 1949–1970, 1974–1976.
Judaica. See especially 51–53 (1937), special issue on Latin American Jewry.
Vida Nuestra (Buenos Aires). Nos. 7, 8 (1919), special issues containing cultural analysis of recent anti-Jewish activities.

Books
Avni, Haim. *Argentina y la historia de la inmigración judía. (1810–1950).* Buenos Aires: AMIA/Comunidad Judía de Buenos Aires/Hebrew University of Jerusalem, 1983.
Beller, Jacob. *Jews in Latin America.* New York: Jonathan David, 1969.
Cohen, J. X. *Jewish Life in South America: A Survey Study for the American Jewish Congress.* New York: Bloch, 1941.
Cohen, Martin A., ed. *The Jewish Experience in Latin America: Selected Studies From the Publications of the American Jewish Historical Society.* 2 vols. Waltham, Mass.: American Jewish Historical Society/KTAV, 1971.
Dujovne, Miriam S., Ana Bercz, Abraham Miller, and Jaime Barylko. *Los judíos en la Argentina.* Buenos Aires: Betenu, 1986.
Elazar, Daniel J., with Peter Medding. "Argentina." *Jewish Communities in Frontier Societies: Argentina, Australia, and South Africa,* 61–134. New York: Holmes and Meier, 1983.
Elkin, Judith Laikin. *Jews of the Latin American Republics.* Chapel Hill: University of North Carolina Press, 1980.
———. *Latin American Jewish Studies.* Cincinnati: American Jewish Archives, 1980.

Elkin, Judith Laikin, and Gilbert W. Merkx, eds. *The Jewish Presence in Latin America.* Boston: Allen and Unwin, 1987.

Isaacson, José, et al. *Comunidades judías en Latinoamérica.* See volumes listed under Isaacson, "Social History."

Itzigsohn, José A. *Una experiencia judía contemporánea: Memorias y reflexiones.* Buenos Aires: Paidós, 1969.

Itzigsohn, Sara, et al. *Integración y marginalidad: Historia de vidas de inmigrantes judíos en la Argentina.* Buenos Aires: Pardés, 1985.

Kaufman, Edy, Yoram Shapira, and Joel Barroni. *Israeli-Latin American Relations.* New Brunswick, N.J.: Transaction Books, 1979.

Klein, Alberto. *Cinco siglos de historia argentina: Crónica de la vida judía y su circunstancia.* Buenos Aires: Comité Judío Americano, Oficina Sudamericana, 1976; Buenos Aires: private reprinting by author, 1980.

Kleiner, Alberto. *El partido peronista y el antisemitismo.* 2 vols. Buenos Aires: Libreros y Editores del Polígono SRL, 1985.

———. *Notas y documentos sobre las colonias judías en la Argentina.* Buenos Aires: Libreros y Editores del Polígono SRL, 1985-.

Kleiner, Alberto, ed. *Bibliografía argentina sobre temática judía.* Buenos Aires: Instituto Hebreo de Ciencias, 1985-.

Lewin, Boleslao. *La colectividad judía en la Argentina.* Buenos Aires: Alzamor Editores, 1974.

———. *Cómo fue la inmigración judía a la Argentina.* Buenos Aires: Plus Ultra, 1971.

———. *El judío en la época colonial: Un aspecto de la historia rioplatense.* Buenos Aires: Colegio Libre de Estudios Superiores, 1939.

———. *Los judíos bajo la Inquisición en Hispanoamérica.* Buenos Aires: Editorial Dédalo, 1960.

Lieberman, José. *Tierra soñada: Episodios de la colonización agraria judía en la Argentina (1889-1959).* Buenos Aires: Laserre, 1959.

Liebman, Seymour B. *The Inquisitors and the Jews in the New World.* Coral Gables, Fla.: University of Miami Press, 1974.

Marchevsky, Elías A. *El tejedor de oro: Memorias de un colono judío.* Buenos Aires: Bastión, 1964.

Mendelson, José. *Génesis de la colonia judía en la Argentina, 1889-1912.* Buenos Aires: Libreros y Editores del Polígono, 1982; reissue of 1939 work.

Mirelman, Victor A. *En búsqueda de una identidad; los inmigrantes judíos en Buenos Aires, 1890-1930.* Buenos Aires: Milá, 1988.

Monin, José. *Los judíos en América española, 1492-1810.* Buenos Aires: Biblioteca Yavne, 1939.

Muchnik, Mario. *Mundo judío: Crónica personal.* Barcelona: Lumen, 1984.

Ropp, Tuba Teresa. *Un colono judío en la Argentina.* Buenos Aires: Instituto Científico Judío, IWO, 1971.

Rozitchner, León. *Ser judío.* 2d ed. Buenos Aires: Ediciones de la Flor, 1967.

Sable, Martin H. *Latin American Jewry: A Research Guide.* Cincinnati: Hebrew Union College Press, 1978.

Schallman, Lázaro. *Orígenes de la colonización agrícola judía en la Argentina.* Buenos Aires: Instituto Judío Argentino de Cultura e Información, 1964.

———. *Los pioneros de la colonización judía en la Argentina.* Buenos Aires: Congreso Judío Latinoamericano, 1969.

Schopflocher, Roberto. *Historia de la colonización agrícola en Argentina.* Buenos Aires: Raigal, 1955.

Schvartzman, Pablo. *Judíos en América.* Buenos Aires: Instituto Amigos del Libro Argentino, 1963.

Sebreli, Juan José, ed. *La cuestión judía en la Argentina.* Buenos Aires: Tiempo Contemporáneo, 1968.

Senkman, Leonardo, ed. *Gente y sociedad: La colonización judía.* Buenos Aires: Centro Editor de América Latina, 1984.

Senkman, Leonardo, and Eliahu Daniel. *La condición judeo argentina en los años sesenta.* Buenos Aires: Ediciones J. N. Bialik, 1984.

Shijman, Osías. *Colonización judía en la Argentina.* Buenos Aires: Private ed., 1980.

Sofer, Eugene. *From Pale to Pampa: The Jewish Immigrant Experience in Buenos Aires.* New York: Holmes and Meier, 1982.

Szapu, Julio. *El camino de un inmigrante.* Buenos Aires: GEL, 1985.

Timerman, Jacobo. *Prisoner Without a Name, Cell Without a Number.* Trans. Tony Talbot. New York: Knopf (distributor Random House), 1981; Vintage paperback, 1982. Spanish original, *Preso sin nombre, celda sin número* [cover title: *El caso Camps, punto inicial*]. Barcelona: El Cid, 1981.

Weisbrot, Robert. *The Jews of Argentina: From the Inquisition to Perón.* Philadelphia: Jewish Publication Society of America, 1979.

Winsberg, Morton. *Colonia Baron Hirsch: A Jewish Agricultural Colony in Argentina.* Gainesville: University Press of Florida, 1964.

Wolff, Martha, and Myrtha Schalom, eds. *Judíos y argentinos: judíos argentinos.* Buenos Aires: Manrique Zago, 1988.

Yagupsky, Máximo, and Mario Diament. *Conversación con un judío.* Buenos Aires: Jacobo Timerman, 1977.

Zago, Manrique, ed. *Pioneros de la Argentina, los inmigrantes judíos* [*Pioneers in Argentina, the Jewish Immigrants*]. Buenos Aires: Manrique Zago, 1982.

Articles and Entries in Books

Avni, Haim. "Argentine Jewry: Its Socio-Political Status and Organizational Patterns." *Dispersion and Unity* 12 (1971): 128–62; 13/14 (1971–1972): 161–208; 15 (1972–1973): 158–215.

Elkin, Judith Laikin. "Goodnight, Sweet Gaucho: A Revisionist View of the Jewish Argicultural Experiment in Argentina." *American Jewish Historical Quarterly* 67 (1978): 208–23.

Horowitz, Irving Louis. "The Jewish Community of Buenos Aires." *Jewish Social Studies* 24 (1962): 195–222.

———. "Jewish Ethnicism and Latin American Nationalism." *Midstream* 18 (1972): 22–28. Also published as "Jewish Ethnicity and Latin American Nationalism," *Israeli Ecstasies/Jewish Agonies,* 121–32. New York: Oxford University Press, 1974.

———. "Organization and Ideology of the Jewish Community of Buenos Aires." *Israeli Ecstasies/Jewish Agonies,* 133–67.

Kitron, Moshe. "Latin American Jewry in Our Time." *In the Dispersion* 4 (Winter 1964–1965): 53–78.

Lerner, Natan. "A Note on Argentine Jewry Today." *Jewish Journal of Sociology* 6 (July 1964): 75–80.

Liebman, Seymour B. "Argentine Jews and their Institutions." *Jewish Social Studies* 43 (1981): 311–38.

Mirelman, Victor A. "Jewish Life in Buenos Aires Before the East European Immigration (1860–1890)." *American Jewish Historical Quarterly* 67 (March 1978): 195–207.

Rosenswaike, Ira. "The Jewish Population of Argentina." *Jewish Social Studies* 22 (1960): 195–214.

Senkman, Leonardo. "Between Revolution and Reaction." *Jewish Frontier* (March 1981): 10–13.

GENERAL BACKGROUND ON JEWISH-ARGENTINE LITERATURE

Periodical Sources
Folio (SUNY-Brockport). Vol. 17 (1987), special issue. Judith Morganroth Schneider, guest ed., *Latin American Jewish Writers*.
Noaj [formerly *Noah*]. 1987–. Leonardo Senkman, ed. Journal of the Asociación Internacional de Escritores Judíos en Lengua Hispana y Portuguesa. Jerusalem.

Books
Aguinis, Marcos. *El valor de escribir*. Buenos Aires: N.p., 1985.
Aizenberg, Edna. *The Aleph Weaver: Biblical, Kabbalistic, and Judaic Elements in Borges*. Potomac, Md.: Scripta Humanistica, 1985. (Also published as *El tejedor del aleph: Biblia, Kabala y judaísmo en Borges*. Madrid: Altalena, 1986.)
AMIA (Asociación Mutual Israelita Argentina)/Comunidad Judía de Buenos Aires. *Pluralismo e identidad: Lo judío en la literatura latinoamericana*. Buenos Aires: Milá, 1986.
Gardiol, Rita M. *Argentina's Jewish Short Story Writers*. Muncie, Ind.: Ball State University Monographs No. 32, 1986.
Kleiner, Alberto. *La temática judía en el teatro argentino*. Buenos Aires: Polígono, 1983.
Senkman, Leonardo. *La identidad judía en la literatura argentina*. Buenos Aires: Pardés, 1983.
Sosnowski, Saúl. *Borges y la cábala*. Buenos Aires: Hispamérica, 1976; Buenos Aires: Pardés, 1986.
————. *La orilla inminente: Escritores judíos argentinos*. Buenos Aires: Legasa, 1987.

Dissertations
Glickman, Nora. "The Image of the Jew in Brazilian and Argentinian Literature." Ph.D. diss., New York University, 1977.
Goodman, Robert. "The Image of the Jew in Argentine Literature as Seen by Jewish Writers." Ph.D. diss., New York University, 1972.

Articles and Entries in Books
Aizenberg, Edna. "Sephardim and Neo-Sephardim in Latin American Literature." *Sephardic Scholar Series* 4 (1979–1982): 125–32.
Borges, Jorge Luis. "El estilo de su fama." Introductory essay to *Mester de judería*, by Carlos M. Grünberg. Buenos Aires: Editorial Argirópolis, 1940.
García, Germán. "Los judíos." "El chauvinismo racista." *El inmigrante en la literatura argentina*, 62–64, 93–99. Buenos Aires: Hachette, 1970.
Gardiol, Rita. "Jewish Writers: An Emerging Force in Contemporary Argentina." *Hispanófila* 91 (1987): 65–76.
Horn, José. "Los nuevos escritores judíos de la Argentina." *Judaica* (Buenos Aires) 70 (1939): 123–29.
Lindstrom, Naomi. "Problems and Possibilities in the Analysis of Jewish Argentine Literary Works." *Latin American Literary Review* 18, no. 1 (1983): 118–26.
Lipp, Solomon. "Israel and the Holocaust in Contemporary Spanish-American Poetry." *Hispania* 64 (1982): 536–43.
Minc, Rose S. "*El mal metafísico*: Hacia una revalorización." *Hispamérica* 34–35 (1983): 139–44.
Nesbit, Lewis. "The Jewish Contribution to Argentine Literature." *Hispania* 33 (1950): 313–20.
Noé, Julio. "La poesía." In *Historia de la literatura argentina*, ed. Rafael Alberto Arrieta, 4:122–24. Buenos Aires: Peuser, 1959.

Onega, Gladys S. "Martel. *La Bolsa*. El judío." "Lugones: La tetralogía del Centenario." *La inmigración en la literatura argentina 1880–1910*, 63–72. Santa Fe: Universidad Nacional del Litoral, 1965.

Orgambide, Pedro. "¿Existe el escritor judeoargentino?" *Nueva Presencia* (Buenos Aires) 441 (13 de diciembre de 1985): 1–2.

———. "Notas sobre un poema de Humberto Costantini." *Hispamérica* 36 (1983): 45–54.

Pineta, Alberto. *Verde memoria: Tres décadas de literatura y periodismo en una autobiografía, los grupos de Boedo y Florida*, 95–103, 164–76. Buenos Aires: Antonio Zamora, 1962.

Sadow, Stephen A. "*Judíos y gauchos:* The Search for Identity in Argentine-Jewish Literature." *American Jewish Archives* 34, no. 2 (1982): 164–76.

Schwartz, Kessel. "Antisemitism in Modern Argentine Fiction." *Jewish Social Studies* 40 (1978): 131–40.

———. "The Jew in Twentieth-Century Argentine Literature." *American Hispanist* 3, no. 19 (1977): 9–12.

Senkman, Leonardo. "La cábala y el poder de la palabra." *Nuevos Aires* (Buenos Aires) 9 (1972–1973): 39–48.

Sosnowski, Saúl. "Contemporary Jewish-Argentine Writers: Tradition and Politics." *Latin American Literary Review* 6, no. 12 (1978): 1–14.

———. "Gerardo Mario Goloboff: Hacia el décimo mes en la diáspora." *Escritura* (Caracas) 4 (1977): 255–82.

———. "Germán Rozenmacher: Tradiciones, rupturas y desencuentros." *Revista de Crítica Literaria Latinoamericana* (Lima) 3, no. 6 (1977): 93–110.

———. "Ill-at-Ease Outsider." *Forum* (Jerusalem), no. 44 (1980?): 113–18.

———. "Latin American Jewish Authors: A Bridge Toward History." *Prooftexts* 4 (1984): 71–92.

———. "Latin American Jewish Writers: Protecting the Hyphen." In Judith Laikin Elkin and Gilbert W. Merkx, eds., *The Jewish Presence in Latin America* (Boston: Allen and Unwin, 1987).

Tirri, Néstor. *Realismo y teatro argentino*, 117–21. Buenos Aires: Ediciones La Bastilla, 1971.

Winter, Calvert J. "Some Jewish Writers of the Argentine." *Hispania* 19 (1936): 431–36.

AUTHOR BIBLIOGRAPHIES

BARNATÁN, MARCOS RICARDO (1946–)

Imaginative Writing
Ante mí: Poesía del hombre mutable. Buenos Aires: Nuevo Hombre, 1964.
Arcana mayor, 1970–1972. Ill. Peter G. Cohen. Madrid: A. Corazón, 1973.
Diano. Barcelona: Barral Editores, 1982.
Gor. Barcelona: Barral Editores, 1973.
El laberinto de Sión. Barcelona: Barral Editores, 1971; Madrid: Ediciones Anjana, 1986.
El libro del talismán. Madrid: Azur, 1970.
El oráculo invocado: Poesía, 1965–1983. Madrid: Visor, 1984.
Los pasos perdidos. Madrid: Ediciones Rialp, 1968.
Tres poemas fantásticos. Málaga: Librería Anticuaria El Guadalhorce, 1967.

Editions
Antología de la "Beat Generation." Barcelona: Plaza y Janés, 1970.
Narraciones/Jorge Luis Borges. Madrid: Cátedra, 1980.

Criticism and Essay
Borges. Madrid: EPESA, 1972.
Conocer Borges y su obra. Barcelona: Júcar, 1972.
Jorge Luis Borges. Madrid: Júcar, 1972.
La Kábala: Una mística del lenguaje. Barcelona: Barral Editores, 1974.
Las metáforas de Eduardo Sanz. Madrid: Rayuela, 1976.

GERCHUNOFF, ALBERTO (1884–1950)

Bibliographies
Blondet, Olga. "Bibliografía." In Sara Jaroslawsky de Lowy, *Alberto Gerchunoff: Vida y obra: Bibliografía: Antología,* 60–62. New York: Columbia University/Hispanic Institute in the United States, 1957.
Gover de Nasatsky, Miryam Esther. *Bibliografía de Alberto Gerchunoff.* Buenos Aires: Fondo Nacional de las Artes/Sociedad Hebraica Argentina, 1976.

Imaginative Writing
La clínica del Dr. Mefistófeles: Moderna milagrería en diez jornadas. Santiago de Chile: Ercilla, 1937.
Cuentos de ayer. Buenos Aires: Ediciones América, 1919.
Los gauchos judíos. La Plata, Argentina: J. Sesé, 1910; Buenos Aires: Manuel Gleizer, 1936; Santiago de Chile: Ercilla, 1940; Buenos Aires: Sudamericana, 1950, 1957; Buenos Aires: Editorial Universitaria de Buenos Aires, 1964; Buenos Aires: Fraterna, 1983. *The Jewish Gauchos of the Pampas.* Trans. Prudencio de Pereda. New York: Abelard-Shuman, 1955. *Idn gauchn.* Trans. P. Katz. Buenos Aires: Ikuf, 1952.
Historia y proezas de amor. Buenos Aires: Manuel Gleizer, 1926.
El hombre importante. Montevideo/Buenos Aires: Sociedad Amigos del Libro Rioplatense, 1934.

Criticism and Essays
Los amores de Baruj Spinoza. Buenos Aires: BABEL [Biblioteca Argentina de Buenas Ediciones Literarias], 1932. *Baruj Spinoes libe.* Trans. José Mendelsohn. Buenos Aires: Sociedad Hebraica Argentina, 1933.
Argentina, país del advenimiento. Buenos Aires: Losada, 1952.
La asamblea de la bohardilla. Buenos Aires: Manuel Gleizer, 1925.
Buenos Aires, la metrópoli de mañana. Buenos Aires: Secretaría de Cultura y Acción Social, 1960.
Entre Ríos, mi país. Buenos Aires: Futuro, 1950.
Heine, poeta de nuestra intimidad. Buenos Aires: BABEL, 1927.
El hombre que habló en la Sorbona. Buenos Aires: Manuel Gleizer, 1926.
La jofaina maravillosa: Agenda cervantina. Buenos Aires: BABEL, 1922, 1923; Manuel Gleizer, 1927; Losada, 1938, 1945, 1953.
El nuevo régimen. Buenos Aires: Otero y García, 1918.
Pequeñas prosas. Buenos Aires: Manuel Gleizer, 1926.
El pino y la palmera. Ed. Manuel Kantor. Buenos Aires: Sociedad Hebraica Argentina, 1952.
Retorno a Don Quixote. Buenos Aires: Sudamericana, 1951.

Criticism on Gerchunoff
Books
Jaroslawsky de Lowy, Sara. *Alberto Gerchunoff: Vida y obra: Bibliografía: Antología.* New York: Columbia University/Hispanic Institute in the United States, 1957.

Liacho, Lázaro [Jacobo Simón Liachovitsky]. *Alberto Gerchunoff.* Buenos Aires: Colombo, 1975.

Articles and Entries in Books

Agosti, Héctor P. "*Los gauchos judíos.*" *Cantar opinando,* 54–56. Buenos Aires: Boedo, 1982.

Aizenberg, Edna. "Parricide on the Pampa: Deconstructing Gerchunoff and His Jewish Gauchos." *Folio* 17 (1987): 24–39.

Alegría, Fernando. "Alberto Gerchunoff." *Breve historia de la novela hispanoamericana,* 200–201. Mexico: De Andrea, 1959.

Ayala Gauna, Velmira. "Alberto Gerchunoff y su mensaje." *Cuadernos de la Diligencia* (Rosario, Argentina) 2, no. 4 (1961): 14–23.

Barchilón, José. "Alberto Gerchunoff." *Gerchunoff/Bufano,* 13–42. San Juan, Argentina: Editorial Sanjuanina, 1973.

Borges, Jorge Luis. "Prólogo" to *Retorno a Don Quixote,* by Gerchunoff, 7–11. Buenos Aires: Sudamericana, 1951.

Cúneo, Dardo. "Alberto Gerchunoff." *El romanticismo político,* 119–24. Buenos Aires: Transición, 1955.

Dujovne, León. "Una aproximación a su intimidad." *Davar* 31–33 (1951): 26–45.

———. "Introduction" to *The Jewish Gauchos of the Pampas,* by Gerchunoff, trans. Prudencio de Pereda, iii–xiv. New York: Abelard-Shuman, 1955.

Eichelbaum, Samuel. "Su memoria es nuestra herencia." *Davar* 31–33 (1951): 107–13.

Espinoza, Enrique. "Alberto Gerchunoff y *Los gauchos judíos.*" *Davar* 31–33 (1951): 61–70.

García, Germán. *La novela argentina, un itinerario,* 169–98. Buenos Aires: Sudamericana, 1952.

Giusti, Roberto F. "Alberto Gerchunoff." In *Historia de la literatura argentina,* ed. Rafael Alberto Arrieta, 5:502–4. Buenos Aires: Peuser, 1959.

———. "El espíritu y la obra de Alberto Gerchunoff." *Poetas de América y otros ensayos,* 139–49. Buenos Aires: Losada, 1956.

———. "Veinte años de vida: Recuerdos y divagaciones." *Nosotros* (Buenos Aires) 219–20 (1927): 5–51. Available in Kraus Reprints.

Glickman, Nora. "Biografía como auto-reflexión." *Folio* 17 (1987): 23–41.

Goldberg, Isaac. "Escritores judíos en Sud América: Alberto Gerchunoff y Samuel Glusberg [Enrique Espinoza]." *Nosotros* 208 (1926): 136–38.

Herrera, Francisco. "Alberto Gerchunoff." In *Enciclopedia de la literatura argentina,* ed. Pedro Orgambide and Roberto Yahni, 269–70. Buenos Aires: Sudamericana, 1970.

Jaffe, Jean. "The World of Gerchunoff." *Congress Weekly* (New York) 22, no. 12 (1955): 9–11.

Kantor, Manuel. "Alberto Gerchunoff, hombre y escritor." In *Idn gauchn,* by Gerchunoff, trans. P. Katz, 9–69. Buenos Aires: Ikuf, 1952.

———. "Vida y anecdotario de Alberto Gerchunoff." In *El hombre importante,* by Gerchunoff, 137–69. Buenos Aires: Hachette, 1960.

Karduner, Luis. "Misión del escritor judío en la literatura argentina." *Judaica* (Buenos Aires) 16 (1934): 145–49.

Koremblit, Bernardo Ezequiel. "Gerchunoff o el vellocinio de la literatura." *Davar* 100 (1964): 242–47.

Lerner, Isaías. "La obra literaria de Alberto Gerchunoff." *Davar* 63 (1956): 59–66.

Liacho, Lázaro. "Gerchunoff judío." *Davar* 31–33 (1951): 71–95.

———. "Misión del escritor judío en la literatura." *Columna* (Buenos Aires) 2 (1937): 49–56.

Meeroff, Marcos. "El futuro del pueblo judío." *Judaica* (Buenos Aires) 13 (1953): 99–122.

Onega, Gladys S. "Lugones: La tetralogía del Centenario." *La inmigración en la literatura argentina, 1880–1910,* 124–25. Santa Fe: Universidad Nacional del Litoral, 1965.

Pagés Larraya, Antonio. *Perduración romántica de las letras argentinas,* 28–29. Mexico:

Universidad Nacional Autónoma de Mexico, 1963.

Piccirilli, Ricardo-Romay, and Leoncio Francisco L.-Gianello. *Diccionario histórico argentino,* 3:109. Buenos Aires: Ediciones Históricas Argentinas, 1954.

Pineta, Alberto. *Tres décadas de literatura y periodismo en una autobiografía: Los grupos de Boedo y Florida,* 201–5. Buenos Aires: Antonio Zamora, 1962.

Pinto, Juan. "Alberto Gerchunoff." *Panorama de la literatura argentina contemporánea,* 169–73. Buenos Aires: Editorial Mundi, 1941.

———. *Pasión y suma de la expresión argentina: Literatura, cultura, región,* 331–32. Buenos Aires: Editorial Huemul, 1970.

Resnick, Rosa Perla. "La obra literaria de Alberto Gerchunoff." *Judaica* (Buenos Aires) 139 (1945): 12–26.

Salvador, Nélida. "José Isaacson." *La nueva poesía argentina (estudio y antología),* 153. Buenos Aires: Columba, 1968.

Sosnowski, Saúl. "Contemporary Jewish-Argentine Writers: Tradition and Politics." *Latin American Literary Review* 6, no. 12 (1978): 1–4.

Soto, Luis Emilio. "Alberto Gerchunoff." *Diccionario de la literatura latinoamericana: Argentina, primera parte,* 59–63. Washington, D.C.: Pan American Union, 1960.

———. "El cuento." In *Historia de la literatura argentina,* ed. Rafael Alberto Arrieta, 4:343–49. Buenos Aires: Peuser, 1959.

Viñas, David. "Gerchunoff: Gauchos, judíos y xenofobia." *Literatura argentina y realidad política: Apogeo de la oligarquía,* 165–85. Buenos Aires: Siglo XX, 1975. An earlier version constitutes chapter 4 of his *Literatura argentina y realidad política.* Buenos Aires: Jorge Alvarez, 1964.

Weinfeld, Eduardo. "Alberto Gerchunoff." *Enciclopedia Judaica Castellana,* 5:60–62. Mexico: Encyclopedia Judaica, 1949.

Special Issue of Journal

Davar (Buenos Aires). Vols. 31–33 (1951). Special issue presenting Gerchunoff commentary by Jorge Luis Borges et al.

ISAACSON, JOSÉ (1922–)

Imaginative Writing

Amor y amar. Preface by Carlos Mastronardi. Buenos Aires: Américalee, 1960, 1963, 1968, rev. expanded ed., 1972.

Las canciones de Ele-í. Buenos Aires: Lautaro, 1952.

Cuaderno Spinoza. Buenos Aires: Marymar, 1977.

Elogio de la poesía. Buenos Aires: Hachette, 1963.

El metal y la voz. Buenos Aires: Américalee, 1956.

Oda a Buenos Aires. Buenos Aires: Américalee, 1966.

Oda a la alegría. Buenos Aires: Hachette, 1965.

El pasajero. Buenos Aires: Américalee, 1969.

Literary Criticism and Editions

Antropología literaria, una estética de la persona. Buenos Aires: Marymar, 1982.

(Ed., with Enrique Urquía.) *Cuarenta años de poesía argentina: 1920–1960.* 3 vols. Buenos Aires: Albada, 1962–1964.

Introducción a los diarios de Kafka, la escritura como dialéctica de los límites. Buenos Aires: Marymar, 1977.

Kafka: La imposibilidad como proyecto. Buenos Aires: Plus Ultra, 1974.

Macedonio Fernández, sus ideas políticas y estéticas. Buenos Aires: Belgrano, 1981.

(Ed.) *Martín Fierro centenario; testimonios.* Buenos Aires: Ministerio de Cultura y Educación, Subsecretaría de Cultura, 1972.

(Ed.) *Poesía de la Argentina, de Tejeda a Lugones*. Buenos Aires: Editorial Universitaria de Buenos Aires, 1965.
El poeta en la sociedad de masas; elementos para una antropología literaria. Buenos Aires: Américalee, 1969.

Social History
(Ed., with Abraham Monk.) *Comunidades judías de Latinoamérica*. 2d ed. Buenos Aires: Candelabro, 1968.
(Ed.) *Comunidades judías de Latinoamérica*. 3d ed. Buenos Aires: Oficina Latinoamericana del Comité Judío Americano, 1969.
(Ed., with Santiago E. Kovadloff.) *Comunidades judías de Latinoamérica*. 4th ed. Buenos Aires: Candelabro, 1970.
(Ed.) *Comunidades judías de Latinoamérica*. 5th ed. Buenos Aires: Candelabro, 1971–1972.
(Ed.) *El populismo en la Argentina*. Buenos Aires: Plus Ultra, 1974.

Criticism on Isaacson
Articles and Entries in Books
Ara, Guillermo. *Suma de la poesía argentina, 1538–1968. Parte I: Crítica*, 164–65. Buenos Aires: Guadalupe, 1970.
Bernárdez, Francisco Luis. Lecture on Isaacson's work reproduced in part across covers of latter's *Amor y amar*. Buenos Aires: Américalee, 1968.
Canal-Feijóo, Bernardo. "*Spinoza*." *Vigencia* (Buenos Aires) 7 (1977).
Fundación Argentina para la Poesía. *Poesía argentina contemporánea*, 1.3:1021–29. Buenos Aires: Fundación Argentina para la Poesía, 1982.
Guardia, Alfredo de la. "Certidumbre de la poesía." Forward to *El pasajero*, by Isaacson. Buenos Aires: Américalee, 1969.
Martini Real, Juan Carlos. "José Isaacson." *Los mejores poemas de la poesía argentina*, 302. 3d ed. Buenos Aires: Corregidor, 1977.
Mastronardi, Carlos. "Isaacson y la esperanza." *Comentario* (Buenos Aires) 25 (1960): 25–32.
Pinto, Juan. *Pasión y suma de la literatura argentina*, 71, 305. Buenos Aires: Editorial Huemul, 1971.

RABINOVICH, JOSÉ (1903–1978)

Imaginative Writing
Note: The early works of José Rabinovich are not readily available. Between his birth in Bialystok in 1903 and his emigration to Argentina in 1924, he began a Yiddish-language poetic career whose products have been, essentially, lost. In 1928 he published in Buenos Aires a novel entitled *Entre el agua y el fuego*, also listed as *Entre el fuego y el agua*. *Konventisches [Conventillo]* was published privately in Buenos Aires; it is described as a forty-eight-page collection of poems in Yiddish dealing with slum life. In the 1940s, Rabinovich was discovered by the social-realist leader Elías Castelnuovo, who promoted the publication of and wrote enthusiastic prologues to two collections of short stories, *Cabizbajos* (1943) and *Tercera clase* (1944). Currently, the only ready access to these early stories is through the reissue of *Tercera clase* in 1969 by Editorial Linosa of Barcelona, including also Ricardo Baeza's prologue to Rabinovich's 1947 *Los acusados* (Buenos Aires: Editorial Israel; translated from the Yiddish by Adela Shliapochnik). Subsequent to the 1952 novel *Pan duro*, Rabinovich's work was published in relatively accessible editions.

Los acusados. Trans. Adela Shliapochnik. Buenos Aires: Editorial Israel, 1947; Buenos Aires: Biblioteca Humanitas, 1974.
Alas desplumadas. Buenos Aires: El Hombre, 1972.

El arquero de estrellas. Buenos Aires: El Hombre, 1972.
Cabizbajos; cuentos. Preface by Elías Castelnuovo. Trans. Rebeca Mactas de Polak. Buenos
    Aires: n.p., 1943.
Campanas a media asta. Buenos Aires: Fabril, 1969; Buenos Aires: Candelabro, 1976.
Una cana negra. Buenos Aires: El Hombre, 1972.
Canción con cuna. Buenos Aires: El Hombre, 1972.
Cazador de luciérnagas. Buenos Aires: El Hombre, 1972.
Cena para un ayuno. Buenos Aires: El Hombre, 1972.
Con pecado concebida. Buenos Aires: Ediciones Dintel / Argentores / Carro de Tespis, 1975.
Cuentos de pico y pala. Buenos Aires / La Plata: Platense, 1971.
Dios mediante. Buenos Aires: Editorial Autores Argentinos Asociados / Nuevas Ediciones
    Argentinas, 1976.
El gran castigo: Obra en tres actos y un prólogo. Buenos Aires: Ediciones Crisol, 1976.
Hombre escatimado. Buenos Aires: Ediciones Dead Weight, 1969.
Luz de eclipse. Buenos Aires: El Hombre, 1972.
Misa de un play boy. Buenos Aires: El Hombre, 1972.
Los muertos no quieren creerlo. La Plata: Platense, 1969.
Pan duro. Trans. Adela Shliapochnik. Buenos Aires: Siglo Veinte, 1952.
El perro de Maidanek. La Plata: Platense, 1968.
Rapsodia judía. Buenos Aires: Candelabro, 1969.
Rapsodia negra. Barcelona: Editorial Lagis, 1971.
Rapsodia rusa. Barcelona: Editorial Lagis, 1971.
Tercera clase, novela. Preface by Elías Castelnuovo. Trans. Rebeca Mactas de Polak. Buenos
    Aires: Sophos, 1944; Barcelona: Editorial Linosa, 1969.
Trinos y truenos. Buenos Aires: El Hombre, 1972.
El violinista bajo el tejado. La Plata: Platense, 1970.
Yo soy Cristo. Buenos Aires: El Hombre, 1972.
Yo soy Judas. Barcelona: Linosa, 1971.

Autobiography
Sobras de una juventud. Preface by Ulises Petit de Murat. Buenos Aires: Crisol, 1976. Preface
    Enrique de Gandia. Buenos Aires: Crisol, 1977.

Criticism on Rabinovich
Books
Dejemos que hablen los críticos. Buenos Aires: Artes Gráficas Cañuelas (printer), 1972. No
    publisher or editor cited.
Articles and Entries in Books
Baeza, Ricardo. "Prólogo" to *Tercera clase,* by Rabinovich, 2–11. Barcelona: Editorial
    Linosa, 1969. Reprinted from Rabinovich, *Los acusados.* Buenos Aires: Editorial Israel,
    1947.
Canzani, Ariel. "Prólogo" to *Hombre escatimado,* by Rabinovich, 3–6. Buenos Aires: Dead
    Weight, 1969.
Gandia, Enrique de. "Prólogo" to *Sobras de una juventud,* by Rabinovich, 5–11. 2d ed.
    Buenos Aires: Crisol, 1977.
Liacho, Lázaro [Jacobo Simón Liachovitsky]. "Apuntes sobre la vida y la obra de José
    Rabinovich." In *Campanas a media asta,* by Rabinovich, i–v. Buenos Aires: Candelabro,
    1976.
Petit de Murat, Ulises. "José Rabinovich, sobreviviente." In *Sobras de una juventud,* by
    Rabinovich, 3–7. Buenos Aires: Crisol, 1976.

Soto, Luis Emilio. "José Rabinovich." In *Historia de la literatura argentina,* ed. Rafael Alberto Arrieta, 4:358–59. Buenos Aires: Peuser, 1959.
Tiempo, César [Israel Zeitlin]. "A manera de un prólogo: Un diálogo con José Rabinovich." In *El perro de Maidanek,* by Rabinovich, 4–21. La Plata: Platense, 1968.

SZICHMAN, MARIO (1945–)

Imaginative Writing
A las 20.25, la señora entró en la inmortalidad. Hanover, N.J.: Ediciones del Norte, 1981.
At 8:25, Evita Became Immortal. Trans. Roberto Picchiotto. Hanover, N.J.: Ediciones del Norte, 1983.
La crónica falsa. Buenos Aires: Editorial Jorge Alvarez, 1969.
Los judíos del Mar Dulce. Buenos Aires / Caracas: Galerna / Síntesis 2000, 1971.
Uslar: Cultura y dependencia. Caracas: Vadell Hermanos, 1975.
La verdadera crónica falsa. Buenos Aires: Centro Editor de América Latina, 1972.

Essay
Miguel Otero Silva, mitología de una generación frustrada. Caracas: Ediciones de la Biblioteca, Universidad Central de Venezuela, 1975.

Criticism on Szichman
Aizenberg, Edna. "Parricide on the Pampa: Deconstructing Gerchunoff and His Jewish Gauchos." *Folio* 17 (1987): 24–39.

TIEMPO, CÉSAR [ISRAEL ZEITLIN] (1906–1980)

Bibliography
Irizarry, Estelle. "Bibliografía." In *Versos de una . . . ,* by Tiempo, 87–89. Buenos Aires: Editorial Rescate, 1977.

Imaginative Writing
Alfarda, drama. Buenos Aires: Columba, 1935.
Así quería Gardel, novela. Buenos Aires: Bell, 1955.
El becerro de oro. Buenos Aires: Paidós, 1973.
Capturas recomendadas. Buenos Aires: Ediciones Especiales de Ediciones de Librería del Jurista, n.d.
(With Arturo Cerretani.) *La dama de las comedias.* Buenos Aires: Ediciones Dintel / Argentores / Carro de Tespis, 1971.
Libro para la pausa del sábado. Buenos Aires: Manuel Gleizer, 1930.
El lustrador de manzanas, comedia. Buenos Aires: Ediciones Dintel / Argentores / Carro de Tespis, 1958.
Manos de obra. Buenos Aires: Corregidor, 1980.
Máscaras y caras. Buenos Aires: Arrayán, 1943.
Pan criollo: Comedia gravemente cómica o lo que a Vd. le parezca, en cuatro estampas y dos desenlaces. Buenos Aires: Porter, 1938; Buenos Aires: Ediciones Dintel / Argentores / Carro de Tespis, 1968.
Poesía completa. Buenos Aires: Stilman Editores, 1979.
Quiero vivir; drama increíble en tiempo de fuga: Un prólogo, cuatro actos y un epílogo superpuesto. Buenos Aires: Porter, 1941.
Sabadomingo. Buenos Aires: Porter, 1938; rev. ed., Buenos Aires: Centro Editor de América Latina, 1966.

Sábado pleno: Libro para la pausa del sábado. Sabatión argentino. Sábadomingo. Nuevas devociones. Buenos Aires: Manuel Gleizer, 1955.

Sabatión argentino: Antiguas y nuevas dones para la pausa del sábado. Buenos Aires / Montevideo: Sociedad Amigos del Libro Rioplatense, 1933. Incorporates material from the 1930 *Libro para la pausa del sábado.*

El teatro soy yo; farsa romántica en tres actos. Buenos Aires: Anaconda, 1933.

El último romance de Gardel, novela. Buenos Aires: Editorial Quetzal, 1975.

Versos de una . . . [published as a hoax under the name Clara Béter]. Buenos Aires: Claridad, [1926]. Republished with commentary and notes by Estelle Irizarry. Buenos Aires: Editorial Rescate, 1977.

Criticism, Essay, and Journalism

La campaña antisemita y el director de la Biblioteca Nacional. Buenos Aires: "Mundo Israelita," 1935.

Clara Béter y otras fatamorganas. Buenos Aires: A. Peña Lillo, 1974.

Evocación de Quiroga. Montevideo: Biblioteca Nacional, 1970.

(Ed., with Pedro-Juan Vignale.) *Exposición de la actual poesía argentina (1922–1927).* Buenos Aires: Minerva, 1927.

Florencia Parravicini. Buenos Aires: Centro Editor de América Latina, 1971.

Máscaras y caras. Buenos Aires: Arrayán, 1943.

Moravia, Vivian Wilde, y Compañía; retratos intempestivos. Buenos Aires: Argos, 1953.

Protagonistas. Buenos Aires: Editorial Kraft, 1954.

Sábado y poesía. Rosario, Argentina: Escuela Normal No. 2 de Rosario, 1935.

La vida romántica de Berta Singermann. Buenos Aires: Sopena Argentina, 1941.

Yo hablé con Toscanini. Buenos Aires: Anaconda, 1941.

Criticism on Tiempo
Articles and Entries in Books

Barcia, José. "Prólogo" to *Clara Béter y otras fatamorganas,* by Tiempo, 7–9. Buenos Aires: A. Peña Lillo, 1974.

Berenguer Carisomo, Arturo. *Literatura argentina,* 51. Barcelona: Editorial Labor, 1977.

Cansinos Assens, Rafael. "Limen." *Sabatión argentino: Antiguas y nuevas donas para la pausa del sábado,* by Tiempo, 9–16. Buenos Aires / Montevideo: Sociedad Amigos del Libro Rioplatense, 1933.

González y Contreras, Gilberto. "Un ensayo sobre el autor de 'sábado pleno.'" In *Sábado pleno,* by Tiempo, 211–12.

Irizarry, Estelle. "El argentino César Tiempo y sus *Versos de una . . . .*" In *Versos de una . . . ,* by Tiempo, 47–86. Buenos Aires: Editorial Rescate, 1977.

Isaacson, José, and Carlos Enrique Urquía. "César Tiempo." *40 años de poesía argentina, 1920/1960,* 1:291. Buenos Aires: Aldaba, 1962.

Lindstrom, Naomi. "Proletarian / Avant-Garde / Jewish / Christian Balances in Two Poems by César Tiempo." *Hispanic Journal* 4, no. 2 (1983): 85–98.

———. "*Sabatión argentino:* Poetry of Jewish Cultural Possibilities." *Revista de Estudios Hispánicos* 20, no. 3 (1987): 81–95.

Martini Real, Juan Carlos. "César Tiempo." *Los mejores poemas de la poesía argentina,* 165. 3d ed. Buenos Aires: Corregidor, 1973.

Méndez Calzada, Enrique. Preface to *Sabatión argentino: Antiguas y nuevas donas para la pausa del sábado,* by Tiempo, 23–31. Buenos Aires / Montevideo: Sociedad Amigos del Libro Rioplatense, 1939.

Noé, Julio. "La poesía." In *Historia de la literatura argentina,* ed. Rafael Alberto Arrieta, 4:122–23. Buenos Aires: Peuser, 1959.

Orgambide, Pedro. "César Tiempo." In *Enciclopedia de la literatura argentina,* ed. Pedro Orgambide and Roberto Yahni, 595–96. Buenos Aires: Sudamericana, 1970.

Pinto, Juan. "César Tiempo." *Brevario de la literatura argentina contemporánea (con una ojeada retrospectiva),* 72–73, 151–52, 176–81, 276–79. Buenos Aires: Editorial de la Mandrágora, 1958.

———. "César Tiempo." *Panorama de la literatura argentina contemporánea,* 358–59. Buenos Aires: Editorial Mundi, 1941.

———. *Pasión y suma de la expresión argentina: Literatura, cultura, región,* 121–24, 135–36, 202–4. Buenos Aires: Editorial Huemul, 1970.

Salas, Horacio. "César Tiempo." *La poesía de Buenos Aires: Ensayo y antología,* 237. Buenos Aires: Pleamar, 1968.

Walsh, Donald D. "César Tiempo." *Hispania* 29 (1946): 197–205. Excerpted as "La misión poética de César Tiempo." *Davar* (Buenos Aires) 7 (1946): 56–57.

Yunque, Alvaro [Arístides Gandolfi Herrero]. *La literatura social en la Argentina,* 313. Buenos Aires: Claridad, 1941.

VERBITSKY, BERNARDO (1907–1979)

Imaginative Writing

Café de los angelitos. Buenos Aires: Siglo Veinte, 1949; Buenos Aires: Corregidor, 1972.

Calles de tango. Buenos Aires: Vorágine, 1953; Buenos Aires: Centro Editor de América Latina, 1966.

Una cita con la vida. Buenos Aires: Platina, 1958.

Cuatro historias de Buenos Aires. Buenos Aires: Rayuela, 1970.

Enamorado de Joan Baez. Barcelona: Planeta, 1978.

En esos años. Buenos Aires: Futuro, 1947.

Es difícil empezar a vivir. Buenos Aires: Losada, 1941; Buenos Aires: Fabril, 1963.

La esquina. Buenos Aires: Sudamericana, 1953.

Etiquetas a los hombres. Barcelona: Planeta, 1972.

Un hombre de papel. Buenos Aires: Jorge Alvarez, 1966.

La neurosis monta su espectáculo. 2d ed. Buenos Aires: Paidós, 1969.

Un noviazgo. Buenos Aires: Goyanarte, 1956; Buenos Aires: Sudamericana, 1966.

Octubre maduro. Buenos Aires: Ediciones Macondo, 1976.

Una pequeña familia. Buenos Aires: Losada, 1951; Buenos Aires: Centro Editor de América Latina, 1968.

La tierra es azul. Buenos Aires: Losada, 1961.

Vacaciones. Buenos Aires: Amigos del Libro Argentino, 1953; Buenos Aires: Ediciones de la Flor, 1967.

Villa Miseria también es América. Buenos Aires: Kraft, 1957; rev. ed., Buenos Aires: Ediciones de la Universidad de Buenos Aires, 1966; and Buenos Aires: Paidós, 1967.

Literary Commentary

Literatura y conciencia nacional. Buenos Aires: Paidós, 1975.

El teatro de Arthur Miller. Buenos Aires: n.p., 1959.

Criticism on Verbitsky
Articles and Entries in Books

Alonso, Fernando Pedro, and Arturo Rezzano. "Bernardo Verbitsky." *Novela y sociedad argentina,* 150–61. Buenos Aires: Paidós, 1971.

Barcia, José. "Bernardo Verbitsky." In *Enciclopedia de la literatura argentina,* ed. Pedro Orgambide and Roberto Yahni, 616–18. Buenos Aires: Sudamericana, 1970.

Bonet, Carmelo M. "La novela." In *Historia de la literatura argentina,* ed. Rafael Alberto Arrieta, 4:211–13. Buenos Aires: Peuser, 1959.

Escardó, Florencio. "Visión de América en una novela [*Villa Miseria también es América*]." *Cuadernos Americanos* 154 (1967): 223–29.

Foster, David William. "Bernardo Verbitsky." *A Dictionary of Contemporary Latin American Authors.* Tempe: Center for Latin American Studies, 1975.

Freitas, Newton. "*Es difícil empezar a vivir.*" *Ensayos americanos,* 181–85. Buenos Aires: Schapire, 1942.

García, Germán. Discussion of Verbitsky in *La novela argentina: Un itinerario.* Buenos Aires: Sudamericana, 1952.

Lichtblau, Myron I. "The Young Jew in Buenos Aires: Bernardo Verbitsky's *It's Hard to Begin Living.*" *Modern Jewish Studies Annual* 5, no. 4 (1984): 82–86.

Mallea Abarca, Enrique. "Dos novelistas jóvenes [Verbitsky, Juan Carlos Onetti]." *Nosotros,* 2d ser., 66 (1941): 307–17.

Martini Real, Juan Carlos. "Los libros de Bernardo Verbitsky." *Macedonio* 6–7 (1970): 65–77.

Mastrángelo, Carlos. "Bernardo Verbitsky." *El cuento argentino,* 78–82. Buenos Aires: Hachette, 1963.

————. "Bernardo Verbitsky: Novelista porteño." *Ficción* (Buenos Aires) 10 (1957): 52–60.

Pinto, Juan. Discussion of Verbitsky in *Breviario de la literatura argentina,* 121. Buenos Aires: La Mandrágora, 1958.

Sánchez Sivori, Amalia. "Un argentino de primera generación: Pablo Levinson, personaje de Verbitsky." *Comentario* 46 (1966): 33–40.

VIÑAS, DAVID (1929–)

Bibliography
Valadez, Gustavo. "David Viñas y la generación del 55." *Vórtice* 1, no. 1 (1974): 93–102.

Imaginative Writing
Los años despiadados. Buenos Aires: Letras Universitarias, 1956; Buenos Aires: Ediciones de la Flor, 1967.

Cayó sobre su rostro. Buenos Aires: doble p, 1955; Buenos Aires: Jorge Alvarez, 1964; Buenos Aires: Centro Editor de América Latina, 1967.

Cosas concretas. Buenos Aires: Tiempo Contemporáneo, 1969.

Cuerpo a cuerpo. Mexico City: Siglo XXI, 1979.

Dar la cara. Buenos Aires: Cooperativa Poligráfica Editora, 1962; Buenos Aires: Jamcana, 1966; Buenos Aires: Centro Editor de América Latina, 1967.

Un dios cotidiano. Buenos Aires: Kraft, 1957; Buenos Aires: Centro Editor de América Latina, 1968, 1981.

Dorrego. Túpac-Amarú. Buenos Aires: Galerna, 1985.

Los dueños de la tierra. Buenos Aires: Losada, 1958; Buenos Aires: Schapire, 1964; Buenos Aires: Sudamericana, 1966; Buenos Aires: Galerna, 1970; Buenos Aires: Editorial Librería Lorraine, 1974; Madrid: Orígenes, 1978.

En la semana trágica. Buenos Aires: Jorge Alvarez, 1966.

Los hombres de a caballo. 2d ed. Buenos Aires: Siglo XXI, 1968.

Jauría. Mexico City: Siglo Veintiuno, 1979.

Lisandro. Buenos Aires: Merlín, 1971.

Lisandro, Maniobras. Buenos Aires: Galerna, 1986.

Las malas costumbres. Buenos Aires: Jamcana, 1963.

Teatro. Dorrego. Maniobras. Túpac Amarú. Buenos Aires: Cepe, 1974.

Ultramar. Madrid: Edascal, 1980.

Criticism and Social History

(Ed.) *Contrapunto político en América Latina: Siglo XX.* Mexico City: Instituto de Capacitación Política, 1982.

Grotesco, inmigración y fracaso: Armando Discépolo. Buenos Aires: Corregidor, 1973.

Indios, ejército y frontera. Mexico City: Siglo XXI, 1982.

Laferrère: Del apogeo de la oligarquía a la crisis de la ciudad liberal. Rosario: Universidad del Litoral, Facultad de Letras y Filosofía, 1965; Buenos Aires: Jorge Alvarez, 1967.

Literatura argentina y realidad política. Buenos Aires: Jorge Alvarez, 1964; rev. ed., *Literatura argentina y realidad política: De Sarmiento a Cortázar.* Buenos Aires: Siglo Veinte, 1971.

Literatura argentina y realidad política: Apogeo de la oligarquía. Buenos Aires: Siglo Veinte, 1975.

Literatura argentina y realidad política: La crisis de la ciudad liberal. Buenos Aires: Siglo Veinte, 1973.

Obras escogidas de Armando Discépolo. Ed. and commentary, David Viñas. 3 vols. Buenos Aires: Jorge Alvarez, 1969.

Qué es el fascismo en Latinoamérica. Barcelona: La Gaya Ciencia, 1977.

Criticism on Viñas
Books

Tealdi, Juan Carlos. *Borges y Viñas: Literatura e ideología.* Madrid: Orígenes, 1983.

Articles and Entries in Books

Agosti, Héctor P. "Viñas: Política y literatura." *La milicia literaria,* 163–66. Buenos Aires: Sílaba, 1969.

Alonso, Fernando Pedro, and Arturo Rezzano. "David Viñas." *Novela y sociedad argentina,* 193–209. Buenos Aires: Paidós, 1971.

Borello, Rodolfo A. "Texto literario y contexto histórico-generacional: Viñas y los escritores liberales argentinos." In Instituto Internacional de Literatura Iberoamericana, *Texto/contexto en la literatura iberoamericana,* 33–40. Madrid: Instituto Internacional de Literatura Iberoamericana, 1981.

Bottone, Mireye. "Del libreto cinematográfico a la novela: *Dar la cara.*" *La literatura argentina y el cine,* 27–31. Rosario, Argentina: Universidad Nacional del Litoral, 1964.

Brushwood, John S. "Las novelas de David Viñas: Mensaje y significación." *Taller Literario* (Los Angeles) 1, no. 1 (1980): 1–10.

Campos, Julieta. "*Los hombres de a caballo.*" *Oficio de leer,* 21–24. Mexico: Fondo de Cultura Económica, 1971.

Cano, Carlos José. "Epica y misión en *Los hombres de a caballo.*" *Revista Iberoamericana* 96–97 (1976): 561–65. Also in *Actas del Simposio Internacional de Estudios Hispánicos,* 505–8. Budapest: Akadémia Kiadó, 1978.

Castillo, Abelardo. "*Dar la cara:* David Viñas o Martínez Suárez." *El escarabajo de oro* (Buenos Aires) 15 (1962): 19–20.

Foster, David William. "David Viñas." *A Dictionary of Contemporary Latin American Authors,* 107. Tempe: Center for Latin American Studies, 1975.

———. "*Literatura argentina y realidad política:* David Viñas and Sociological Literary Criticism in Argentina." *Ibero-Amerikanisches Archiv* 1, no. 3 (1975): 253–77.

Glickman, Nora. "Viñas' *En la semana trágica:* A Novelist's Focus on an Argentine Pogrom." *Modern Jewish Studies Annual* 5, no. 4 (1984): 64–71.

Grossi, Héctor. "Angry Young Argentine: David Viñas Speaks His Mind." *Américas* 12, no. 1 (1960): 14–17.

Herrera, Francisco. "David Viñas." In *Enciclopedia de la literatura argentina,* ed. Pedro Orgambide and Roberto Yahni, 625–26. Buenos Aires: Sudamericana, 1970.

Jitrik, Noé. "David Viñas." *Seis novelistas argentinos de la nueva promoción,* 68–72. Mendoza: Cuadernos de Versión, 1959.

Kerr, Lucille. "La geometría del poder: *Los hombres de a caballo* de David Viñas." *Revista de Crítica Literaria Latinoamericana* (Lima) 9 (1979): 69–77.

Larra, Raúl. "David Viñas o el terrorismo literario." *Mundo de escritores,* 23–27. Buenos Aires: Sílaba, 1973.

Lindstrom, Naomi. "David Viñas: The Novelistics of Cultural Contradiction." *Ibero-Amerikanisches Archiv* (Berlin) 2d ser., 10, no. 1 (1984): 87–102.

López Morales, Eduardo E. "De levita (de esos de caballería) [*Los hombres de a caballo*]." *Cuadernos Americanos* 46 (1968): 186–92.

Lyon, Ted. "El engaño de la razón: Quiroga, Borges, Cortázar, Viñas." *Texto Crítico* 4 (1976): 116–26.

Masotta, Carlos. "Explicación de *Un dios cotidiano.*" *Comentario* (Buenos Aires) 20 (1958): 78–88. Also in Masotta, *Conciencia y estructura,* 120–44. Buenos Aires: Jorge Alvarez, 1968.

Mattarollo Benasso, Rodolfo. "Para una crítica de la crítica [*Literatura argentina y realidad política*]." *Latinoamérica* (Buenos Aires) 1 (1972): 137–40.

Pereira, Teresinha Alves. "*Túpac Amarú.*" *La actual dramaturgia latinoamericana,* 31–36. Bogotá: Tercer Mundo, 1979.

Portantiero, Juan Carlos. "Literatura argentina: Una lectura de *Cosas concretas.*" *Realismo y realidad en la narrativas argentina,* 91–96. Buenos Aires: Procyón, 1961.

Rasi, Humberto Mario. "David Viñas, novelista y crítico comprometido." *Revista Iberoamericana* 95 (1976): 259–65.

Rodríguez Monegal, Emir. "David Viñas en su contorno." *Narradores de esta América,* 2:310–13. 2d ed. Montevideo/Buenos Aires: Alfa, 1969–1974. Published previously in *Mundo Nuevo* (Paris) 18 (1967): 75–86.

Rosa, Nicolás. "Literatura argentina y David Viñas." *Setecientos monos* (Rosario, Argentina) 5 (1965): 9–13.

———. "Sexo y novela: David Viñas." *Crítica y significación,* 7–99. Buenos Aires: Galerna, 1970.

———. "Viñas: La evolución de una crítica." *Los libros* (Buenos Aires) 18 (1971): 10–14.

Silver, Juan A. "Prólogo" to *Los dueños de la tierra,* by Viñas, 5–6. Buenos Aires: Schapire, 1967.

Sirusky, Jaime. "El ejército como última estructura sobreviviente del liberalismo oligárquico hoy sólo tiene como ideología el antipensamiento: Entrevista con David Viñas." *Marcha* (Montevideo) 3–4 (1967): 102–14.

Solero, F. J. "*Cayó sobre su rostro,* por David Viñas." *Ficción* 1, no. 1 (1956): 180–85.

Sosnowski, Saúl. "*Los dueños de la tierra,* de David Viñas: Cuestionamiento e impugnación del liberalismo." *Caravelle* 25 (1975): 57–75.

———. "*Jauría,* de David Viñas: Continuación de un proyecto desmitificador." *Revista de Crítica Literaria Latinoamericana* (Lima) 7–8 (1978): 165–72.

Szichman, Mario. "David Viñas (entrevista)." *Hispamérica* 1, no. 1 (1972): 61–67.

Timossi, Jorge. "*Literatura argentina y realidad política:* Se abre la polémica." *Cuadernos Americanos* 41 (1967): 125–27.

Vásquez Rossi, Jorge. "David Viñas y la crítica literaria argentina." *El lagrimal trifurca* (Rosario, Argentina) 2 (1968): 39–43.

INDEX

Absatz, Cecilia: 41; *Feiguele y otras mujeres,*
46; *Té con canela,* 46; *Los años pares,* 166
Acusados, Los (Rabinovich), 38
Adler, Mortimer J., 114, 124, 126
Aguinis, Marcos: *La cuestión judía vista
desde el Tercer Mundo,* 35; *Refugiados:
crónica de un palestino,* 35; *Carta esperan-
zada a un general,* 164–65
Aizenberg, Edna, 146
*A las 20.25, la señora entró en la inmor-
talidad* (Szichman), 162
Alberti, Rafael, 97
Aleichem. *See* Scholem Aleichem
Alter, Robert, 71–72
AMIA. *See* Asociación Mutual Israelita
Argentina
Años pares, Los (Absatz), 166
Antiparticularism of the Left, 5–6, 9–11,
26–27, 29–30, 34, 40, 162–63
*Anti-Semitic Campaign and the Director of
the National Library, The* (Tiempo), 24
Anti-Semitism: public discussions of. *See*
Aguinis, Marcos; Antiparticularism of
the Left; Comité contra el Anti-Semitismo
y el Racismo; Delegación de Asociaciones
Israelitas Argentinas; Fascism; Gálvez,
Manuel; Holocaust; Israel: debate over
Israeli-occupied territories; Justo, Juan B.;
Lugones, Leopoldo; Martel, Julián;
Mirelman, Simón; Memmi, Albert; Mili-
tary régime of 1976–1983; Military mind:
post-1983 analyses of; Rozitchner, León;
Sebreli, Juan José; Tiempo, César; Timer-
man, Jacobo; Tragic Week; Wast, Hugo
Arcana mayor (Barnatán), 42
Argentina, oscuro país (Kovadloff), 165
Argentine Movement of National Libera-
tion, 29
Argentine Socialist Party. *See* Socialist Party
Asociación Mutual Israelita Argentina
(AMIA), 8, 163
Astarte, 141
Auto-Emanzipation (Pinsker), 54
*Aventuras de Edmund Ziller en tierras del
Nuevo Mundo* (Orgambide), 158–59

B.A.B.E.L. *See* Biblioteca Argentina de
Buenas Ediciones Literarias
Babel, Tower of, 107
Bacon, Francis, 121
Baeza, Ricardo, 38

Balfour Declaration: Argentine reaction
to, 9
Barnatán, Marcos Ricardo: career and
major concerns, 42–44, 49–50; *El laber-
into de Sión,* 130–45
Barylko, Jaime, 163
Beat poets, 44
Benjamin, Walter, 137, 138–39
Beter, Clara. *See* Tiempo, César
Bialik, Chaim Nachman, 15
Biblioteca Argentina de Buenas Ediciones
Literarias (B.A.B.E.L.), 18
Bilik, Dorothy Seidman, 39
Bloom, Harold C., 130, 131, 133, 137, 138,
141, 142
Blyenbergh, G. van, 121
Bonet, Carmelo M., 85, 169*n*5
Borges, Jorge Luis, 21, 44, 57, 62, 127
Bortnik, Aída: *La historia oficial* (with Luis
Puenzo), 165
Brailowsky, Antonio Elio: *Identidad,* 161
Budasoff, Natalio, 31

Caballos por el fondo de los ojos (Goloboff),
58–59
Calas, Nicolas, 156
Calny, Eugenia (pseud. of Fanny Eugenia
Kalmitsky), 46
Caras y caretas, 6
Carta esperanzada a un general (Aguinis),
164–65
Castelnuovo, Elías, 37
Chagall, Marc, 103
Chaplin, Charlie, 15, 67
Chicos de la guerra, Los (Kon), 165
Chudnovsky, José, 31
Clara al amanecer (Calny), 46
Claridad publishing house, 22
Comentario, 28
Comité contra el Antisemitismo y el Rac-
ismo, 23
Contorno, 28, 29
Costantini, Humberto, 43, 161, 165; *De
dioses, hombrecitos y policías,* 161
Cozarinsky, Edgardo, 50; *Vudú urbano,*
167–68
Crítica, 27
Crónica falsa, La (Szichman), 47
Cuaderno Spinoza (Isaacson), 113–29
Cuestión judía en la Argentina, La (Sebreli),
34

Cuestión judía vista desde el Tercer Mundo, La (Aguinis), 35

DAIA. *See* Delegación de Asociaciones Israelitas Argentinas
Dar la cara (Viñas), 88–101
Davar, 14, 27, 28
De dioses, hombrecitos, y policías (Costantini), 161
De este lado del Mediterráneo (Kamenszain), 172
Delegación de Asociaciones Israelitas Argentinas (DAIA), 23
De músicos y relojeros (Steimberg), 45–46
Descartes, René, 121–22
Diano (Barnatán), 42
Dickmann, Adolfo, 5–6, 9
Dickmann, Enrique, 5–6, 9
Dickmann, Max, 21, 26
Dietary laws, Jewish. *See* Kashrut
Dios era verde (Chudnovsky), 31
Disputation with divinity, 103–4
Divina Commedia, 74
Don Quixote, 83
Dueños de la tierra, Los (Viñas), 30
Dujovne, León, 13, 21, 98

Eichelbaum, Samuel, 20
Eichmann, Adolf, 32
Einstein, Albert, 96
Elkin, Judith Laikin, 163
En búsqueda de una identidad (Victor Mirelman), 169
Es difícil empezar a vivir (Bernardo Verbitsky), 79–87
Espinoza, Enrique. *See* Glusberg, Samuel
Estrella de la mañana (Fijman), 19
Etiquetas a los hombres (Bernardo Verbitsky), 34–35
Exposición de la actual poesía argentina (1922–1927), 14

Falkland Islands Conflict. *See* Malvinas Conflict of 1982
Fascism: Argentine, 12, 22–24, 99–101
Federación Israelita Argentina, 8
Feierstein, Ricardo, 165; *La sinfonía inocente*, 166–67
Feiguele y otras mujeres (Absatz), 46
Fernández, Macedonio, 61
Fijman, Jacobo, 19–20
Francis of Assisi, 74
Franco, Francisco, 138
Freud, Sigmund, 136
Frondizi, Arturo, 30, 96

Gálvez, Manuel: relations with Gerchunoff, 12; conversion, 12, 19

Gauchos judíos, Los (Gerchunoff), 4–5, 7–9, 46–47, 51–60, 146–52. *See also* Viñas, David: polemical commentary on *Los gauchos judíos*
Gematria, 138
Gerchunoff, Alberto: early life and entry into Buenos Aires literary scene, 5–7; shifts in public stance, 9–11; and younger Jewish writers, 17, 21, 25, 27, 61, 79; later Jewish writers express differences with, 31, 43, 46–47, 49, 98; compared to Isaacson, 40–41; *Los gauchos judíos*: 51–60; ideology in, 4–5; publication of, 7–9; parodied by Szichman, 46–47, 48, 146–52
Girondo, Oliverio, 61
Gleizer, Manuel, 18
Glickman, Nora: as creative writer, 41, 46; as critic, 79–80; research on white slave trade, 171
Glusberg, Samuel (aka Enrique Espinoza), 18–19
Glusberg, Santiago, 18–19
Goloboff, Gerardo Mario: 41, 45, 158–59, 163, 165; *Caballos por el fondo de los ojos*, 58–59
González Lanuza, Eduardo, 62
Gor (Barnatán), 42
Grandmontagne, Francisco, 6
Grünberg, Carlos M., 20–21

Halakhah, 139–40, 144
Haya de la Torre, Raúl, 97
Hebrew: revival as literary language, 15, 52; in Spanish-language literature, 17, 147; as modern national language, 38; religious value of alphabet and script, 71, 133–34, 135, 144. *See also* Scribes
Hecate, 141
Hecho de estampas (Fijman), 19
Heine, Heinrich, 143
Heschel, Abraham Joshua, 77
Hirsch, Baron Maurice de, 3–4, 169n2
Historia oficial, La (Bortnik and Puenzo), 165
Hitler, Adolf, 83
Holocaust, 35, 39, 104
Horowitz, Irving Louis, 54

ICA. *See* Jewish Colonization Association
Identidad (Brailowsky), 161
Identidad judía en la literatura argentina, La (Leonardo Senkman), 188
Immigration to Argentina, Jewish: Sephardic, 2–3; Western European, 3; Eastern European, 3–4
Isaacson, José: career and role in Argentine intellectual life, 36, 39–42, 43, 49; *Cuaderno Spinoza*, 113–29

Israel: emigration to, as theme in Argentine literature, 21, 158, 166–67; debate over Israeli-occupied territories, 33–35, 40, 150, 166–67. *See also* Zionism

Jan es antisemita (Palant), 26
Jauría (Viñas), 160
Jewish Colonization Association (ICA), 4
Jews of Argentina, The (Weisbrot), 169
Jews of the Latin American Republics (Elkin), 169
Job, Book of, 103, 104
Jolson, Al, 15, 65–66
Judaica, 14
Judeo-Spanish language (Ladino), 135
Judío Aarón, El (Eichelbaum), 20
Judíos del Mar Dulce, Los (Szichman), 146–57
Juno, 141
Junto a un río de Babel (Grünberg), 21
Justo, Juan B., 6, 9, 11, 97
Juventud, 8

Kabbalah, 43, 44, 62, 98, 118, 126–27, 130–45
Kahal, El (Wast), 23
Kalmitsky, Fanny Eugenia. *See* Calny, Eugenia
Kamenszain, Tamara: 46, 165; *De este lado del Mediteráneo,* 172n45
Kantor, Manuel, 14, 169n10
Kaplan, Mordecai M., 63
Kashrut, 65
Katz, Pinie, 8, 21
Kermode, Frank, 130, 145
Kibbutz ideal, 166–67
"Kid Ñandubay" (Kordon), 26
Kon, Daniel, *Los chicos de la guerra,* 165
Kordon, Bernardo, 26
Kovadloff, Santiago, 165

Laberinto de Sión, El (Barnatán), 130–45
Ladino, 135
LAJSA. *See* Latin American Jewish Studies Association
Lange, Norah, 62
Latin American Jewish Studies Association, 163
Lehrmann, Charles C., 143, 152
Lema, Vincente Zito. *See* Zito Lema, Vincente
Lévi, Eliphas, 138
Levita gris, La (Samuel Glusberg), 18
Liacho, Lázaro. *See* Liachovitsky, Jacobo Simón
Liachovitsky, Jacobo Simón (aka Lázaro Liacho): 8; *Siónidas desde la pampa,* 20; *Sonata judía de Nueva York,* 20

Libro para la pausa del sábado (Tiempo), 18, 61
Literatura argentina y realidad política (Viñas), 31, 88
Lost tribe of Israel, 161
Lugones, Leopoldo: as organizer of Centennial activities, 6–7; *Odas Seculares,* 6, 61; denunciation of anti-Jewish violence of 1919, 10–11; conversion to Catholicism and conservativism, 12, 19; befriended by Glusberg, 18

Maccabees, 52, 98
Mafud, Julio, 91
Mal metafísico, El (Gálvez), 12
Malvinas Conflict of 1982, 165
"Manifiesto de Martín Fierro," 61, 64
Martel, Julián (pseud. of José María Miró), 7
Martínez Estrada, Ezequiel, 18, 19
Martínez Zuviría, Gustavo. *See* Hugo Wast
Martín Fierro (avant-garde tabloid), 61
Marx, Karl, 137
Memmi, Albert, 34, 35
Mendelsohn, José, 13
Méndez, Evar, 19
Mester de judería (Grünberg), 21
Military mind: post-1983 analyses of, 160, 162
Military régime of 1930–1943, 16, 25, 86
Military régime of 1976–1983, 40–41, 158–62, 164, 165, 168
Mirelman, Simón, 23
Molino rojo (Fijman), 19
Mundo Israelita, 8, 23
Murena, Héctor A., 119

Nación, La, 4, 6, 38, 41
Nadie la conoció nunca (Eichelbaum), 20
Nazis: hiding in Argentina, 32; in Argentine literature, 35, 83, 105; effects on Yiddish culture, 39; in Francoist Spain, 138
Niborski, Isidoro, 163
Novalis, 123
Nueva Presencia, 33

Oldenburg, Hendrik, 121, 123
Onega, Gladys, 51
Opinión, La, 162
Oráculo invocado, El (Barnatán), 42
Orgambide, Pedro: 41, 45, 158–59, 163, 165; *Aventuras de Edmund Ziller entierras del Nuevo Mundo,* 158–59
Orilla inminente, La (Sosnowski), 188
Oro (Wast), 23

Palacios, Alfredo J., 6, 10
Palant, Pablo, 26

Pan criollo (Tiempo), 23
Particularism. *See* Antiparticularism of the
   Left
Paul VI, Pope, 104
Payró, Roberto J., 6
Perón, Eva, 28, 153–54, 157
Perón, Isabel, 39–40
Perón, Juan Domingo, 24, 28, 29, 39–40, 48
Pinsker, Leo, 54
Pinto, Juan, 79
Pius XII, Pope, 105
Planetarium (Satz), 160–61
Portuguese Jews in Argentina. *See* Immigra-
   tion to Argentina, Jewish
Presse, Di, 36
*Prisoner Without a Name, Cell Without a
   Number* (Timerman), 162
Prophetic harangue, 36, 103
Protocols of the Elders of Zion, The, 23–24
Proust, Marcel, 142–43
Publishing industry: Jewish Argentines'
   involvement in, 8–9, 18–19; 21–22, 28, 162
Pueblo Pan (Chudnovsky), 31

Rabinovich, José: career and reception of
   his works, 36–39, 49; *Tercera clase,* 37;
   preface to *Los acusados,* 38; *Sobras de
   una juventud,* 39; *El violinista bajo el
   tejado,* 102–12
Rabkin, Eric S., 146
Radical government of 1916–1930, 86–87
Radical government of 1958–1962, 30
Radical Party, 30, 86–87
Radical social thought among Eastern Euro-
   pean Jewish immigrants, 6, 8, 10, 22, 30,
   36–38, 53–54
Rasi, Humberto, 88
Refugiados: crónica de un palestino
   (Aguinis), 35
Réquiem para un viernes a la noche (Rozen-
   macher), 31–32
Resnick, Salomón, 14
Rozenmacher, Germán: 31–32, 79; *Réquiem
   para un viernes a la noche,* 31–32
Rozitchner, León, 33–34, 164, 165
Ruth y Noemí (Samuel Glusberg), 18

Sabadomingo (Tiempo), 15
Sábado pleno (Tiempo), 24
Sabatión argentino (Tiempo), 61–78
Samet, Jacobo, 19
Satanowski, Marcos, 13
Satz, Mario: 42–43, 160–61; *Planetarium,*
   160–61
Scholem, Gershom G., 130, 131, 133, 137,
   138, 141, 142
Schultz Solari, Alejandro. *See* Solar, Xul
Schwartz, Kessel, 52, 59, 79

Scribes, 64, 160
Sebreli, Juan José, 34
Semon, Larry, 65–67
Senkman, Beatriz, 163
Senkman, Leonardo: observations on Jewish
   Argentine writing, 22, 37, 114, 116, 128,
   131; and movement to preserve Jewish
   Argentine history, 163
Sennacherib, 76
Sephardic Golden Age: mythified in *El
   laberinto de Sión,* 42, 132, 139, 143, 145;
   disparaged in *Los gauchos judíos,* 53–54,
   152; protrayal in *Cuaderno Spinoza,*
   114–118, 121
Ser judío (Rozitchner), 33–34
SHA. *See* Sociedad Hebraica Argentina
Shekhina, 141
Shelley, Mary, 141
Shliapochnik, Adela, 193, 194
Sholem Aleichem, 103
Sinfonía inocente, La (Feierstein), 166–67
Singerman, Berta, 36, 196
Siónidas desde la pampa (Liachovitsky), 20
Sobras de una juventud (Rabinovich), 39
Socialist Party, 6, 9–10
Sociedad Hebraica Argentina (SHA), 11, 13,
   27
Solar, Xul (pseud. of Alejandro Schulz
   Solari), 62
Sonata judía de Nueva York (Liachovitsky),
   20
Sosnowski, Saúl: commentaries on Jewish
   Argentine authors, 32, 51, 79, 148; par-
   ticipation in Jewish Argentine intellectual
   activity, 165
Soto, Luis Emilio, 38
Soviet graphic art, 111
Soviet literature, 22, 25
Spanish Jewish civilization. *See* Sephardic
   Golden Age
Spanish Jews in Argentina. *See* Immigration
   to Argentina: Jewish
Spinoza, Baruch (Benedict de), 41, 113–29
Steimberg, Alicia, 41, 45, 165; *De músicos y
   relojeros* and *Su espíritu inocente,* 45–46
Su espíritu inocente (Steimberg), 45–46
Szichman, Mario: 41, 42, 45, 46–49, 50; *La
   crónica falsa,* 47; *La verdadera crónica
   falsa,* 47; *Los judíos del Mar Dulce,*
   146–57; *A las 20.25, la señora entró en la
   inmortalidad,* 162

Talmud, 54, 57, 59, 148, 152
Tchernihowsky, Saul, 52–54, 111–12; "They
   Say There Is a Country . . . ," 52–53
Teatro soy yo, El (Tiempo), 22–23
Té con canela (Absatz), 166
Tercera clase (Rabinovich), 37

Tiempo, César (pseud. of Israel Zeitlin): 12, 14–18, 22–24; and "Clara Beter" hoax, 14, 170n16; Sabbath poetry, 5–18; *Sabadomingo,* 15; *Libro para la pausa delsábado,* 18, 61; relations with contemporaries, 20, 21; *El teatro soy yo,* 22–23; *Pan criollo,* 23; *The Anti-Semitic Campaign and the Director of the National Library,* 24; relations with nationalists and Peronist régime of 1946–1955, 24, 25, 28, 171n16; *Sábado pleno,* 24; contrasted with subsequent Jewish writers, 30, 43; contrasted with Gerchunoff, 46–47; *Sabatión argentino,* 61–78
Timerman, Jacobo, 162
Tolstoy, Leo, 111
Torah, 133, 137, 138, 141, 144
Tragic Week, 10–11, 18, 20
Translation by Argentine Jews, 21–22

Uno de sus Juanes (Glickman), 41, 46

Vanguardia, 14
Verbitsky, Bernardo: as writer and public figure, 24–25, 27–28; relation to contemporaries, 26–27; *Etiquetas a los hombres,* 34–35; contrasted to Gerchunoff, 47; contrasted to Tiempo, 69; *Es difícil empezar a vivir,* 79–87
Verbitsky, Gregorio, 27–28
Verdadera crónica falsa, La (Szichman), 47
Versos de una . . . ("Clara Beter"). *See* Tiempo, César: "Clara Beter" hoax
Vida nuestra, 8, 10–11
Vignale, Pedro-Juan, 14
Viñas, David: early career and involvement in *Contorno* group, 28–31, 34; *Los dueños*

de la tierra, 30; *Literatura argentina y realidad política,* 31, 88; influence on Szichman, 42, 47–48; commentary on *Los gauchos judíos,* 47–48, 49, 51, 55–56, 58, 148; *Dar la cara,* 88–101; period of exile, 160; *Jauría,* 160; resumption of career in Argentina, 164; rediscovery of Tiempo's "Clara Beter" poetry, 170n16
Violinista bajo el tejado, El (Rabinovich), 102–12
Vudú urbano (Cozarinsky), 167–68

Wandering Jew, 159
Wast, Hugo (pseud. of Gustavo Martínez Zuviría), 23–24
Weisbrot, Robert, 169n1

Yerushalmi, Josef Hayim, 117
Yiddish Argentine culture, 22, 36–39
Yiddish language: translation of, 8, 21–22, 37, 185; in Argentine newspapers, 8, 36, 150; in Spanish-language Argentine literature, 17, 48, 70, 147, 149
Yidische Tsaitung, Di, 8, 150
Yidisher Wisnshaftlecher Institut Archives and Library, 36

Zangwill, Israel, 84, 123
Zeitlin, Israel. *See* Tiempo, César
Zion, Argentina as: general concept, 3–4; advocated by Gerchunoff, 4–5, 9, 51–55, 58; in Liachovitsky's poetry, 20; notion questioned by subsequent Jewish Argentine writers, 43, 148, 150, 151
Zionism: Israel as modern Jewish state, 3–4, 9, 35, 158, 166
Zito Lema, Vicente, 19–20
Zweig, Stefan, 84